THE HUNGRY SEASON

THE HUNGRY SEASON

A Journey of War, Love, and Survival

LISA M. HAMILTON

Little, Brown and Company

New York   Boston   London

Little, Brown and Company
Hachette Book Group
1290 Avenue of the Americas, New York, NY 10104
littlebrown.com

First Edition: September 2023

Little, Brown and Company is a division of Hachette Book Group, Inc. The Little, Brown name and logo are trademarks of Hachette Book Group, Inc.

The publisher is not responsible for websites (or their content) that are not owned by the publisher.

The Hachette Speakers Bureau provides a wide range of authors for speaking events. To find out more, go to hachettespeakersbureau.com or email hachettespeakers@hbgusa.com.

Little, Brown and Company books may be purchased in bulk for business, educational, or promotional use. For information, please contact your local bookseller or the Hachette Book Group Special Markets Department at special.markets@hbgusa.com.

Maps by Kevin Sprouls

ISBN 9780316415897
LCCN 2022952001

Printing 1, 2023

LSC–C

Book design by Marie Mundaca

Printed in the United States of America

CONTENTS

AUTHOR'S NOTE

While this book is rendered in English, most of the dialogue originally occurred in Hmong. I have worked hard to ensure that the translated phrases are as close as possible to what was said, and that the core meaning of the spoken words remains true. Conversations I witnessed firsthand are in quotation marks. Dialogue that was recounted to me after the fact is set in italics. Additionally, Hmong words are rendered in italics to distinguish them as belonging to a language that evolved from a place and tradition vastly different from the place and tradition that produced the English language, and which therefore are not always interchangeable with English words.

Some names of people and identifying places that appear in the book have been changed to protect individuals' privacy.

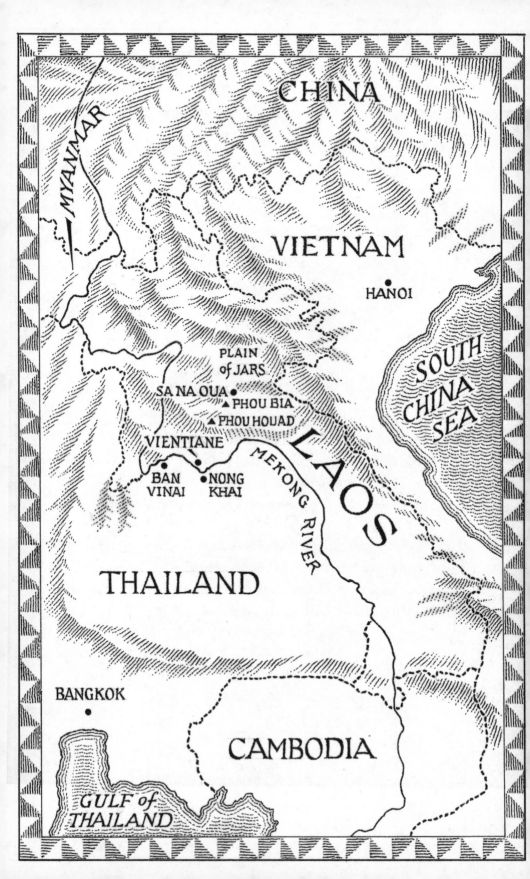

THE HUNGRY SEASON

PROLOGUE

They call this particular rice *nplej niam tais,* "grandmother rice." Some say it's named for the person it came from: The farmer got the seed from her brother, who got it from a friend, who got it from his wife, who got it from her mother. That mother has a name, but no one would have used it since before she was married. As an old woman, she would just be called "grandmother." Grandmother's rice.

Others say that the rice was given this name because it yields so much, taking care of you with its bounty the way a grandmother's love softens the sharp edges of life. And it's true: this year all the farm's rice grew tall and thick, but none like the grandmother rice. In mid-October, when the wands of ripe grain have bowed under their own weight and curved back down toward the earth, the arc of the grandmother rice is taller than anyone on the farm. Below, its long, sword-shaped leaves have plaited together in such a tangle that the spaces between rows disappear. Entering this thicket, the farmer must first push with her shoulder, then draw her arms through as if opening a heavy door. As she passes inward, the vegetation rejoins behind her. Were she to release herself and fall backward, the grandmother rice would hold her up.

When the farmer is enclosed like this, the only view is straight up, to the blank, blue sky. The road running alongside the field disappears; the din of traffic fades. As the honeyed fragrance of rice fills her head, she can imagine herself back to the place of her memories. The village where she was born was swallowed up by the jungle in the years after the war, but it is still alive in her mind. All around are steep mountains shrouded in clouds. The village itself is level, set amid gentle green hills with blue skies above. It is never too hot there, never too cold. The air is sweet with sugarcane, the land thick with wild fruit trees. Every morning, a choir of birds. Even today, forty years later, standing in this grandmother rice can transport her back to there, then. It's almost as if she could reach into the tangle of leaves and touch her parents, close to her once again. An orphan no more.

Were the sky to look back down on her, though, it would tell the biting truth of where she stands, alone. Her field is a crooked little square within a larger square within a grid of rectangles, alternating irrigation-emerald and dusty beige to the edge of the flat earth. This is the great agricultural matrix of California's San Joaquin Valley, land of vast, silent plantations growing fruits and nuts measured in the tons and by the thousands. Eastward, the grid subdivides into squares that are smaller and gray: the concrete of Fresno.

Farther east, where the ground is no longer flat, the grid does finally concede to the earth's natural contours. Beyond that are mountains, and in the blue light of dawn their jagged horizon can resemble the mountains she remembers. By midmorning, though, the likeness is gone, the range erased by the hot yellow smog. Anyway, there is work to be done.

Where the rice has already been harvested the plants are ragged and short, with a clear view of the cars smoking by at fifty-five miles an hour. Yesterday the hired workers cut it down one stem at a time. They bundled the stalks of rice into sheaves the width of a woman's grip and impaled each one on the plants from which they came, to dry in the sun. This morning the farmer walks the rows collecting the bundles, dropping each one behind her head into the basket on her back. Even after it is heavy and full she continues dropping more rice gingerly on top, even as the load threatens to spill. The straps cut into her shoulders, but the skin there is tough. Not like when she was young, when the weight of the basket would grind into her flesh until it blistered, broke, and peeled away.

Back then, her name was Ai, written *Aiv*. Her birth name had been Yer, meaning something like "precious youngest daughter," but that didn't last. She was a sickly infant, failing to grow, and so people began calling her by the generic nickname Me Aiv, "small one." It stuck. As she grew into a child and then an adolescent, people dropped the first half and called her just Ai, "small."

Now she calls herself fat—fat like an emperor. She is still only four foot eight, but her belly is a pumpkin inside her elasticized pants. Her cheeks are round and full, and under her chin is a crease so deep the center is pale white, like a second smile. Under the crease, a gold pendant with rubies in the shape of a heart. A matching gold watch on her wrist. Today a hip sack is clipped in the narrows above her waist; the money bag attached to it, tense with a roll of bills, hangs down over her bulge.

Her name has changed, too, though she's not sure exactly when. Definitely after the Thai military police collected her on the banks of the Mekong River, still damp from her desperate escape out of Laos. Maybe it was during the fingerprinting, when they asked for her name and her husband answered for her. Or later, when that Thai script was turned into English—perhaps some aid worker with a pen deciding that what sounded like "I" couldn't possibly be a person's name, so adding a letter to produce the closest thing that made sense: Ia. In her language, *Iab,* meaning "bitterness." A common name for girls.

It was the third time she had been named, but the first time she had been written down on paper, made official. The name stuck. It would follow her through fifteen years in the refugee camps, then across the Pacific Ocean to California. It would be the name printed on her United States passport, surrounded by words she could not read and set against a drawing of an eagle and a sheaf of wheat. "Ia Moua." With it, a new chapter of her story began.

She knew it would never be possible for her to go back and undo the beginning of that story—once a person becomes an orphan, she can never not be one again. But there was no law that said she couldn't be the one to compose the rest of the narrative. And perhaps in doing so she could imagine herself into something bigger than an orphan. Something more valuable. Something less alone.

PART I

DAUGHTER

When the news came, they were planting rice. It was May, after all—nearly everyone in Laos was doing the same. In March, as the days grew hot again, the forest had been burned down to clear room for their crop. In April, the climax of the dry season, the air became so parched that the bamboo around the field's perimeter split open at its brittle seams, the sound of it crackling like gunfire. But now was May, and rain was on its way. Fed by the forest's ashes, the bare yellow earth was succulent. Across the hillside moved a line of a dozen men, each one methodically stabbing the soil with a sharpened stick. Behind them, a bent-over army of wives and daughters seeded the holes the men had made with rice. Any children who were old enough to be helpful toddled in the rear, reaching into their own pouches of seed to plant the spots that had been missed. Food for another year.

But then a young man emerged from the forest and quickly approached the field. He found his father and spoke softly into the man's ear. That man told the other men, and the phalanx of them stopped in a jagged line. The husbands told their wives, then the mothers told their children. The youngest ones were given the news in words simple enough for them to understand: *The Americans have deserted us. General Vang Pao has fled to Thailand. As of today, Laos be-longs to the communists.*

As both a child and a girl, Ai was among the last to be informed. The news didn't scare her. She had been born in 1964, the year the fragile peace established by the second Geneva conference fell apart and Laos once again disintegrated into armed conflict, alongside the rest of Indochina. Now eleven years old, Ai had never lived *not* during war, but all she had ever known was that her parents kept her safe; she had no reason to think that would change now. With dry eyes, Ai watched as the adults around her began to wail with the grief of orphans, distraught over losing the great military leader they regarded as a father to them all. With General Vang Pao there had been war, but also hope of winning. Without him, the battle was un-equivocally over. What came next, they feared, would be far worse.

The men laid their sticks on the ground and began walking to the village. There they would hold a counsel to decide what every-one should do. Ai stayed with the women, who bent back toward the earth and resumed slipping seed into the soil. When all the holes were filled, the women turned away from the half-planted field and followed their husbands home. Ai walked with them.

There were few choices for how to proceed, none of them good. Nobody wanted to leave the village. And yet already the new gov-ernment had launched a searing propaganda campaign against "the bandit General Vang Pao" and his followers, who were said to be sabotaging the nation's fragile peace. Government radio broadcasts sizzled with headlines like "The Patriotic Forces' Liberated Zone Must Be Resolutely Defended with Blood" and "Vang Pao 'Special Forces' Must Be Liquidated."

"Clearly," one radio announcer boomed, "the people have the right to search for and exterminate such people from our beloved and respected fatherland."

Word was spreading that the communists would hunt down those who had served in Vang Pao's army, which in Ai's world effectively meant any male from puberty to old age. Ai's older brothers and father would be prime targets. Women and children might be spared, but without men to protect and lead the families, how would the rest survive? It became clear that there was only one choice: they must all follow Vang Pao to Thailand.

They had left once before. It was during the height of the war, when orders came for the whole village to relocate to an internal refugee camp several days' walk to the south. Ai's family had brought their livestock: an ox, cattle, pigs, even chickens. The animals all died, but the people were back home in six months, in time to plant the year's rice crop.

This departure would be different. The journey to Thailand was long and uncertain, and if they made it over the border they would probably not return. And so the long night before they left was marked by a cacophony of crying and killing, the family plucking and gutting and roasting and mincing as much meat as they could carry on the journey ahead.

Nobody slept—there was too much to do. Over the course of those dark hours, Ai finally began to feel scared. When she asked her parents what Thailand was like, they said they didn't know. They hadn't even been to Vientiane, the capital of Laos, much less across the Mekong River and into another country. Still, Ai watched them prepare to leave their home behind, baskets packed with only the barest possessions: meat and rice, the family's three cooking pots, the father's hunting rifle, all the money they had. In her child-size basket, Ai packed meat and rice for herself, plus the traditional Hmong outfit her mother had sewn for her to wear at New Year's. She dressed herself in the same tired skirt and blouse she would have worn to go to the farm, flip-flops on her feet. And that was it. After breakfast, the family walked out of the village single file: Ai's father first and mother last; between them her older brothers and their families; her younger brother, Tong, who was too small to carry anything; and Ai.

When General Vang Pao and those closest to him left Laos, they

rode in U.S. Air Force aircraft. Their departure had been not unlike that of the American allies fleeing Vietnam and Cambodia the
month before, although like everything about the war in Laos, the
airlift had been intentionally discreet and miserly in scale—maybe
2,500 people evacuated compared to 140,000 out of Vietnam and
Cambodia. In the days that followed Vang Pao's departure, other
high-level military men had hurriedly driven their families to Thailand. The masses, though, once they heard the news, traveled by foot.

In Ai's village, only a few families stayed behind; they were
known to be opium addicts, and thus too poor to afford a journey
away from home and to another country. The rest of the village
followed the one narrow footpath that led into the forest, heading
southward over and around one mountain after another. It was the
same across much of northeastern Laos, entire communities pouring
out down the slopes to follow their own unnamed paths. Gradually,
each group would merge onto common trails woven through the
jungle, joining with the other travelers to form ever larger streams of
people. By the time they reached the one main road heading toward
the capital city, the frantic migrants were a river of thousands.

The first night, Ai's family slept in the forest. In the dark, her
parents cut down a few leafy boughs and fashioned a lean-to. Protected under its cover, Ai slept with her mother and father and
little brother, just as they always had at home. After another full
day of walking, they stopped in a village that, like theirs, had been
abandoned. They found an empty house and moved in for the
night.

Here, as in much of the country, there were few true cities. Ai's
family and the majority of the migrants planned to travel by way
of the settlements that had mushroomed during the long war, as
military bases sprung up and people displaced by fighting clustered
around them by the thousands. Ai's family was headed for a settlement called Muong Cha, and from there, gradually west and south
to Thailand. But that night in the abandoned village, other travelers

delivered news and warnings. The government had closed the border with Thailand. The communists' fear was that if Vang Pao's followers made it out of the country, they would reconstitute their army and attack anew. To prevent people from fleeing, military checkpoints had been erected along the roads.

Before first light, Ai's father called a family meeting. He told everyone that the journey ahead was too uncertain. Equally, he had left behind a wealth of livestock. If their family didn't make it over the border, by the time they returned home all his animals would have been stolen or eaten. He and Ai's mother would be going back to the village.

Ai's little brother, Tong, too young to be apart from his mother and a sickly child besides, would return with them. Ai's older brothers, who were technically still Vang Pao's soldiers, were in the greatest danger of retribution and would have to forge ahead; their wives and children would naturally join them. The only person whose path was not obvious was Ai. Her parents asked her to choose what she would do.

In the growing light of dawn, Ai looked at the circle of her family. She pictured her village now empty of people. She imagined how lonely their house would feel with most of its inhabitants gone. If she returned, her life there would be the same drudgery as before, her days devoted mostly to feeding her father's livestock. Even yesterday, the morning they walked away from the village meaning to leave forever, her parents had still made her feed the damned pigs. The decision before her felt easy. Physically, she was smaller than other girls her age, but she was one who saw possibility. Even after hearing her father describe the challenges of the journey ahead, Ai hoped maybe she would be one of the few to make it to Thailand. She told her parents that she wanted to try her luck.

Ai's father concluded the meeting by assuring the group that their separation would be temporary: If Ai and her brothers made it to Thailand, he and Ai's mother and Tong would follow. If they didn't make it, he and the others would be waiting at home. Either way, the family would end up together. Meeting adjourned.

Ai's mother pulled her daughter aside. In the night she had sewn money inside a pouch. Now she gave the bag to Ai and explained that it was meant to support her during the time that her parents would not be there to do so. As Ai clutched the pouch, her father, her mother, and Tong gathered their things and began walking back the way they had come.

The morning was bright now, and in the new light, Ai watched her parents grow smaller as they moved down the path. At last her tears burst through and she ran after them.

I've changed my mind, she called out. *I want to go back with you!*

Her parents continued walking, gently telling her to stay with her older brothers.

Ai cried, *Why don't we all go back together?*

Father shushed her and repeated his promise that they would reunite eventually, told her to turn around. Ai slowed down, obediently, then sped up to close the growing distance. Mother looked back over her shoulder to say, *Go back and be safe until we see each other again.* Like this, over and over: Ai stopping as she was told to, then starting again in a fever; her mother telling her to go back, each time from a little farther away. Finally, the pattern was broken by a rise in the hill and the three of them—mother, father, son—sank down on the far side, disappearing from sight.

––––––––––

Ai's older brothers decided to pause for two days, so that their children could rest but also so the brothers themselves, now in charge, could determine how to proceed. At night, Ai slept with her young nieces. During the day, she stayed close to the abandoned house. In earlier times, she might have sought out the girls her age who were also stopped in the village, but her brothers had warned her that they might need to run. She could not risk being separated from them.

When the journey resumed, Ai's family banded with three other households to make a group of roughly forty people. The route to Muong Cha was familiar—in better times, even Ai had gone there—but the landscape through which they traveled was now empty, most everyone in these parts having left already. Hurrying, they walked through tangled forest and past half-planted farms, down into the valley of the Naxang River, then steeply up one mountain and down another.

When they had nearly reached the road that would take them into Muong Cha, behind them appeared a man, walking briskly. He approached Ai's oldest brother and spoke a few words. Then the two men turned to Ai. She knew the man from her village—his family had been one of those too poor to leave. Ai's brother explained that their mother and father had sent this man to come get her. They needed her to help feed the livestock.

Ai stood there, hands gripping the one of the family's three cooking pots that she had been entrusted to carry. Her brother told her she could choose whether to follow the man or continue on with them, but really, this time there was little choice. Her parents wanted her to return, and they had paid the man a lot of money to retrieve her. Knowing she could not delay the larger group with her own hesitation, Ai nodded and turned to face the man. In a seeming act of kindness, he took the cooking pot from her. Carrying it with one hand, he began walking back the way he had come.

They traveled in silence, he first and Ai behind. He was fast—a full-grown man compared to an undersized eleven-year-old—and Ai had to jog to keep up with him. As they retraced the steps she had walked earlier in the day, the landscape felt somehow more empty. After two hours of going downhill, they came to where the broad Naxang River cut the landscape in two. Just before the man stepped onto the bridge, Ai stopped and spoke.

Will you give me my pot back?

The man stopped. *Huh?* he said.

I'm going back to my brothers.

Are you serious? It's half a day's walk to the city! You'll be scared.

I won't be scared, Ai told him solidly. *I'll be fine.*

What she did not say was that what scared her more than traveling alone was going forward with him. She knew that before long it would get dark, and eventually they would stop somewhere to sleep. She knew what a man could do if he wanted to, and that her twiggy strength would be no match for his. The fear was not hypothetical: her older sisters had all been married and gone before Ai was born, but their mother still told the story of how, at the age Ai was now, her eldest daughter had been raped so violently she nearly died from the injury. Seeing the Naxang River, Ai had realized just how far she had traveled in the opposite direction of her brothers. This was her last chance to turn around and catch them.

What am I supposed to tell your parents? the man asked.

Tell them I changed my mind, Ai said. *Tell them I didn't want to come back.*

Fine. He shrugged and handed her the cooking pot. *But I'm not going to give them their money back because I found you already.*

Fine, Ai said. *Tell them when we make it to Thailand we'll come back for them.*

Ai turned around, faced the path up the mountain she had just descended, and began running. She kept her head down, eyes fixed on the dirt path, watching for rocks but more so trying not to see what else might be here with her. In this deserted landscape, which would be worse: to see no one at all, or to see someone appear from the undergrowth? A soldier, a demon lurking in the trees, an ordinary man. In the softer ground on the trail's edge were the footprints of a *tsov liab,* a fearsome wildcat known to be accompanied by ghosts.

Each of these frightening possibilities fueled an even greater fear that pulsed in Ai's head as she ran: what if she did not catch her brothers? She knew that once they reached Muong Cha, they would shell out precious silver to hire a car that would drive them many hours away toward the border. If they left before she got there...That was the unthinkable danger. She would not be able to continue on to Thailand because she did not know the way. Even if she made it over the border, what then? The point was not Thailand; the point was safety. Family was what kept a person safe. If she missed her brothers, she would be alone as never before. The threat propelled her.

For hours she ran up and down craggy slopes, panting, stumbling, walking, then always running again. Her eyes stayed focused on the ground before her, but the edges of her vision increasingly tracked the sun, which was sinking ever lower toward night.

Only once did she stop, at a place whose name translates roughly as "Mountain of Starvation." Long in the past, a family fleeing its own dangers had traveled this way; here was where their bodies were said to have given out, and the group had died from hunger. Ai knew to gather a bouquet of leaves to offer the spirit of the place. Nobody wise would skip this ritual—the pile of greenery grew so continuously that every so often the nearest farmer would have to burn it. Holding her bouquet in the air, Ai spoke a careful request for protection that she had learned from listening to her mother on previous trips. She placed her own bright bundle on top of the wilted leaves of those who had come before, and resumed running.

The sun was heavy on the horizon when at last Ai emerged from the veil of mountains and stumbled into Muong Cha. She had only ever known this to be a crowded, noisy place, more cars and airplanes than she would see in a lifetime back in her village. Today it was nearly empty, most residents having left for Thailand; even the migrants like her had already passed through. Facing the puzzle of dirt roads before her, she knew only which direction she had gone in the past. But what good was that now?

A voice called out to her.

Girl, where are you going? It was an old man. *You're so little. Why are you alone?*

Something about his words—Ai cracked open like an egg. Through sobs she told this stranger how the man from her village had come for her and she had had to leave her brothers but then she had left the man and run the whole way to try to catch her brothers before they drove away, and did he—Grandfather, she called him respectfully—did he know where her brothers were and how she could find them?

And somehow, he did. The old man had spoken with her brothers earlier in the day, when they were asking around for a car. He knew just where they would be—if they hadn't left yet. Pointed Ai up the road and down a side street, told her to hurry. She ran, and right where the old man had said her brothers would be, they were.

Her oldest brother greeted her with a look of confusion, then amazement. Almost in the same breath, the truck that had been hired to take them away pulled up.

Do you realize how lucky you are? her brother said, as the family loaded in. *If you had come just a little later, you could have been lost forever.* Here she was instead, though, squeezing along with the rest onto a bench in the back of the truck, then speeding off down the road, every minute a bit closer to Thailand.

Never in her life had she traveled beyond Muong Cha. Never in her life had she ridden in an automobile. What might have been exciting in a movie felt, in reality, relentless. Motion sickness nauseated her. Wind whipped her ears. For hours they rattled forward into places she had never been, but Ai kept her eyes shut tight the whole time, save for the moments when she had to throw up.

There is a saying in Hmong, *"Ntuj dub ntuj tib txig,"* which translates essentially as "The sky is black." It means that because the sky is dark, no one knows what lies ahead—the future is uncertain. As they rode through the night, the sky above them was black as a hole.

———

At last the truck stopped in Ban Xon. Formerly the operations center for American relief efforts in the region, this vast compound had had a working hospital and warehouses full of rice. Around it had grown a settlement called Na Sou, built by the thousands of refugees who had arrived here after the war forced them from their true homes. Scores of little houses of bamboo and thatch were packed together wherever there was room, some right along the airstrip. When Ai and her brothers arrived, though, the place felt even more vacant than Muong Cha had. In the quiet, her family chose an empty house and tucked inside.

They woke in the morning with no more of a plan than to talk to the other migrants gathered there and determine how to go forward. Without bushwhacking through the jungle for weeks there was really only one way from here to Thailand: west to the country's main highway, south to the capital city of Vientiane and then the Mekong River, on the far banks of which lay Thailand. But between Na Sou and the highway, the only road bottlenecked in a place called Hin Heup, at a narrow bridge over an unswimmably big river. Word had it the military was blocking the bridge; those people who had already moved west from Na Sou were stalled there, unable to cross.

Ai's family stayed where they were, collecting information as it dripped into the encampment. In the capital, anti-American demonstrators were sacking official buildings to drive out any remnants of the USAID workers and the Lao administrators who supported them. "Only by overthrowing these archpirates who have plundered our country can our nation prosper and our people live in peace and happiness," the radio broadcasts boomed. "Each of us must heighten the revolutionary spirit of continuous, all-out attack." There was now a dusk-to-dawn curfew in Vientiane. Soldiers had orders to shoot anyone attempting to cross the Mekong in the dark.

Ai's brothers were days into figuring out how to proceed when a stream of people came into Na Sou traveling in reverse, as if to return to the mountains they had all just left. Hurried and scared, these people told the story that would change everything: How thousands of people had amassed at the bottleneck in Hin Heup, the crowds camped along the road backing up for miles behind the bridge. How those in the very front, thinking their numbers gave them safety, had finally pushed forward against the military barricade. How the soldiers had opened fire on the crowd with machine guns.

On the airwaves, the government told a story of how the migrants had actually attacked the soldiers, who then fought back only in self-defense. While there were no reporters on the scene, in the days that followed, newspapers in Bangkok and New York would publish anodyne accounts with death tolls in the single digits. Those migrants who had been there, however, told their fellow refugees in Na Sou of a massacre: How so many people were shot that the cement underfoot turned red. How the soldiers dumped bodies into the river, where they disappeared beneath the swirling waters. How the living flooded backward on the narrow road, trampling one another in their frightened retreat.

Over decades to come, many Hmong would come to see the event at the Hin Heup bridge as the opening shots in an assault that would last for years. The story would be passed down like a folktale, the horror of it seared into the memories of even those who hadn't been present. It's not that these people were strangers to armed conflict; after decades of war there was hardly a person in Laos who had not experienced violence. But this was different. This was the vested government attacking its unarmed citizens—all the belligerence of the radio broadcasts come to life. Fearing this reality was exactly why tens of thousands of Hmong had suddenly left behind everything they owned and fled for an unknown country. Because of the shooting at Hin Heup, now thousands would flee back to their villages. They did not know that the violence to come would eventually send at least a hundred thousand of them over the border to Thailand, nor that at least fifty thousand more would die before they made it there. At this moment, they thought only of their immediate safety.

Ai's brothers picked up as much information as they could from the people retreating through Na Sou. Ai, at their elbows, listened with horror. She was just eleven years old, thinking she would be one of the few to reach Thailand. Suddenly, it felt as though her choice had nearly led to her death. When Ai's brothers announced that they would all turn around, she grabbed her cooking pot and her basket and ran behind them, now in the direction of home.

At young Ai's eye level, the road out of Na Sou was a sea of people, all stampeding to find a vehicle that could get them out of there. On the edge of town, Ai's group plunged into a traffic jam of frenzied drivers and terrified people squeezing through the cracks between cars, climbing over the truck beds, clambering to charter any vehicle that had not already been taken.

Ai still had the pouch of money her mother had given her. Her brothers used it to win a driver who would bring the group all the way past Muong Cha, to a village where relatives took them in. At dawn the next day they began retracing their steps, walking deeper and deeper into the mountains on trails used by fewer and fewer people. With their back baskets now empty of food, they moved faster than when they had walked in the other direction the week before. Still, the night was deep into darkness by the time they wound up the path that led only to their village.

They went straight to their house. Inside, circled around the fire, were Ai's father, mother, and brother Tong, and when the travelers entered all three jumped to their feet. While everyone in the village would eventually return, Ai and her brothers were the first group to make it back. Later that night, her older brothers would recount the horrors at the bridge and the mad scramble to escape, and the adults would begin to nervously speculate about what terror might come next. But in those first moments there was only the euphoria of reunion.

Ai ran straight to her mother and pressed herself into that familiar bosom. Safe at last, Ai let go all the tears she had had to keep inside since they had left this house a week before. When at last she paused to breathe, she could feel that her mother was crying, too. Every member of the family was. Tears of relief and of anguish. Tears of fear over what had just happened. Tears of joy. *I thought I'd never see you again,* Ai's mother said to the daughter in her arms. And yet here they were, every one of them, together again, just as Ai's father had promised.

In northeast Laos, flat land is the exception, not the rule. The region is part of a larger mountainous zone stretching from northeast India to China's Yangtze River, created over millions of years of tectonic upheaval that crumpled the land into innumerable geological folds. Over time, the syncopated landscape was covered in thick forests and crosshatched by rivers of snowmelt and monsoon rain until there was little smooth, open surface left.

In recent centuries, humans have overwhelmingly chosen to occupy the limited flatlands—the river deltas and coastline, the occasional plateau—so much better were these lands for growing grains, and thus populations, and thus power. But that is not where Ai was born. Her village was more or less invisible to the people in Vientiane, Bangkok, and Hanoi, tucked as it was into a green valley within a bowl of jagged mountain slopes. It was not marked on maps, but the local people knew it was called Sa Na Oua. For Ai, it was a sanctuary.

While some villages would clear a hillside bald, the forest surrounding Sa Na Oua was thick right up to the edge of each house's yard. It began as a small settlement, with just six or eight families living there. Ai's parents had been among the first to arrive, before Ai was born. After building their thatch-roofed house, they surrounded it with a hip-height berm of soil. On top of that they planted trees, to further enclose the home. The trees quickly grew tall enough to act as a wall around the property, but it was never dark within. Each day, sunshine filtered through their leaves to light up the yard around the house.

By local standards Ai's family was wealthy. Livestock was a kind of currency, and her father had more than most men. Even with this advantage, though, the family still spent most of their time growing and gathering food to eat. The livestock was mostly saved for rituals, so Ai's father hunted and fished to put meat in their bowls. Salt, which could only be bought, was a luxury. Cooking oil was all but unheard of. Every summer, the family scrabbled its way through the hungry season, those thin months after last year's rice crop had been eaten but before this year's crop had been harvested.

Despite the family's lean existence, Ai's parents kept a sunny attitude. The time that insects decimated the rice crop, they said, *It's okay. We'll only be hungry for a year.* When Ai's mother accidentally set one of their rice fields on fire, Ai's father consoled her, then together they threshed the charred stalks to get what they could. Always they carried this underlying sense of abundance and ease.

Ai believed the source of their strength was each other. With the exception of her father's time at war, Ai's parents were always together. When her father wanted a hunting companion, instead of bringing his sons, he brought his wife. If Ai's mother had to feed the animals in the morning, her husband would man the hearth and cook the rice for breakfast. It was plain that they loved each other. They didn't kiss or hold hands—no one did—but he never beat her, and in their world that was notable. Indeed, the one time Ai witnessed them quarrel, the whole thing ended in laughter.

Ai had seen how it could be otherwise. There were families whose fathers were addicted to opium and grew so lazy their families were forced to beg for food rather than grow it. Worse, there were kids who had lost their parents. Ai grew up with the story of two cousins of hers, a boy and a girl, who were not even school-age when they lost their mother. Their stepmother, wanting to direct the family's resources toward her biological children, condemned her two stepchildren to live by themselves on the periphery of the family's farmland. Knowing only how to catch crabs but not how to cook them, the young siblings subsisted on the raw meat until the girl died.

The story was chilling, but not altogether unusual. To lose one or both of your parents was to be orphaned, the worst of all fates. In basic terms of economy, people simply did not have any fat around the edges to share with someone outside their own bloodline. It was deeper than that, though. There's a Hmong saying: "Orphans have a lot of lice"—not because they are inherently dirty, but because they are neglected. While being orphaned didn't necessarily mean one would be banished to the wilderness as Ai's cousins had been, it nearly always meant being abandoned on some level—and that was its curse. In this lean landscape, each person's survival depended on the supportive web of family and clan. Being cast out of that larger group meant being consigned to a life of struggle.

From a young age, Ai was aware of her place within the larger group. She understood that her body—anyone's body—was merely a vessel for a soul, and that those souls cycled between worlds: first being born into a body, then passing into the land of the ancestors for some years, until being reborn into a new body. This life of Ai's was just one of many that her soul would live. Knowing this, she understood that her self was not freestanding or paramount—it wasn't the thing her life was meant to serve. Instead, there was an order to things much greater than her or any other individual person. Ai was part of a family, and her family was part of a clan; each group worked as a single organism, both practically and spiritually. The larger and more cohesive the group, the greater its collective prosperity.

Orders within the group came from a clearly established hierarchy: Leading the clan were the elder men, because, as the saying went, "They have eaten more rice, they have seen more things, and they have done more thinking." Within each family, the leader was the father. He was the conduit to the rest of the clan, which provided critical support with rituals and practical help with farming. Equally important, the father was the person who tended to the needs of the ancestors.

This was not an abstract concept. Laid over the "seen world" of the living was an unseen world of spirits that was just as real. When parents or grandparents passed away, they migrated to the land of ancestors but remained present in earthly life, inhabiting the same houses and farmland as the family they had left. Survival for the living depended heavily on protection and fortune granted by this world beyond. In a certain sense, the ancestors were the most powerful tier in the social hierarchy. Because the man of the house was the sole person who communicated with them, he was essential. Without a father, even the most capable people were considered to be orphans.

In the social hierarchy, after the father came the sons, who were valued in large part because they would one day assume the role of caring for their parents in the afterlife. Ai, as a child and a female, was on the bottom of the pile, even lower than her little brother, Tong. From the start, she knew the deal: Unless one was a leader, personal opinions were to be discarded. Hard work was prized. Obedience was vital.

Ai was not afraid to ask for things. She wanted to go to school as her next-oldest brother did, so she could become a teacher herself. But when she asked and her father said no, she did not ask again. Few parents sent their daughters to school, knowing that eventually every girl would be wed into a different clan, at which point any investment that had been made in her education would be lost. Instead, most girls stayed home, and so did Ai. When her mother needed water, Ai placed a bamboo yoke over her shoulders and walked half an hour to fill a set of jugs from a stream. When her father wanted to smoke, she rolled cigarettes for him. When harvesttime came and Ai's mother filled her daughter's child-size back basket with rice to carry down the mountain, Ai shouldered the heavy load without complaint. Indeed, she stayed silent even when her mother then loaded more rice on top of the full basket, in a special sack she had sewn for just this purpose. Only after hours of carrying the load, when Ai could no longer stand the pain, did she speak out that the weight was too much. Only then did her mother lift up Ai's shirt and see that her skin was raw, too painful to touch.

Ai's sisters had similar youths, but by the time Ai was born, they had already moved to their husbands' homes. To fill the gap, Ai's parents had made a practical calculation. Just before their first son left for the army, they had married him to a girl in the village. While the boy was serving General Vang Pao, his wife had remained in Ai's parents' house, where she fed the livestock and cooked the rice and swept the floor.

In time, this girl became a woman with several children and thus a little more stature. As Ai edged toward adolescence, she gradually took the daughter-in-law's place. By the time the war ended, it was Ai who swept the floors and cooked the rice. Ai who fed the livestock.

After the family returned from the aborted trip to Thailand, Ai resumed this role without questioning. In the familiar order of daily life there was safety, and for the time being that was all she wanted. Throughout the summer that followed, the rest of her family would empty out of their house in the village to live at the rice farm for days at a time. At home alone, Ai would hike into the forest to fill her back basket with the leaves and tubers that comprised the bulk of the pigs' diet. When she returned, she would grind corn for them using the family's hulking seesaw mortar. Too light to weigh down the mortar's heavy arm, Ai would put on her basket, fill it with pumpkins, and hang off the long wooden lever until the other end finally raised. When she let go, the arm would slam down into the basin and crack the corn in half. Over and over she went, rising up and slamming down, until the pigs were fed.

She never complained—but then, there was no one to complain

to. At the end of the day, with what energy she had left, Ai made dinner and ate it in silence. As the hearth fire died out and she went to sleep in the empty bed she normally shared with her parents, Ai soothed herself by imagining the day when she would get married. After that, she would never be alone like this again.

———

When Ai's family went to farm in the mountains, it didn't look the way most people today would imagine. In the lowlands of Laos, people grew "wet rice" in flat paddies with standing water—the classic image of rice cultivation from across Asia. But Ai's family and most others who lived in the uplands planted their seed on mountain slopes, in dry soil watered by rain. While both lowland and upland farmers relied on rice for most of their calories, the different ways of farming represented separate strata within the social hierarchy: generally speaking, the higher in elevation a group lived, the lower its status. Ai's family and other Hmong like them lived nearly in the clouds.

The disparity between the two growing systems and the social classes they supported was rooted in ecology. The rice paddies dominating the lowlands had a unique microbiome in their wet soil that allowed farmers to plant on the same plots year after year without having to rotate in other crops to renew the soil's fertility. As a result, wet rice produced a stunning amount of grain on a small amount of land. The trade-off was that building and operating the systems to collect, store, and deliver water for paddies required a great deal of labor. But then, because wet rice made so much food, it was able to support the workforce. Over centuries, the proliferation of the wet rice system was self-perpetuating—enabling large, concentrated populations and at the same time necessitating them. Beginning two thousand years ago, wet rice gradually blanketed the lowlands of Southeast Asia and underwrote the creation and expansion of the societies that ruled them: first the kingdoms, then the states, then the nations like Laos.

If wet rice was defined by its abundance, the rice that Ai's family grew was defined by its resilience, born out of an adaptation to scarcity. The mountains lacked the flat land necessary for wet rice paddies. To clear land, upland farmers would cut down trees from the slopes and burn away the remnants of forest. The seed they planted was nourished by only what nutrients lay in the soil, and what rain fell from the sky. This "dry rice" yielded much less. But it also took less work, leaving more time for growing other crops, hunting, and foraging. The resulting food system was extraordinarily diverse; if one food failed, there was nearly always something else to eat.

However, because the dry upland soils quickly lost their fertility, farmers had to clear new fields every few years—which meant the system required far more land than the concentrated wet rice paddies did. So while lowland states steadily multiplied their populations and expanded laterally, upland people were forever segmented into smaller, often itinerant, clans, which couldn't coalesce into a counterweight to empire. As lowland states grew in size and power, overall the non-state people in the uplands grew proportionally weaker. It was because of this imbalance of power that Ai and other Hmong ended up in the highest reaches of Laos, and on the lowest rungs of society.

When the Hmong first enter written history, it is in the chronicles of the largest wet rice state in history, imperial China. Originally, the empire had been built on millet, the grain best suited to the arid plains where it began. But it was when the Han expanded into the rice lands of the Yangtze River Valley and southward, beginning in the T'ang dynasty, that they became a dominant regional power. As a tax base, wet rice underwrote the empire's massive bureaucracy and its opulent court life. As a food, wet rice enabled vast population growth and fed the armies that seized ever more territory.

Ai's forebears first appear not as part of the expanding state, but rather as people who had occupied these southlands for millennia before the empire came to claim them. Linguists trace Hmong back through their ancestral language, proto Miao-Yao, to around 300

BCE. At this time, their ancestors were living in the southern half of what is now China. Hmong oral tradition fills out the picture, telling of an original Hmong kingdom that was as sophisticated as any other. Led by a benevolent king, this society had wise men who interpreted the world through a complex cosmology, and a script that allowed them to write it all down.

But the stories go on to tell of how the Hmong king was ultimately vanquished by the conquering Han empire. The kingdom was lost, as was the written language. The people fled. Their downfall followed a pattern that repeated over time as imperial China expanded its territory: When the Han armies arrived, the ancestors of the Hmong and other people outside the state faced a choice between two bad options. They could join the advancing power and live by its rules: pay the taxes, perform forced labor, drop their beliefs, and assimilate to the dominant culture and religion. Or they could leave, moving onto lands the state didn't want—land that was undesirable precisely because it was less productive for farming. Over centuries, Ai's ancestors were repeatedly pushed south in latitude and up in elevation, their settlements scattered across the territory of imperial China like drops of water. *Ntsuag teb ntsuag chaw,* they called themselves. "Orphans of country."

By the seventeenth century, Hmong and other Miao-Yao people had settled in the flinty frontier lands of Yunnan and Guizhou, in far southern China. There they lived on lands so undesirable and so far away from the empire's center of power that they could exist relatively undisturbed. This began to change in the late eighteenth century, when the British and other Europeans gradually encroached from the south. Threatened by these prospecting nations, the Han state appraised the southern frontier with new urgency in the early nineteenth century. Using a strategy that calls to mind the U.S. government's conquest of Native American land, Han settlers were sent in to homestead the brittle lands and thus claim them for the empire.

The Hmong and others who already lived there tried to defend their lands, but the Han state buttressed its expansion with ruthless military force. As had happened so many times before, Hmong responded by moving south and west, across the mountains into the highlands of what would later be called Vietnam and Laos; by the early 1900s, some had migrated as far as northwest Siam, or Thailand. Within this new landscape, Hmong mostly ended up in the highest reaches, where often it was too cold to grow rice. In order to plant a crop, they had to travel down the mountain to farmland that was hours, perhaps days, away from home. And while their migration succeeded in putting them beyond the reach of imperial China, ultimately it only subjected them to a different lowland ruler.

Shortly after the waves of Hmong began arriving from southern China in the mid-1800s, the French began colonizing what they called *Indochine,* a region that ran from the Mekong Delta north to the border of China. They saw little intrinsic value in the mountainous, landlocked space in the middle, soon to be known as Laos. However, because it was geographically strategic—as a bulwark against Siam to the west, as a possible pathway to the ultimate prize of China—the French claimed the space as well. In the early 1900s, they built the *routes coloniales,* roads that connected Laos's royal and administrative capitals, Luang Prabang and Vientiane, with colonial hubs along the coast. In many ways, these roads would change the course of Hmong history.

The *routes coloniales* ran over old trade routes through the northern mountains, where the majority of Hmong in Laos had entered from Vietnam and then stopped and settled. They had chosen this place in part for its seclusion, but now the roads brought the colonial state right to their doors. The French forced Hmong men to do the backbreaking, unpaid work of building more roads—*ua qhev,* the men called it, "slave labor." At the same time, the Hmong's primary cash crop, opium, was taxed heavily, and doubly so: first by the French, then by the Lao bureaucrats who mercilessly administered colonial rule. If one could not pay, there was prison, possibly death. Family stories tell of parents forced to sell a child in order to meet the tax collectors' demands.

Hmong oral tradition speaks of a day when the Heavens will decree that Hmong have a mandate to rule themselves again. The celestial kings will vest their powers in an earthly prophet. Following this powerful leader, the Hmong people will finally restore the kingdom they lost so long ago. As Hmong in Vietnam and Laos suffered under French colonial rule, several times the prophecy seemed to be coming true: a leader believed to be divine would lead the Hmong in challenging their oppressors, and for a period they would triumph.

Inevitably, each new uprising was brutally defeated. But out of the crucible of their discontent, Hmong in Laos began to forge a more earthly path toward power. In the first years of the twentieth century, Hmong began building a political identity within the colonial state. By World War II, the Hmong political class had grown its power so much that it had split, along clan lines, into rival factions that vied against each other for government positions.

When World War II ended, almost immediately a new war began in Indochina: the restored French colonialists now fighting against the communist Viet Minh and their offshoot in Laos, soon to be known as the Pathet Lao. In Laos, a central theater for what has been called the First Indochina War was in the mountains where northwest Vietnam met northeast Laos—right where the majority of Hmong in the two countries were settled. Suddenly, to both the French and the communists, the Hmong in these mountains were seen as valuable assets. Both sides scrambled to win them over.

What most written histories fail to mention is that at the same time, Hmong in Laos were making their own calculations. Each of the rival Hmong political factions sought greater power for itself by banding with a larger entity: one stuck with the French; the other backed the communists. These alliances would hold fast through thirty years of nearly continuous bloodshed, up through the war that forced Ai to flee Sa Na Oua—and ultimately Laos—for good.

When the Viet Minh won the war in 1954 and the Geneva Accords were written, France agreed to relinquish its claim to Indochina, and Laos became a newly independent nation. From the start, the right and left jockeyed for control. For years already, the American government had been meddling in the region's power struggles, supporting first the Viet Minh and then the French. Now, under President Eisenhower, the United States would become the central benefactor of the right-aligned Royal Lao Government.

Like the French, the Americans held little material interest in the nation itself. Laos had fewer than three million people and was only slightly larger than Utah, but because it ran like a line up the center of Indochina, Eisenhower is said to have considered it the region's most strategically important country—"the key to all Southeast Asia." He predicted that if communists won Laos, adjacent countries would fall like dominoes: South Vietnam and Cambodia, then Thailand; perhaps the Philippines and Taiwan. Worst-case scenario: India.

During the 1950s, the American government tried from many angles to turn Laos rightward, using military funding and political intervention, infrastructure development, and humanitarian aid. But after the communist influence proved too strong for the Americans to overcome, they pivoted toward a next-best approach: the United States helped engineer a new Geneva conference, whose agreements, when finalized in 1962, established a coalition government and reinforced Laos's designation as a neutral nation; all foreign military was to be withdrawn.

Similar provisions had been signed into agreement in 1954, at the end of the First Indochina War. North Vietnam had largely ignored them then, and now they did the same. The North Vietnamese Army had had soldiers on the ground in Laos since the beginning of 1960, and there they would remain for more than a quarter century. The United States, however, wanting to at least appear to take the diplomatic high ground, found a work-around: conducting their battles not with American troops but with native-born soldiers. Chief among them were the Hmong.

The man who led these soldiers was Vang Pao. He was a bold, brave army major, still in his early thirties when the Americans first contacted him but fast on his way to becoming the leader of the right-aligned Hmong in Laos. During the First Indochina War, he had fought for the colonial government in the country's northeast. After the French lost and left, he had kept fighting the Pathet Lao and then the North Vietnamese Army troops that came to back them up. On their own, Vang Pao's soldiers were no match for the communists. Not only did the enemy have exponentially more fighters on the ground, but they had better weapons, communications, and training, thanks largely to the patronage of the Soviet Union. If Vang Pao was going to win—and he never had any other intention—he needed backing of his own.

History books in the United States recount how the Americans were thrilled to discover and enlist this sharp, bullish "hill tribe" leader. Vang Pao's main CIA contact, Bill Lair, famously called him "a miniature Genghis Khan." Told from the Hmong perspective, though, Vang Pao saw in the Americans a means to his own desired end. With American aircraft, weapons, training, and seemingly unlimited money, Vang Pao could wage the war he envisioned. At the meeting that solidified his partnership with the United States, he promised to produce ten thousand men to fight. Fueled by the CIA's military machine, he believed he would finally be victorious.

———

In 1964, the year Ai was born, the U.S. Air Force began bombing Laos. Their strategic goals were straightforward: In the east, ravage the Ho Chi Minh Trail, which North Vietnam used to funnel soldiers and materiel to South Vietnam. In the northeast, tie up the North Vietnamese Army so they would have fewer troops and resources for the fighting in their own country. Over the course of the war, American planes would strike Laos in what averaged out to a planeload of ordnance every eight minutes, twenty-four hours a day, for nine years—the most bombing per capita in history, greater even than what befell Japan and Germany in World War II.

The United States government did it all covertly. Laos was still technically neutral, and foreign troops were prohibited. So the Department of Defense used USAID to quietly underwrite the Royal Lao Army, under the 1962 Geneva conference agreement's provision allowing material assistance "necessary for the national defence of Laos." At the same time, the CIA equipped, trained, and paid General Vang Pao's "irregular" army of mostly Hmong soldiers. These ground troops worked in conjunction with the bomber pilots, which included both Hmong and other Lao-born pilots flying within Laos, and clandestine American pilots flying in and out of Thailand. For the hidden nature of the United States' involvement, Americans would come to call this the Secret War. To people in Laos, however, the fighting and its violence were painfully manifest.

It must be said that while the arrangement satisfied the Geneva conference agreement's prohibition of foreign troops, it was also just less expensive for the U.S. government: using Hmong and other Lao-born fighters meant no lifetime veterans' benefits, no sending them to college after the war. While the lowest-ranking American soldiers in Vietnam were paid $78 a month, Vang Pao's ground soldiers would take just $3 or $14 or $30—whatever the general decided to pay them—and still do more or less the same work, from armed combat and intelligence gathering to directing air strikes. Using "irregular" troops was also cheaper in terms of political cost: while in Vietnam the sons and daughters of American citizens were dying, in Laos the casualties were people who few in the United States knew or cared about. When one American pilot went down in enemy territory, ten of Vang Pao's men were sent to rescue him.

The Western media regularly portrayed Vang Pao's soldiers as mercenaries, but in doing so they misunderstood why Hmong went to battle. The average Hmong family was not motivated by a desire for the money soldiers were paid. At the same time, most had little interest in the larger geopolitical battles taking place in their midst. What mattered to them—what could galvanize them into action—was protecting their homes. It was a matter of livelihood: like 85 percent of the people in Laos, the vast majority of Hmong were subsistence-level rice farmers. If they lost their land they would not be able to feed their families. It was the most essential reason that General Vang Pao and his soldiers had been fighting the communist incursion for years already before the Americans arrived.

When the North Vietnamese Army entered Laos in 1960, they did so on the *routes coloniales* the French had built over the mountains from northern Vietnam to northeast Laos. With their arrival, more and more Hmong who lived in the region were drawn into the now transnational conflict by virtue of location. When the Vietnamese coming from the east gained territory, that territory was commonly Hmong villages and farmland; again and again, it was their possessions that were ransacked, their homes that were burned, their loved ones who were killed. Each time the army advanced, Hmong families faced a choice that echoed their long history of dispossession and dislocation in China: they could submit to the invaders, they could fight, or they could leave. As the USAID mission that organized relief for internal refugees explained, "Entire villages were evacuated in what was to become a slow, 15-year withdrawal to the south." By war's end, six hundred thousand people in the northeast had been displaced from their homes.

It is true that some Hmong men did enlist with Vang Pao's army for the rare opportunity to receive cash wages. Others joined out of sheer devotion to the cause. However, likely a far greater number would have preferred to stay out of the war altogether. Indeed, had the conflict not come to them, most Hmong might have never taken sides, much less sent their fathers and sons to battle. Each time a Hmong man left for the army, his family was deprived of critical manpower that was needed on the farm.

Knowing this, Vang Pao instituted an unofficial draft. Sending word through village chiefs and recruiters, he let it be known that each family was required to send one man to his army. Rich families could hire a man to fight for them or bribe the officials in charge. But poor families, which were the vast majority, had virtually no way around the sacrifice. If they stayed neutral, they would be suspected of sympathizing with the communists.

By the time Ai was born in 1964, the North Vietnamese Army had advanced steadily along the *routes coloniales,* capturing territory deep into northeast Laos. The fighting now centered on a roughly ten-mile-wide plateau called the Plain of Jars. As the largest flat area in northern Laos and a major intersection of the French-built highways, it was a strategic prize that both sides hungered to win; indeed, the front lines for Vang Pao's army would pulse back and forth across this region essentially until the war ended in 1973.

Ai's village was roughly thirty miles from the plateau, in the folds of earth extending out from Laos's highest mountain, Phou Bia. The rough terrain there was all but impenetrable, and for most of the first decade of Ai's life the region was untouched by active combat. Still, when she was not yet one, her father had no choice but to join Vang Pao's army.

Ai was too young to remember this herself, but years later her mother told her a story about that time. Without her husband, Ai's mother was left to feed the family by herself. She had two adolescent boys, a toddler, and an infant, all hungry. When the previous year's rice ran out, she rolled baby Ai against her chest, took her toddler by the hand, and hiked to the farm, where there was at least the first of the corn to eat. That night, Ai's mother lay down with her babies to sleep in the farm's little hut. In the dark, she heard an unfamiliar noise—then felt the bamboo sleeping platform sink down. The intruder was not a human but a tiger, front paws pressed on the edge of the bed. Ai's mother grabbed her machete, roared up to her knees, and struck at the beast with the sharpened blade. Somehow, she won. The tiger disappeared into the darkness.

After that, Ai's father quit the army and headed home. The family was not absolved of its obligation, however. To take his place in the war, Ai's father sent their oldest son, who was thirteen years old. His job would be to help protect Road 7, the old *route coloniale* to Vinh and, beyond that, Saigon to the south and Hanoi to the north. Not yet strong enough to carry his M16, the boy dragged it behind him into battle.

Almost three years later, in 1968, the family's next-oldest son joined his brother in the army. He was thirteen as well. Young Ai watched her mother agonize over her sons' safety. More than once, her mother talked her way onto a military airplane and rode to Vang Pao's headquarters at Long Cheng, just to try to reach her sons by telephone. Back at home, Ai's mother stopped sewing; following the belief that using sharp tools could put a loved one at war in harm's way, she would not risk using a needle.

Things like this signaled to Ai that something was not normal in her life. And yet life during war was all she had ever known; in a sense, it *was* normal. There was a fort across the valley, and her young ears were accustomed to the noise of artillery rounds being fired in the distance—the sound of killing, her mother told her. Because it was believed that any attack would come early in the morning, Ai knew to sleep fully clothed, so she would be ready to run.

When Ai was seven years old, the North Vietnamese Army had gained so much ground in Laos that it captured the fort across the valley from Sa Na Oua. Ai's family and their neighbors were ordered to abandon the village and relocate to an internal refugee camp several days' walk away. Her brother Tong rode on top of the family's ox, and when Ai got tired, her mother suggested she hold on to its tail for support. Walking like this, away from her family's home and into an unknown land, Ai understood for the first time that the world around her was not as it had always been. None of this was normal. They were in the middle of a war.

But still Ai was not afraid. The simple reason: she had her parents. They had always protected her, always given her anything they had. If they had meat, she got some, too. If she went hungry, it was because no one had food. Even now, as they left their home and all that was familiar, her parents were right beside her. Ai trusted that as long as she stayed with them, she would be safe. Because of that, there was nothing to fear.

———

Those Hmong who were fighting under General Vang Pao might have been disillusioned to hear their American allies behind closed doors. From the start, the Americans predicted that their army of "irregulars" would lose to the North Vietnamese. When the CIA first decided to support Vang Pao, they did so with the understanding internally that probably the best they could ultimately offer the Hmong in the northeast would be to relocate them to the northwest, closer to Thailand. By the early 1970s, actually winning rightist control of Laos was a bygone priority of the Eisenhower administration. To the Johnson and then Nixon administrations, U.S. involvement in Laos was merely a means to fight the war in Vietnam.

Still, General Vang Pao fought with unrelenting conviction. At the war's height in 1968 and 1969, he had forty thousand men enlisted, plus an uncounted number of women who served as nurses and other noncombat support. Reinforced by colossal American airpower, his ground troops were able to hold the North Vietnamese to largely the same battle lines in the northeast for ten years. The price was bodies, mostly Hmong. "By 1971," a classified U.S. Air Force report noted, "many families were down to the last surviving male (who was often a youth of 13 or 14)." Despite the casualties, General Vang Pao continued to recruit.

In 1971, half a million people marched on Washington, DC, to protest American involvement in the wars in Vietnam, Cambodia, and, for those who were aware of it, Laos. As the federal government began drawing down forces and looking for an exit, the air support that had enabled Vang Pao's army dwindled. The North Vietnamese advanced deeper into northeast Laos.

Many Hmong had grown skeptical of the war. For years now, combat had robbed them of their fathers and increasingly their sons, leaving some villages shrunken down to just orphans and widows. Had they stopped fighting, it would have been understandable. But the reality was that they were no closer to winning back the lands from which the war had displaced them. Across the northeast, Hmong were still being relocated as refugees, thousands at a time. What's more, General Vang Pao was still fighting. *If we die, we die together.* That's what his soldiers remember him saying. *Nobody gets left behind.* Despite all they had lost, Hmong continued to follow him into battle.

Ultimately, though, it was the Americans and the North Vietnamese who ran the show. The two governments had begun secret talks in 1970 and continued to negotiate until calling a cease-fire in January 1973. One month later, the Royal Lao Government signed a cease-fire and power-sharing agreement with the communist Pathet Lao. The Americans took the opportunity to discontinue military aid and quietly begin extracting themselves from Laos. But the North Vietnamese supporting the Pathet Lao did not. Their army continued to gain ground through military campaigns while the Pathet Lao quickly drained the Royal Lao Government of what power it had left.

General Vang Pao stood his ground, trying to hold back the communists from taking over Laos. Even as his army was rolled into the dysfunctional and barely funded Royal Lao Army, and even as the battles became increasingly futile, he refused to give up his defensive positions. He persisted for two years after the cease-fire, until finally the Americans sent the message that it was time to stop. In May 1975, after fighting for more than twenty years, General Vang Pao was forced to recognize that the war had been lost.

The price had been great all around. Roughly one-quarter of Laos's population—776,000 people—had been uprooted by the fighting and now lived elsewhere in the country; four out of five of those displaced people had originated in the northeast. In a nation of just three million people, two hundred thousand had died. Among the dead were thirty thousand Hmong who fought under General Vang Pao, and an uncounted number of Hmong civilians lost to warfare and disease. In the decades to come, the unexploded ordnance left behind from the Americans' bombing campaigns would kill tens of thousands more people.

On May 14, 1975, General Vang Pao escaped to Thailand. In the following weeks, Ai and her family ran for the border, too. By the first days of June they were back in Sa Na Oua, planting rice. There at home, they tried their best to return to normal—what else could they do? At the backs of their minds, though, they were bracing for what would come next.

The end of the war in Laos began a time of hunger and fear. Without American aid to prop up the economy and deliver food rations, this nation of farmers struggled to feed itself. In places where masses of refugees had been resettled, farmland was exhausted; elsewhere, fields were mined with unexploded ordnance from the U.S. Air Force's bombing campaigns. With most oxen and buffalo long since dead, in some places men had to pull the plows themselves. The central government responded with attempts at collectivization, which only exacerbated the challenges.

The communist leaders' response was, "The people must understand." They promised that in a decade's time, the wounds of war would be healed, the nation would be self-sufficient in rice, and the work of converting the country's abundant natural resources into a thriving export-oriented economy would have begun. They said the real problem was the lackeys of U.S. imperialism, who were already plotting against the new nation. In newspapers and on the radio, government spokespeople offered amnesty to their former enemies, inviting them to help bring lasting peace to the nation.

In truth, the government was intent on eradicating all dissent. Even as the talking heads offered "splendid treatment" to Hmong who had previously served Vang Pao, the armed forces were rounding up those same men and shipping them to prison camps. The stated purpose was to reeducate former rightists about the new communist model, but the means for teaching were unforgiving: forced labor, torture, starvation. Roughly forty thousand people were sent for reeducation of some kind; ten to fifteen thousand of them endured the prison camps for up to fifteen years. Many others, including the king of Laos, were never seen again.

Somehow, Sa Na Oua seemed to be insulated against the suffering and the terror. When Ai's family returned to the farm, the land was as rich as it had ever been. When far-reaching droughts parched much of the country in 1977, Ai's household still managed to grow a decent crop. And while countless other villages had been raided by the communists and had their young men stolen away to prison camps, no soldiers ever hiked all the way up to Sa Na Oua. Life proceeded as it always had. And yet any sense of normalcy was crippled by the feeling that it would not last.

Some Hmong rooted themselves in the faith that General Vang Pao was in a war room in Thailand, plotting for when he and the Americans would storm back across the skies. Indeed, the faith that people invested in the possibility of his return echoed the hope many drew from the character in Hmong stories known as the king. This recurring hero of the folktales was a divine incarnation of the original king of the original Hmong kingdom. In story after story, he is sent to earth to deliver the people to freedom; as a theme, the repetition of his return acts as a sort of promise that it will happen again, in the present. All over northeastern Laos, Hmong people believed Vang Pao would return to liberate them now.

And yet the ground truth: the general was gone. While the people of Sa Na Oua and others like them were back at home in the same place as they had always been, life felt fragile in a new way. Without their father Vang Pao, they were orphans, all of them at once.

It was a good time for the elders to draw on an alternate set of stories to tell their children around the hearth fire. These concerned a different kind of hero—one for the meantime. His name is Ntsuag, "orphan." In some stories his parents have died; other times they have cast him out. Sometimes his mother is alive but he is considered an orphan because he has no father. Always, though, the character Ntsuag is defined by being alone and homeless in a harsh landscape, forced to survive on his own. The poorest of the poor. More than one scholar has suggested that Ntsuag is a metaphor for the Hmong, these people who have identified themselves as "orphans of country."

But Ntsuag is not a hero for being a victim; he is a hero for being an underdog. While his challenges vary widely, from wicked kings to magical tricksters, his trajectory is unchanging: Through some combination of hard work, obedience, and cunning, Ntsuag overcomes his desolation and poverty. He gains wealth. He acquires farmland. He secures a wife. With this partnership, he restarts his lineage, rebuilding that essential web of family and the survival it enables. In each story, he goes from powerless to empowered, from the margins to the center. If Ntsuag were a rice plant, he would be the one that persevered through the hail and the heat and the terrible drought. On the other side of those tragedies, his heroic seed would multiply and lay the foundation for stronger, more resilient offspring.

In the months after the war officially ended, Ai's parents were both alive. Already, though, Ai seemed to carry the spirit of Ntsuag in her. That autumn, she decided she wanted her own farm. She had been watching people in the village growing crops to sell in addition to the crops they ate. She saw their money and wanted her own. Her parents told her she didn't need her own—she was eleven years old—but she stood her ground. It wasn't that she wanted to buy anything in particular. She wanted the money itself, and the respect that came with it.

What girl has her own farm? her parents said. And besides, she was too small.

I've got two hands and two feet just like everybody else, Ai told them.

I'll do it slowly, little by little. Watch me. She pleaded and cried until they gave in and helped her find a steep hill that no one else was using. Ai cleared it of trees that were as thick as her skinny legs. She hoed the ground and picked out the rocks. And toward the end of the wet season, when the time was right, she planted: opium.

The poppies rose up and blossomed. When the petals fell away, she scored their green seed heads, scraped up the tar-like sap, and amassed it into a sticky ball of pure, smokable narcotic. Ai gave the harvest to her father to sell to the addicts in the village, with instructions that she wouldn't accept paper bills, only silver coins and bars. With some of the profits she had her father buy precious salt, which she then shared with her family. She bought herself her first pair of real shoes. The rest of the silver she had her father bury, for a time in the future when she might need it.

————

In June 1977, exactly two years after Ai and her brothers returned from Thailand, Ai's aunt visited her with a secret. The rice had been planted and the family was back at home, Ai's mother in one corner of the house and the visiting aunt in another. Because Ai was hard-working, this aunt had always treated her fondly. Now she called out that her scalp had a strange itch and loudly asked Ai to come examine it. Ai obliged, and while bent over the woman's head, she heard her aunt whisper, *You're going to be married.*

The aunt explained that Ai's parents had arranged for her to marry Ai's mother's brother's son. Ai was stunned. It was not un-usual to marry a relative. In fact, it was considered a safe bet: while marriage would transfer a girl to a different clan, marrying a cousin would keep her within the protective circle of family. What appalled Ai was that this particular cousin was old enough to be a grand-father. He wasn't, however, because neither of his two current wives had been able to bear children. Ai, his third wife—his thirteen-year-old wife—was imagined as the solution.

Ai rushed to her mother. *How could you do that to me, Mom? He's so old!*

It was your father's idea. That was all her mother said, but Ai understood. She had not had any say in the matter either.

It's your life, the aunt said to Ai. *I'm telling you because you should be the one to choose your husband.*

The aunt explained that once the rice had been harvested, the man's clan would come to collect Ai. This meant that she had a few months to save herself. They both knew Ai would not be able to plead her way out of the planned marriage; once men made an agreement like that, it was irrevocable. The sole way out was for Ai to marry someone else first.

Ai had only recently become interested in boys. There was no time during the day for courting—the endless work of farming consumed a girl's daylight hours. Instead, after dark, a boy would go to a girl's house, position himself outside where she would be sleeping, and whisper to her through the woven bamboo walls. But Ai was always bone-tired by nighttime, and she went to bed knowing she would have to rise at dawn. When a boy stood outside her wall, she was usually already asleep. If she ignored his calls, he might jab a stick through the bamboo slats to see if he could rouse her that way; she learned to crawl to the far side of the bed to avoid being poked. If he persisted, Ai would usually tell him to go home. If he insisted on staying, she often dozed off during the conversation. She had her own bed now, but when her parents were at the farm she would sleep in their bed to avoid the nuisance altogether.

Still, Ai understood that if she was going to find a husband her age, this was how it would happen. And while her interest in boys was still new, already some had drawn her attention.

Every so often the voice outside her house was that of Chou Lor, a sixteen-year-old whose family had moved to Sa Na Oua after the war. With a heavy brow and mostly expressionless face, he was handsome in a basic way. He spent most nights courting, often ranging out to other villages, but despite his efforts he was far from slick. Even as he showed up specifically to talk to Ai, he spoke little, mostly repeating the same topics from night to night. *What did you do at the farm today? Does your rice field have a lot of weeds? What did you eat for lunch?*

Rice, she would answer sleepily.

Then one night he whispered, *I tried to marry a couple of other girls but they won't marry me. So, do you want to marry me?*

Are you joking, Ai whispered back, *or are you serious?*

I'm serious.

Okay, she replied, thinking of the old man who was waiting for her. *Sure, let's get married.*

———

Ai's parents had had an exciting engagement. Forbidden to wed, one night the young lovers had snuck into his bed and remained there as his family awoke in the morning, intentionally getting caught so their union would be unavoidable. But they were special. For most people in a village like Sa Na Oua, marriage was less an act of love and more a practical arrangement between families. The betrothal could take various forms, but in Ai's case it was as perfunctory as the proposal had been: Chou Lor asked his father for permission, and in granting it, his father chose an auspicious date to begin the procedure.

When that day came, various ceremonies would be performed to transfer Ai out of her clan of birth, Moua, and into her husband's clan, Khang. When complete, her husband's parents would take the place of her birth parents, and Chou Lor's ancestors would become hers. The children Ai bore would be vessels for the rebirth of Khang ancestors' souls. When she died, the living members of the clan would feed her soul and make sure she was not forgotten.

But until the day the wedding began, Ai's parents would know nothing of her clandestine engagement—they thought *they* were keeping a secret from *her*. So once Ai learned the date that Chou Lor's father had chosen, she alone bore the agony of the marriage equation's second half: being dismissed from her father's clan would mean she was no longer part of the family. Daily events became bloated with despair. *These are the last times I'll eat with them at this table,* she thought during meals. *These are the last times I'll cook rice in this pot.* She would still live in the same village as they, but the severance was nonnegotiable. Once the offerings were made, there would be no grace period for second thoughts. Should Ai come to the Moua family house on the verge of death, her birth parents would let her die in the dirt yard rather than risk the curse of letting someone from outside the clan perish under their roof. As she counted down the days, she would sneak away from her house to wail and grieve and wish she had been born a boy.

When the appointed day came, Ai snuck away from her house for the last time and entered Chou Lor's house for the first. Had Ai thought about it in advance, she would have considered that the Khang clan was small, and that fewer families in turn meant less wealth, especially compared with her own dominant Moua clan. Whereas her family's house was big and filled with people, surrounded by livestock, Chou Lor's house was dark and empty, the air filled with loss. There had been nine children in all. The oldest girl had died of illness during the war, the next had been lost to a land mine. The oldest son had died in combat. One after another they had passed away or been married off, until now the only people who lived here were her new husband and his parents—Ai's new parents.

The father was an opium addict, happy and talkative after he smoked, a tyrant during withdrawal. He ruled his dominion without tolerance for dissent, enforcing his law with a violent hand. The mother turned her grief for all the lost children into verbal abuse, scorning her remaining son for, in her words, being dumb as a pestle. She had had her own plans for Chou Lor to marry her brother's daughter. Chou Lor's father had rejected the idea, arguing that that

particular clan did not produce enough boy children, but his mother
was still attached to the idea. As soon as Ai arrived, she could feel
that her new mother did not want her.

Nonetheless, the rituals proceeded and by dusk Ai had been
made part of the Khang clan. That night, Ai went to bed on a bamboo platform beside her new husband. Chou Lor had instructed her
that she would not lie on the side against the wall, he would—he
didn't want to be disturbed if she got up in the night, or when she
rose first to start a fire in the morning. Instead, Ai lay on the exposed
side of the bed, facing away from him, terrified. She had never been
touched by a man. She had not begun menstruation. She didn't
really even know what sex entailed or how it worked. That first
night, when Chou Lor whispered to the back of her head, asking
permission to put his hands on her, Ai quickly said no. *Okay, then,* he
replied. *I'll just wait.* For hours she lay awake on her side, careful not
to relax onto her back, eyes looking toward the door.

That same night, envoys from the Khang clan notified Ai's parents
of the marriage, and the two families agreed to complete the ceremony three days later, as was customary. Their house was only fifty
yards away from Chou Lor's, but Ai stayed out of sight, certain that
her father would be furious about the shame she had brought to him
by undermining the engagement he had arranged. And yet, when she
arrived on her parents' doorstep three days later, her father simply
began crying. Her mother's tears had begun even before she arrived.

Ai was overcome with regret. She had laid the plans for the rest
of her life using only her judgment as a thirteen-year-old girl. Indeed, one of the reasons parents arranged marriages was to employ
their adult wisdom and prudence in making that eternal choice. At
the same time, her father's approach still didn't make sense. The man
to whom he would have married Ai was easily thirty years older
than her, and would probably die while she was still young. What
future was that, to be a lowly third wife for the start of your life and
a poor widow for the rest?

Through tears, Ai asked her father, *Why?*

He explained. When he and Ai's mother fell in love, Ai's mother's mother forbade their marriage. After they defied her and wed, she went beyond the ritual separation and disowned her daughter. A cold distance settled between the two families. But when the old woman died, the division died with her. Ai's mother's brother sought to reunite the households through marriage.

Yes, Ai's father knew that this meant marrying his thirteen-year-old daughter to a much older man. He knew that the two senior wives would make her life hell. But the marriage was about something more than Ai: it was a means of fortifying the larger group. Ai's mother's brother had envisioned it as a way to pay back his sister for all the years their own mother had stood between them. All the love he had been prevented from giving to her, he would now give to Ai, as his daughter-in-law. Ai's father felt he could not reject this effort to reunite the family. Further, he saw it as a way to protect his daughter: Ai would inevitably leave his household when she got married. This way, though, she would stay within his circle.

Ai's father was a calm and reasonable man—for this he was a leader in the clan. After explaining his own predicament, he told Ai he understood that she didn't choose to marry in secret in order to disrespect him. *I did what I did because I didn't have a choice,* he told her. *But this is your life, and you had to make the decision that was right for you. If you think this is the best choice, then I support you.*

Of course it was not the best choice—there were no good choices. But because a choice had been made, the rituals were performed and fate was sealed. Ai's parents gave their daughter a gift: two silver bars, to be saved for her funeral, when the money would buy a cow on their behalf to feed her in the afterlife. Chou Lor's father paid her parents a bride-price, a standard sort of insurance policy to ensure that he and his family would love and take care of Ai. At last, following her new father, Ai walked away from her birth parents and her siblings and the house where she had been born. By dark, she was back in the grim Khang house, lying beside her new husband, stiff with fear and remorse. Years later, Ai and her girlfriends would nod ruefully and agree: getting married is the saddest day of your life.

———

With the wedding, Ai was renamed again. People stopped using her given name and instead called her *Niam Chou Lor*—"Chou Lor's wife."

This new life was not what she had imagined it would be during all those nights spent alone in her parents' house. Her new husband quickly turned cold and began to ridicule her. One day, Ai asked him to accompany her to the farm in the dark early morning, saying she was scared to go by herself.

Oh, don't worry, he said. *You're so ugly a tiger wouldn't waste its time eating you.*

The next day she asked again, but he was no more kind. *If a tiger mauls you,* he said, *I'll make sure to come get your body.*

Chou Lor found a girlfriend and began sneaking off with her. Alone at the farm, Ai would tweak her skin until it bruised and turned black. Already she knew that she did not want to be married to this boy, but she also knew marriage was a commitment involving entire clans; the group was not designed to accommodate the individual unhappiness of a union gone sour. Divorce was not really an option. Ending a marriage would sever a woman from her husband's clan, and to be without a clan was to be spiritually homeless—in some sense, a fate worse than death. So instead of trying to leave their husbands, many women chose actual death.

Already at thirteen years old, Ai knew this. Her aunt had committed suicide. So had Chou Lor's sister. Indeed, in this very house, the wife of one of Chou Lor's brothers had killed herself years before. But the one that really stuck with Ai was her older sister Ka Yang. She had endured her husband's beatings until they became unbearable, then overdosed herself with opium. For the funeral, Ka Yang's body had been laid out in the house, and relatives had taken their proper turns mourning her. For an entire day, Ai's mother wailed to her daughter's corpse. Her grief was so thick that she did not notice when Ka Yang's baby daughter crawled onto the body, nor when the baby dug into the clothing that lay over her dead mother's chest and rooted into her breast to nurse. To try.

Ai had been too young to have a memory of this day—she couldn't even remember what Ka Yang looked like. From a young age, her mother had told her the story like a parable, always with the same message: *Don't do it.* It was not up to Ai to decide when she would die.

By the time a soul is born into a human body, its destiny on earth has already been determined by the celestial parents: whether a person will be rich or poor, whom she will marry, how she will die—the story has been written even before it starts. When a person dies naturally, the surviving relatives grieve the death and thus guide the person's soul to the land of the ancestors, where it can rest. For generations, the living feed the soul and tend to its needs. That's how it is meant to happen. Should a person tragically die in a way that deviates from the divine plan, the soul instead wanders for eternity, hungry and cold. But if a person causes her own untimely death, her soul does not just wander; it is cursed. Were Ai to commit suicide, her mother warned, in the afterlife she would haunt the living for generations. After years of hearing the story of Ka Yang from her mother, Ai understood the moral clearly: choosing her own immediate relief over the fortunes of others would be selfish.

Rather than succumbing to the bad, Ai was told to rise above it. Her mother explained that in life there are things you can control but far more that you cannot. Even when something is out of your control, though, you still have the choice to not allow other people's actions to hurt you—that's what her mother would say. Forgive those who wrong you, and it will help them recognize the error of their ways. Good would prevail. And yet while Ai had always trusted in her mother's wisdom, how could she forgive this cruel man across from her? The situation certainly felt out of her control, but there were no signs that good would win this time. Ai's fantasies of suicide continued.

As Chou Lor's mother observed her daughter-in-law's collapse, it was familiar enough that she enlisted the help of a female shaman. The woman found several spiritual causes, including a demon that had commandeered Ai's thoughts—this was the reason given for her desire to kill herself. Chou Lor's father was too poor to offer a cow, so the shaman negotiated for Ai's release in exchange for the soul of a goat. Ai figured that the demon must have been appeased, because while Chou Lor did not magically change, her suicidal thoughts abated. In the coming months, she tried her best to make life with her new husband work. Really, there was no other choice.

———

It was during the fall of 1977, around the time when Ai married Chou Lor, that people in Sa Na Oua began hearing the big guns go off. Even before Ai saw the threat with her own eyes, she knew this meant their time of normalcy was over; Vang Pao had not come to save them. The uncertainty that had nagged at them for the two years since the war ended now gave way to panic.

Immediately after the communists had taken over in 1975, pockets of armed resistance formed throughout Laos. Some were composed of former military aiming to topple the new government. There were others who followed messianic leaders waging battle to win a new Hmong kingdom. Still others were simply loose bands of people who wanted to prevent the communist regime from imposing its will on their particular corner of the country.

Because most high-level military had fled to Thailand or been sent to prison camps, the rebels were composed mainly of low-level soldiers armed with whatever ammunition had been squirreled away after the war; instead of bombers, they now had boulders that they launched down slopes at the enemy. In the northeast, rebels began with isolated attacks around Vang Pao's former headquarters and on the nearby roads. It was assumed that at best they could harass the Lao soldiers they targeted, never win a full-scale war. But the new government's armed forces were weak, and they were spread across the country putting out the many fires of resistance. In the northeast, rebels were able to claim small victories. Gaining momentum, they spread southward and began attacking targets in the vicinity of Phou Bia, the towering mountain on whose flanks lay Sa Na Oua. People began to talk of liberating the entire region.

The story changed midway through 1977, when Laos called for backup. In July, the Lao People's Democratic Republic and the Socialist Republic of Vietnam signed a Treaty of Friendship and Cooperation, which formalized what was less a partnership between the two countries and more a conservatorship. Vietnam and its Soviet backers propped up the struggling nation in exchange for implicit control of its territory and its politics. Vietnamese troops had been on the ground in Laos continuously since 1960; in many ways, it was Vietnam that fought Laos's civil war on behalf of the communists. (Indeed, the phrase many Hmong use to say "communist" is *Nyab Laj,* which means "Vietnamese.") With the signing of the treaty, that military presence became legal. By year's end, there were as many as thirty thousand Vietnamese soldiers in Laos. With these partners and their big guns, the government of Laos set out to crush the Hmong resistance simmering around Phou Bia.

The government-backed assault that began in late 1977 was uncompromising. Bulldozers cleared the way for Soviet tanks to penetrate the mountainous terrain. Search and destroy units raided some villages while heavy artillery shelled others. From the air, machine gunners strafed the hillsides and bombers dropped all manner of munitions, not just explosives but darts and nails, tear gas, and napalm. When the human targets escaped into the thick cover of forest, the Vietnamese military found them with Soviet chemical weapons.

Ever since Ai's family had returned from their attempt to flee to Thailand in 1975, all they had wanted was a return to the life they had lived before; the same was true of Chou Lor's family. Some men from the village joined the rebels, but otherwise the people of Sa Na Oua kept their heads down and continued farming—or trying to, at least. Initially, the village was just small and high and remote enough to stay outside the fighting. But as the violence grew and spread, a new reality dawned: there was no more neutral ground. Hmong rebels looked just like Hmong farmers. Not taking any chances, the *Nyab Laj* began attacking them as one and the same. Until people had formally sworn allegiance to the Lao People's Democratic Republic and moved to a communist settlement, they were suspect.

The people of Sa Na Oua tried to continue farming, but it became increasingly dangerous to venture away from the village. At the same time, stories trickled in of people Ai knew being murdered by the communists: A young man forced to kill his brother. A father and a mother shot point-blank in front of their children. Those children's skulls then crushed in a rice mortar. During that time, without General Vang Pao there to protect them, such atrocities were unfathomably common.

In desperation, in spring of 1978, Ai and the remaining villagers made a move: The women, children, and elders would hide out at the farmland. The men, who could not risk being found by the *Nyab Laj,* would join the rebels for sheer protection. Ai's little brother, Tong, now twelve, went with the men. So did Chou Lor. Before leaving, he offered Ai no words of encouragement or promises of reunion; he simply left her in the care of his mother and father and disappeared into the forest. At least her real parents were still part of the larger group.

One older man stayed behind in Sa Na Oua. He had been a high-level military officer under Vang Pao, but now he was hobbled by gout and chose to rest in his house rather than camp out at the farm. He was there when the government agents arrived. They came like missionaries, all smiles and promises, purring about the

glorious new nation that was being built. The man was instructed
to retrieve his fellow villagers from wherever they were hiding and
share the news. And so the man limped his way to the farmland, at
which point the villagers hiding there had no choice but to follow
him home—their refusal would have marked them as insurgents.

At around this time, the government delivered them another
serious blow, this one bloodless but no less devastating. The prime
minister sought to modernize the country's agriculture by moving
rice farming exclusively to lowland plots, which could be cultivated
in the irrigated, Green Revolution style. As part of his program announced in April 1978, the prime minister banned the clearing of
forest that was an integral part of upland farming—effectively out-
lawing the method of rice cultivation that Ai's family relied on for
subsistence. Economically, it made no sense. Already Laos was not
growing enough rice to feed its people. To prohibit the kind of
farming practiced by roughly half the population of Laos would
mean a vastly greater deficit. Strategically, though, the ban was cru-
elly precise: As long as people lived in the uplands, they could maintain a fair amount of independence from the government—and
continue to breed resistance. However, if they could no longer feed
themselves, they would be forced to move into the lowlands and
submit to communist rule.

It would have been nearly impossible to enforce this policy
throughout the nation's mountainous expanse. Nonetheless, in Sa
Na Oua the message was clear: people could register with the communists and farm under their direction, or they could cease farming and slowly starve. Ai's family had planted rice that spring, but
now it was too dangerous to bring the crop to maturity. When the
grain from their previous harvest ran out, the hungry season came
as never before. There were no grocery stores or marketplaces, no
traveling traders. There was wild food in the forest, and yet it was too
dangerous to venture far from the village because of the big guns.
By submitting to the totalitarianism of Laos's new rulers, Hmong

would surrender the independence that they and their ancestors had spent generations defending and migrating to preserve. And yet how else could they survive?

The old man with gout decided to take the government at its word. With his family of fourteen, he sought out the agents who had come to the village and asked to be accepted into the nearby settlement. At first it seemed he and his family had been granted safe passage. Then there was a misunderstanding, after which the officials searched the old man's belongings and found evidence of his former military position under Vang Pao. Soldiers proceeded to kill him and his entire family.

When word got back to Sa Na Oua, Ai and the rest felt the walls closing in. Weakened by malnutrition, their bodies were no longer functioning properly. Their sweat was no longer salty. Depleted of energy, they moved wearily through their days. The elder men discussed bringing everyone to hide with thousands of other Hmong on the upper slopes of Phou Bia, where at least they would have the armed protection of the rebels. Before they left, though, Ai's father and her father-in-law each killed and boiled a chicken as a sort of oracle. The signs they received changed their minds at once: On one bird, the toes of both feet were tangled together, indicating there would be no way out of Phou Bia. The other chicken had one foot strangely crossed over its neck, a sign that they would be killed.

As their hunger grew by the day, it appeared that the safest route was one that relied on a lot of good luck: they would surrender to the communists and move to a government-run settlement, staying there for as long as it took the young men hiding with the rebels to find an escape to safety. As they packed their few belongings into baskets and filed onto the path down the mountain, no one thought they were leaving forever.

———

The communist escorts were suspiciously friendly. The villagers played along, and as they walked together in the rain, everyone smiled at one another as if the nation had been reborn. Ai, posing as an unmarried daughter, even managed to attract the affection of a soldier, who carried her cooking pot. After days of traveling they reached the settlement: an abandoned village called Nou Tao, located in the foothills below the fort that Ai's brothers had once defended for Vang Pao. In Nou Tao there was rice to be eaten. Ai even sweet-talked her way into getting two cans of salt, something her family had not had since the war ended two years earlier.

One night Ai's mother came to her in the dark. *Tomorrow your father and I will be gone,* mother said to daughter. *But don't miss us. Don't cry for us. You just stay here.* The next day one of Ai's older brothers crept into the settlement and snuck their parents out to hide in a different area of the mountains. Where? Ai was not sure. When Chou Lor had left, he had given her no assurances to hold on to; her mother's words were little more comfort. Now Ai was alone, with only Chou Lor's volatile father and sour mother to bind herself to. The weeks passed.

The moment things changed, Ai heard it: rebels posing as farmers attacked the *Nyab Laj* outside the settlement. After a firefight killed numerous communist soldiers, the government agents stormed into Nou Tao for punishment. Accused of colluding with the rebels, the village's chief was executed. The bullet entered one side of his abdomen and left through the other, tearing him open like an envelope.

As Ai watched the man's life hang from his middle, she didn't know if he was guilty or innocent. In a way, that ambiguity was the point: no one was safe anymore. It felt to her that the government had led them into this trap of a village like animals into a pen, taming them before slaughter. Ai and the rest had thought they would stay in Nou Tao indefinitely, but now it was clear they had to leave.

Their next move was to embrace what had always been the last resort: living in the jungle, subsisting on what wild food they could scrounge. The men of Sa Na Oua who had embedded with the rebels were contacted, and they took up a new hiding place in the nearby forest. One by one, the villagers were to disappear from Nou Tao, and Ai did as she was told. While working at the settlement's rice farm, she slipped away as if to pee in the bushes. Once out of sight, she just kept walking, first into a field of tall corn, then into the trees, then deep into the forest. Right where they said they would be, the men from the village were camped out, waiting.

Ai was relieved to have escaped Nou Tao and its communist overlords. But to reunite with Chou Lor here in the forest brought her no solace. They had been married only one year, and while her thoughts of suicide had abated, his cruel demeanor had not. And now her parents were gone.

Ai and the rest moved through the forest, never staying in one place for long. Every time she came to a clearing that allowed a view of the valley below, her mind wondered where down there her parents might be hiding. That is, if they were still alive; she didn't know. At the same time, her fourteen-year-old body began to bulge with a child that had somehow been conceived amid the terror and uncertainty—an accident, that was sure. In all her life, she had never been more *kho siab:* "lonely," yes, but deeper than that. Isolated. Incomplete. Homesick.

After all the people had left Sa Na Oua, the village was occupied by Vietnamese soldiers, though only briefly. Afraid that rebels would attack them there, the *Nyab Laj* abandoned it. While no one can say exactly what happened after that, the accepted story is that the land itself naturally repossessed the site, vines climbing up the house posts as the thatch roofs fell apart and blew away—the reclamation would have begun almost immediately. As Ai looked over the hills that autumn, she pined only for her parents. Little did she know that, already, the only place she had ever called home was effectively gone.

One morning, when Ai needed to relieve herself, she went searching for a secluded place to do so. That's when she found the cave. She walked through the dark opening and, after her eyes adjusted, marveled at what she had found.

As caves go, this one was ideal: spacious, with high ceilings and sectioned space in which several families could coexist with some privacy. There were two separate entrances, one in front and one in back, offering an escape route if such became necessary. Ai thought it strange that the cave was empty, given the times that were upon them. Men like her father had hunted in these mountains for decades, and over the past few years, more and more people had moved into the surrounding forest. How could it be that no one was living in this cave? She received it as a divine intervention.

Without delay, Ai, her husband, his parents, and five other families moved in. They were still in hiding. Fires were lit long before dawn so that the smoke leaving the cave would dissipate before daylight; when they left the cave, they covered their footprints with leaves. But the cave afforded comfort that those living fully outdoors in the jungle did not have. Inside, they could burn torches at night rather than cower in darkness. They built beds and stools from bamboo. They could cook without fear of discovery.

By then there was rice: not their own, but that left behind by other farmers who had surrendered their own villages and abandoned their own fields. Ai's group had moved into the cave at the end of the rainy season, just before the rice crops turned from green to gold. As soon as the first grains tinged brown, showing that their insides had thickened to grain, Ai snuck out to pick it.

To simply walk into the open and harvest rice meant risking one's life. Out of necessity, Ai and Chou Lor became a team. He wove a basket, which Ai strapped onto her front. While he stood guard on the road, clutching his rusty old gun, Ai would disappear into a field and snap the rice off its stalks with both hands. There was no time for knives or bundling or drying sheaves in the sun. She filled the basket with grain, emptied it into a bag, and repeated this until she had all that the two of them could carry. When she called out with a tiny whistle like a birdsong, Chou Lor arrived to escort her out.

Outside of making the birdcall, they made sure to stay silent from the time they left the cave to when they covered their footsteps upon return. Then again, even inside the cave, the two spoke only as necessary. Really, what was there to talk about? Every morning, using water she collected from the dripping of the dank ceiling, Ai cooked their rice and served it to her husband, his father, and his mother. Same the next day and the one after that, as they waited anxiously for their chance to escape—still with no word from Ai's parents.

———

Ai and Chou Lor were not the only ones who gleaned rice. It seemed as though the whole world had abandoned their crops to go into hiding, and so anyone who was brave enough swooped in like birds to collect what they could. One day, a man who also lived in the cave found that some of his rice was missing, and he accused Ai of taking it. Without hesitation she told the man he was wrong, that she would never do that. Then she suggested that the true thief was another woman living there.

When Ai's father-in-law learned of Ai's reply to the man, his anger was incandescent. Not because of the stealing—he did not even explore whether Ai was guilty or not. What enraged him was the insubordination: that this fifteen-year-old girl would challenge a full-grown man; that she would feel authorized to point the finger at someone else; that, even if she *was* innocent, she would not accept the blame when it was handed to her. What's more, Ai's accusation had offended the accused woman. There must be a penalty.

With a fury that could only have been born of people and events much older and more haunting than Ai and her quick mouth, Chou Lor's father yelled to his son to beat his wife. When Chou Lor hesitated, his father yelled that if he wasn't man enough to do it, then to get out of the way—he would pummel Ai himself and throw her off a cliff. *Who's going to punish us if she dies?* the old man raged. *We own her.* Ai, terrified, took off running up the slope from the cave.

In spite of his cruel words, Chou Lor had never physically abused Ai. Just as she was only a girl, he was only a boy. And yet the instant she ran, the father's wrath seemed to pass down to his son, where it materialized as the strength of a man. Chou Lor chased down his wife and clawed his hand onto her shoulder. He dragged her back down the wild mountain, smacking her body against rocks and brush. He grabbed a stick as thick as the handle of a shovel, and there in front of the cave he beat her until she was bruised, until her skin split and bled. He beat her so many times that the stick itself broke down into a tattered switch. When he was finished, she lay motionless on the ground, in too much pain to move. Chou Lor simply stood there looking down at her. To his mind, there was no call for pity or apology. By his father's ruling, she was the guilty one.

The next morning, Ai resumed her daily work with a quietness deeper than usual. For fifteen years she had been surrounded by war and never had the trauma of it touch her skin, had never bled. The first violence of her life had just come by the hand of the man to whom she was bound for this lifetime and the next. Chou Lor had not said a word to question his father's mandated punishment or to call for an investigation, much less to defend her. Instead, he had silently shown his wife the laws by which their life together would be lived. And so, as Ai made her way through her chores that day, she held an idea in her mouth like a spoonful of rice, ready to swallow: this time, she would kill herself.

For two nights and two days, Ai clutched the opium in her hand. But every time she readied herself, she thought of the baby inside of her, now evident to the world, and how killing herself would mean the child would not have a chance to live. She thought of how if she didn't die from the overdose, she might miscarry and thus further incur the wrath of her father-in-law. More than anything, she thought of her parents. She believed they were still hiding somewhere in the vast jungle. If she killed herself, they might never learn the whole truth of what happened to her. Instead, they would be left with only the burden of grief and the madness of having another daughter fail.

On the third day after Chou Lor beat her, Ai heard noises in the dark at the far end of the cave, where the second entrance led into the jungle. *My daughter?* a voice called. *My daughter, are you there?* The sound shot through her. She had known it since birth.

Dad? she called.

From the blackness, the lines of a figure emerged. Her father, who had hunted these mountains his entire life, knew this secret cave, had come looking for her. He and her mother and brother Tong had left their earlier hiding place and were now in the forest beside the family's old farm site, as close as they could get to going home. Ai hugged her father and cried—happy, sad, scared, suddenly safe again. *Don't cry,* he said gently. *Your mom and I are here now.*

The wounds on Ai's back strained as she clasped her arms around her father, but still she didn't tell him about the beating. He could stay only a few hours because he had left her mother and Tong alone at their camp. Ai feared that if she described what had happened, he would explode at her father-in-law, and then after he was gone she would be left to suffer the repercussions alone. At least now she knew where he and her mother were.

Two days later, she convinced Chou Lor to trek with her to where her parents were hiding out, near the family's old farm. An aunt joined the trip, and together they hiked three hours across rocky slopes and thorn-lined paths. When at last they arrived, Ai liquefied in her mother's arms. Before Ai could find her own words, the aunt lifted the girl's shirt to bare the evidence.

Ai's mother said little. As a woman, she understood the immutable reality that a daughter-in-law belongs to her husband and his clan. But Ai's father was unrestrained. He unwound a coil of rage toward Chou Lor, cracking it with a verbal ferocity Ai had not known her mild-mannered father to possess. How could anyone beat a child this way? And why had no one investigated the theft before exacting punishment? Did Chou Lor's father truly believe that just because he had paid a bride-price for this girl her life was his to end? *Had I known you had done this,* Ai's father roared at Chou Lor, *I would have taken my daughter back.*

Despite the finality of wedding rituals, there was a way to annul them. In an egregious case like this, in which most witnesses would agree that Ai's father-in-law had acted unjustly, clan leaders would conduct a sort of trial. They would question the perpetrator and the victim, call to account the husband's relatives who had sworn to protect Ai as part of the marriage ritual, come to a settlement and ensure that restitution was made. Ai's father could have paid back the bride-price and brought his wounded daughter home. Except that right now, home was a secret shack tucked into the forest; the clan leaders and wedding observers were hidden throughout the mountains, fighting off starvation and searching for escape. Justice was a luxury of earlier times.

When Ai's father's fury finally burned out, unable to catch anything aflame, Chou Lor turned away and began walking back to the cave. Ai had no choice but to follow. Along the way, he scolded her for snitching.

Ai did visit her father near the old farm once more—this time, by herself. He was ill, and for medicine she brought him the opium that she had held in her hand but not swallowed those weeks before. She found him in the shack, with her mother and her younger brother, the three of them always a unit.

As they sat together, her father brought up the only topic there was: the future. It was winter, and they were still able to survive on rice they had gathered from the abandoned fields. But because, like themselves, the farmers had all fled their villages, those fields would not be planted again the next year. When Ai's and her family's existing stores ran out, the hunger would come without relief. Once the rice was gone, the family would have to make a final decision: flee to Thailand, or stay in Laos and join the communists.

Her father didn't know which they would choose—didn't know if Thailand would even be an option—but he promised this: If they stayed, they would all stay together. If they left, they would leave as one. Ai didn't care much which place, Thailand or Laos, was chosen to be their home. What mattered to her was the staying together. Everything else in this life that made her feel safe and whole had been lost. But as long as she remained in arm's reach of her parents, she believed she would survive.

———

Ai and her husband's family had lived in the cave for six months when at last, in March, they got their chance to escape to Thailand. There were roads, of course, but they couldn't use them. At this point, any clear path to the border was studded with mines and patrolled by soldiers who had orders to kill. To leave, one needed a guide who knew the way and could carve a new path across the mountains south or west to the Mekong River, which served as the border. Mostly, that meant an enterprising person, often ex-military, who had already made it out, then risked returning to shepherd others back. Escaping with someone like that was a privilege accorded mostly to relatives, and even then it was not free.

Opportunity came through some other residents of the cave, members of the Lee clan whose relatives had made it to the United States and were able to pay for a man to guide them and others from their clan. Such chances came rarely, and anyone who could talk his way into the group would do so; families glommed on until the groups grew to include hundreds of people. When the guide arrived at their cave, Chou Lor's father negotiated the inclusion of his four-person family for the fee of one precious silver bar.

Chou Lor was gone at the time. Ai knew she had most of the day before he returned, so she cooked up a plan and presented it to her father-in-law: she would walk to her parents' shack, collect some rice stored there, give them the news that it was time to leave, and return immediately. Her father-in-law responded that she would stay put; an uncle who was going that way would bring her parents the message instead. The decision was not up for discussion.

The Lee clan had other family members to gather, so they left, promising to wait at a designated point where Ai's group could catch up to them. Late that day, Chou Lor returned. The group he was with had stopped at Ai's parents' shack on the way home. He told Ai that they had been packing up and had assured him they would leave in the morning, meeting the group the following day. Of course Ai would have liked to wait for her parents and walk with them. They would be traveling with her brothers and their wives; all told, their group would be half a dozen households, all Moua clan. But one day of separation wouldn't matter. *If we leave, we will leave together.* Her father had promised that.

This time, packing was straightforward: most everything they owned had already been left behind. Ai had had a pair of flip-flops, but they had broken so many times that eventually Chou Lor could no longer fix them for her. As she walked away from the cave for good, her feet were bare. She had no clothes other than the ones she wore. The only money she and Chou Lor had was forty silver coins that remained from her opium profits, plus the two silver bars her parents had given her at the wedding. Ai's basket held what remained of the rice they had gleaned, and her hands clutched a cooking pot over her belly, now bulging. She was seven months pregnant.

While there was still a bit of daylight left, Ai, Chou Lor, and his parents joined more than one hundred from the Lee clan. With the guides cutting a path across the forest, they walked through the dark of night and all the next day. As they went, Ai and an older man marked the way with little signals for her parents' group to follow: a branch bent to point the way, a set of leaves folded to mark a turn.

When they reached the second night's designated spot in the jungle, they received the news that the party preceding them had not made it to Thailand. Soldiers had slaughtered them. A few people from the group had escaped and managed to hide, among them a woman whose husband had been killed in the ambush. The story went that this woman could not control her mourning, and her cries exposed the group. When soldiers tracked the noise to where they hid, this time no one got away. In total, five of Chou Lor's relatives had died. Ai and the others wrapped themselves in that knowledge as they huddled under makeshift shelters in the darkness.

Through the night, the encampment swelled with new arrivals. At dawn, Ai excitedly went to find her parents among the crowd. She asked a man if he knew where her father was.

What's his name?

Nhia Pao Moua.

The man didn't need to know her father, could tell by the name that the man she sought was not there. He had heard that the Moua clan had followed the guidance of a man who told them that the rushing was unnecessary, that they could go to a place called Thong Nhai and meet the group there.

The air left Ai's chest. Her group had taken the road around the other side of the mountain, which meant they would not be passing through Thong Nhai. *How could this be happening?* she thought. *Why would that man tell them to go a different way?* It made no sense that their chance to escape could be derailed by a careless misunderstanding like this.

And yet, even as she strained to figure out what had gone wrong, Ai could feel the dense weight of a new certainty in the space where her father's promise had been. The rest of her family had stayed together, yes, but she was now alone. As she pushed her way into the tangled wilderness that morning alongside Chou Lor and his family, Ai knew the separation would be forever.

———

The guides knew the general direction, but the path itself was made fresh each day. When they lost their way, one would climb a tree with a compass and search the view for familiar features of the land to orient himself. The guides always held the front of the line, followed by anyone who had shoes and therefore could tamp down the raw forest enough so that the others behind, in their bare feet, could step more easily. Even so, there was no avoiding the rocks and the briars, and after days, the pain in everyone's feet howled. After many days more, though, the same pain became white noise, buzzing alongside hunger and exhaustion.

They walked in silence. If there was an urgent message, such as to stop at the sign of danger, it would be passed in a whisper from the person in front to the person behind, all the way down the line of two hundred people snaking through the jungle. Otherwise, no one spoke from the time they began walking at dawn until the light evaporated from the forest and they could stop to sleep in the underbrush. Babies were given opium to mute their cries, the parents meting out as small a dose as they could, hoping it would not be fatal. The lead guide had no tolerance for their fears. When one teething five-month-old could not be quieted, the guide instructed the parents to deliver a lethal dose. *When we get to Thailand you can fuck all you want and make more,* he told them. *But if you don't off this kid, he's going to get the rest of us killed.*

Even after hiding in the jungle for months, they hadn't imagined terror of this saturation. All through the region, the Vietnamese army was still attacking Hmong without restraint. In desperation, thousands of people were fleeing across the Mekong River each month; perhaps just as many were dying or being killed along the way. With every step through this unfamiliar landscape there could be land mines hidden in the dirt, mortar shells that dropped from the sky, soldiers that materialized through the trees. One day a deer appeared before them. The leader stopped, whispered over his shoulder to halt the line. As the message passed backward, the tawny creature walked across where the guide had been cutting their path. Ai couldn't see it—she was too far back—but when the person in front of her stopped and the message reached her ears, she knew what it meant: an ancestor had sent the creature as a warning that danger was ahead; they needed to wait until it was safe to proceed. Standing there, still, her bare feet on the earth, it was a moment of comfort. This time they had been protected. The rest of the time, though, Ai's mind crackled with a chilling thought: *Who will be the next to die?*

———

By the time the group neared the border with Thailand, Ai was eight months pregnant. The procession of staggering bodies had walked up and then down countless small mountains and crawled for hours on their bellies, all in silence. Most people had run out of rice and begun to subsist on wild plants they found along the way. Somehow, no one had been killed.

As the group prepared to emerge from the forest and make their final run to the Mekong River, Chou Lor's father pulled his son and daughter-in-law aside. He and Chou Lor's mother would not continue with them. Their bodies were too frail to risk entering the frigid, wild Mekong, so they would wait for a boat sent back by those who made it across. There was not enough money for Chou Lor and Ai to ride a boat, so they would have to swim.

Chou Lor and Ai left his parents what little they had on their backs: the remaining rice, the pot to cook it in. Chou Lor kept his gun and the money belt. Ai kept only the clothes she wore.

The group was now thinned out by similar attrition of the elderly, the infirm, and the well-off. Before those who remained lay a series of tactical stops on the way to the river, planned out by the head guide. First they were herded to a grove of bamboo and shown how to weave small, makeshift rafts from the hollow wood: six stems about two feet long were laid vertically and crossed by six more stems horizontally; young shoots were peeled apart and wound into rope, which was used to lash the stems together. Each person would need two of these squares, tied together and placed one under each arm, like bat wings. If fashioned correctly, these rafts would float them across the river. Chou Lor, a prodigal tinkerer, quickly made two for his wife and two for himself. They strapped the rafts onto their backs and kept moving.

The next stop was a pool where they would be able to drink once more before the long night ahead. Life, like that of animals, had been stripped down to such necessities. The head guide led the way, so he was the first to see what lay at the pool: A family of bodies flat on the ground, motionless but taut in their final moves, some as if trying to grab for the people beside them. The food in their hands was uneaten. Blood was sprayed across the rice, across their bodies and faces and ragged clothes, pooled black behind some heads. There was the horror of it, of course, the primal distress of seeing human carnage. The anguish of knowing they could not help the dead, with no shovels for burying or time for mourning. And then the torment of seeing the blood slicked across the surface of the pool of water that Ai and the others could now not drink. The sheer thirst.

Then the creeping terror in realizing that the campfire at their feet was still smoldering—the killing fresh enough that the killers might still be near. When the guide told them to wait, they sat down, stiff and still. If they went anywhere they might encounter military patrols, and yet there, near the sight of this massacre, they felt surrounded by the unmoored souls of the newly dead. They gave their babies opium without hesitation. They ached for nightfall.

When at last the sky was black, the guide led them to their final traverse before the river. It was chosen as a place where no soldier would set foot: a grove with briars packed as densely as plants in a rice field, ripe with thorns down the length of their canes. As the group pushed forward, barbs snagged their clothes and clawed through to their skin. The bamboo rafts on their backs caught on the stalks. They tried to clear the space before them with waving arms, but the night was so dark and the spines so many that still the thorns found their faces, their eyes. Chou Lor whispered to Ai to hold on to his shirt so they wouldn't be separated. *With what hands?* she hissed back, palms spread across her face in protection.

When they finally broke into the open air, before them was the river. They had been told what to do: how to tie the wings under their arms with an X across their chests, how to paddle to move their bodies forward. That was small comfort for Ai. She did not know how to swim. What's more, she had been told that most pregnant women did not make it across, that her bulging body would sink. Still, when the guide gave the motion to go, there was only one thing to do.

Ai and Chou Lor and the rest of the band knew that this was the moment when they would make it to Thailand or they would die trying. They needed to enter the water together, to make as little noise as possible, but that would be their final act as a group. From now on they would survive only as individuals.

They stepped into the water and felt the soft dirt between their toes. Another step and they were up to their knees, then the ground seemed to drop off. The water was cold and it set fire to the countless angry scratches from the briars. No one made a noise. They disappeared into the river until only their heads poked above the water, like crocodiles.

Their minds burned with borrowed memories of this place. The very first night of the journey, the same night they learned that everyone in the preceding group had been killed, they heard a story: A man they knew was towing his wife across the river while she carried their baby on her back. As he swam, she was shot in the head. The baby could do nothing but drown. When at last the man reached the shores of freedom, his reward was to haul the corpses onto the riverbank and dissolve into grief.

Tonight, though, there was no sign of soldiers. The water was calm, the floats were sturdy. They paddled as the guides had shown them, scooping the river's surface with their hands and beating their legs beneath. Ai opened her cottony lips to drink blessed water, thrilling as the liquid seeped across her shriveled insides. Soon everyone felt the ground underfoot—just like that. It was so easy. Up and down the banks people stood up, shook off, and walked away from the water. Ai watched some around her drop their bamboo floats, but she and Chou Lor held on to theirs. This had not been the struggle of which they had heard. They could not feel the triumph as they should have. They hadn't walked far before they realized why: a massive river lay before them. The branch they had just swum was a rillet by comparison.

There was no time for disappointment or fatigue. Chou Lor knew how to swim, and felt sure that as long as they were not separated, he could get them across. He tied a rope under his arms and lashed it to Ai's bamboo wings.

As they approached the water, beside them was a family they knew from Sa Na Oua: two brothers with their mother and frail, older father, already shivering from the first leg of the swim. For floats they had limp plastic tubes they had bought from the guides, which even on land appeared untrustworthy. The brothers worriedly approached Chou Lor and Ai, confiding that they feared their parents would not make it.

One brother asked, *For safety, could we join you in swimming across?*

Chou Lor assented, then pulled Ai close to him and told her, *Do not let them hold on to you. I can't get all of us across.* She agreed.

They slipped into the new river, and its deep current pulled them away from the shore.

So, do you want to marry me? He had asked her so casually through the walls of her parents' home. They had been children. In so many ways, they still were. Now the river's dark water swallowed them up to their chins. Above, the blackness hung vast and unsparing. As if suspended in the night sky itself, Ai and Chou Lor were each more alone than they had ever been in their young lives. At the same time, they were bound together. Ai clung to her bamboo wings while Chou Lor paddled with all the strength he had left, clambering on blindly in the dark until at last his feet touched something. Land. Thailand.

As they stumbled onto the muddy banks, this time they could feel that the triumph was real—they had finally found refuge. Ai knew they had not done it alone. Before they had parted at the edge of the forest, Chou Lor's father promised to ask the ancestors for protection as his only remaining son crossed the Mekong. But Ai knew there must have been something more powerful at work. There were just too many times this journey could have gone wrong, when they could have been discovered in the forest or spun by the river current right back into the net of a vengeful army. Her parents, wherever they were, must have made their own entreaties to their own ancestors. Ai felt sure that it was their mighty force that had delivered her to safety at last.

There on the banks, Chou Lor saw that the family from Sa Na

Oua had climbed out of the water with them. He was aghast. Had Ai let them grab on after all?

They just sort of held on, she told him sheepishly.

In her mind, though, it was clearer than that: without her help, the old man likely would have died, maybe even dragged his wife and sons with him. When a person was in need, Ai could not turn away—this was a fundamental piece of her parents' teaching. But she had not considered that for the sake of these other people's safety, she had imperiled them all.

In stinging disbelief, Chou Lor removed the rope from his torso and showed her the raw flesh fanning from chest to armpit, his body literally worn away. In the darkness, though, she couldn't see him or his wounds. So with hours left before daylight, they silently ditched their floats by the water's edge, crawled under some bushes, and sank into sleep.

———

When Ai and Chou Lor awoke, they were still alive. Looking at the river in the light, they saw for the first time that its waters were yellow and putrid. They thought about how the night before, they had quenched their thirst by drinking as they swam, how the waters had felt like a gift; now their empty stomachs heaved.

People who lived near the river found them, gave them rice, and brought them to the police. While Ai and Chou Lor had spent years fearing anyone in a government uniform, they were not scared. This was where General Vang Pao had told the Hmong people to come to join him. If they were where he was, they would be safe—just as they had been safe in Laos until he left. They did not know that by then General Vang Pao was living in Orange County, California. Perhaps that didn't matter. The din of artillery and mourning had always been a radio playing in the background of their lives; in Thailand, it was finally quiet.

The police loaded them in a truck and carted them to one of the many austere government facilities along the border that were performing the clerical processing of sometimes thousands of desperate refugees each week: the questioning, fingerprinting, and paperwork necessary to feed these people into the stream of international bureaucracy that would determine their fate. Men in uniforms bearing clipboards wrote down the vital pieces that composed each person's story. Ai spoke only Hmong, but Chou Lor had learned some Lao in school. Lao was close to Thai, and he was able to communicate enough to speak for both of them.

Up to now, no state had ever recorded Ai's existence. There was no official record of her birth, no passport verifying citizenship. She had been counted only as part of a population enumerated in abstract, as a resident in a village or a member of an ethnic minority. When the Thai official asked Chou Lor their ages, he puffed them up to twenty-six and twenty-three, having heard that the older one was, the greater the rice rations one received. When asked their names, he told the truth: Chou Lor Khang and Ai Moua.

His name was recorded correctly, but there was something about her name, destined to change when in other people's hands. Perhaps it was an error of translation or pronunciation, or simply messy handwriting that muddied the letters. Ai would never know. Indeed, she didn't even know, in the moment, that anything was different. Weeks later, in a hospital waiting room, she heard it for the first time, another person in a uniform calling, *Ia Moua? Ia Moua?* She herself looking around the room to see who this "Ia Moua" was. Not realizing, until the woman with the clipboard explained, that this strange, unknown person was her.

PART 2

MOTHER

The processing center wasn't set up as a place to live. There were no shelters, no food distribution. With the silver coins from Ia's opium profits, they bought a handful of sticky rice twice a day. They slept under two big trees, alongside all the other waiting bodies. To wash, they walked to the river and did their best with the cloudy water.

One day, there on the banks, Ia noticed a man—a grandfather, she would learn, though he was middle-aged at most. With him were a boy and a girl, young enough that they should be playing in the sand. Instead, the children sat next to the man and did exactly as he: looked out over the river, tearfully calling the names of the dead one by one and lamenting each person's death. It was their family that had been slaughtered by the campfire at the water hole. This man had been away from the fire with his grandchildren when the soldiers arrived. Hearing gunshots, he had tucked himself and the two kids out of sight and waited breathlessly until long after there was no more human noise. Every member of the family had been killed except for them. Now here they were, safe and alive but dead inside.

Ia was overcome by the hopelessness she saw in the man, the loneliness in each of the two orphan children's calls. She walked over, touched the man's head, and said with all the warmth she had, *Don't cry. I, too, have lost my family, my mom and dad. I left them behind in Laos.*

The man replied, not unkindly, *Yes, but mine have all died and so they are gone forever. Yours are still alive, so surely you'll see them again.*

Standing at the edge of this vast, yellow river, the sting of his words made Ia cry. Her parents were still alive, and yet she knew they, too, were gone forever. Looking at the smudgy horizon of Laos on the distant banks, she reached her arms out, in vain. *This river is as big as the sky,* she wailed through her tears. *How will we ever meet again? How long will I have to miss you?*

Every day after that, Ia would go to the river, look back toward her homeland, and call to her parents. As she poured the murky water over her body to bathe, she keened their names and the litany of sorrows for which they stood. Yes, her parents were still alive, but she was already an orphan.

———

Weeks later, after Chou Lor's parents finally made it across the Mekong in a boat, the four of them were shipped to the Nong Khai refugee camp. In theory, at least, they would be taken care of there.

Nong Khai was already way over capacity, with twenty-six thousand people stuffed into quarters for sixteen thousand. No housing was available, and because the four of them had no relatives with whom to stay, they were left homeless. And broke. The silver coins had trickled through their fingers: for rice to eat, water to drink, paperwork, and fingerprints. They still had the two silver bars that Ia's parents had given her at the wedding, but that was currency she was meant to never spend.

In desperation, Chou Lor's father convinced one already crowded household from Ia's birth clan to allow them in. Ia's job was to cook for the family there, while Chou Lor did his best to catch fish that they could sell for a meager income. One day in April, as Ia was scaling one of the fishes, a pain shot through her pregnant belly. She had never felt this before, and yet she knew what it meant. She called for Chou Lor, told him the baby was coming.

What are we going to do? he said feverishly.

I don't know!

A woman couldn't give birth in a home that was not of her own clan. To do so would disturb the spirits of that house, bringing misfortune to its inhabitants. Chou Lor rushed to his father, who directed them into the alley behind the house. As Ia remembers it, she walked there, sat down, under a tree, and felt the baby slide out of her body and onto the bare ground. In her shock, she yelled for Chou Lor: *We have a baby!* Chou Lor yelled for his mother.

Women came, knowing what to do: Find a blanket to wrap around the baby. Bring thread to draw tight around the umbilical cord until it severed. Prepare the placenta to be buried—this was the most important step. Each baby was a vessel for rebirth. In this body, an ancestral soul of the Khang clan would be given new life. When in time the body died, the funeral ritual would guide the soul back to its birthplace to find the placenta or *tsho tsuj tsho npuag,* the "birth shirt," the garment to be worn on the journey to the spirit world. When a son was born, the placenta was buried under the central column of the house. This child born into the dirt was a girl, so its placenta would be buried under the parents' bed in the family house. There, protected by the clan's resident spirits, the mother and child would rest for thirty days, the mother eating a special diet of fresh chicken and medicinal herbs to cleanse her body and restore her strength.

But of course there was no family house, no resident spirits, just an alleyway in a refugee camp in a country that was the whole world of the Mekong River away from their actual home. Because a new mother could not live in another clan's house, Ia's father-in-law built a lean-to: two bamboo poles stuck in the ground, with a thin plastic tarp spread between them and attached to the side of the building. The women buried the placenta right where the child was born, under the tree. For thirty days, Ia and her baby lay there on a bamboo mat in the shade of the tarp, this new mother living on a diet of government-issue rice and water.

The baby was neither a comfort nor a burden. Mostly, she was one more way for Ia to miss her parents. Lying there all those days, Ia imagined how if her mother were there she would bring chicken to nourish her daughter, blankets to keep her warm, new clothes to keep her clean. Sharing this moment with her parents would have allowed it to feel special instead of just hard.

As was the custom, after three days had passed, Ia's father-in-law performed the ceremony to call the soul into the baby's body. He christened her *Hlau,* "metal," a boy's name and a strong one at that.

Still, within weeks, the baby faded to the edge of death. Her stomach was distended and hard, a symptom seen in many of the camp's children. Because some of those children who had been treated at the camp's hospital had died, Ia and Chou Lor were warned not to take her there. Instead, they did what they could with the little they knew and the nothing they had: made poultices from the leaves of a nearby tree and fashioned simple treatments with bamboo and smoke. In an agonizing pattern that continued for weeks, Hlau would revive miraculously, only to dim again days later.

At last, in desperation, Ia removed from her money bag the silver bars given by her parents when she married Chou Lor. They were meant to be used only when Ia died, to ensure that she would have a cow for her funeral—a final act of love between parents and child. In the refugee camp, Ia cashed one in for a stack of Thai paper money and bought medicine for the infant. Hlau revived once more. When the child fell ill again, Ia cashed in the second silver bar to pay for a shaman's ritual. Again the girl came back to health.

But the day the bus arrived to move them to a different refugee camp, the baby began slipping away. There was no time to hunt down a remedy—the transport was not scheduled on individuals' time. When Ia frantically asked her father-in-law what they should do to save the child, he replied that they would leave it up to fate. If she didn't survive, then it wasn't her time.

They boarded the bus, Chou Lor carrying their few possessions and Ia carrying the baby. As the diesel engine roared to life, the face in Ia's arms turned ashen. Ia touched her daughter's feather of a body: still warm, still hopeful. Then she put her mouth next to the lips: nothing. Ia realized that beneath her hand, there was no heart beating.

I think she died, Ia said.

Hold her for a bit, the father-in-law replied. *If she doesn't come back, we'll tell the bus driver to stop and we can bury her by the side of the road.*

Fear—that was Ia's first reaction, because here death was coming to claim the child in her arms and there was nothing she could do to stop it. If Chou Lor was worried about the child, she was not aware of it; her agony that day was solitary. In the confines of the bus seat, Ia wrapped her own small, weeping body around the baby's. She did not notice the foreign country rolling past the windows, did not imagine what lay ahead in their new home. Instead, numb with anguish, she disappeared into herself, touching her mouth to those tiny, still lips, over and over. Miles passed. Time evaporated.

Then, as suddenly as Ia had felt the girl's life extinguish, she felt it return: a wisp of breath, little more than a pulse of heat. Peering through her tears, Ia saw a trace of pink in the lips. She put a breast in the mouth and felt the baby begin to draw.

———

It was dark by the time Ia's bus and the nine others transporting people like her arrived at the Ban Vinai Holding Center. Both the refugee camp itself and the family's stay within its confines were meant to be temporary. When Ia arrived, she had no idea how much would have changed by the time she left: That the baby she held in her arms would be fifteen years old, the same age Ia was in that moment. That she herself would be thirty, the mother of not just this girl but seven more children. That life's established hierarchy would have been shuffled, irreversibly; that she would find herself much closer to the top. Instead, as she stepped down off the bus into the red dirt of Ban Vinai, all Ia knew was that she was that much farther from the place she still called home.

Until just before Ia and Chou Lor arrived, the Ban Vinai Holding Center had been seen as apart from the other camps in Thailand. Initially funded by the CIA, the camp was conceived as a waypoint on the route to international resettlement for the elite, mostly high-ranking military Hmong who were able to flee Laos immediately in 1975. The original director was a man named Vinai, meaning "discipline"; honoring him, the camp came to be known as Ban Vinai, "village of discipline." Concerned international visitors who arrived in helicopters and sanitized tour buses described it as livable, friendly, productive—the "country club" of refugee camps.

But that was before Laos and Vietnam waged their all-out assault on the resistance at Phou Bia that ultimately sent Ia and countless others flooding over the banks of the Mekong beginning in 1978. In 1979, Ban Vinai's population jumped from twelve thousand people to more than thirty-two thousand. Packed into a space not even three-quarters of a square mile, the camp assumed the density of a single-story urban slum. Soon international visitors would remark on open sewers and overcrowded housing.

When Ia and Chou Lor arrived, they and other members of the Khang clan made themselves a home by doing as they had back in Laos: the men cut down trees to use as posts and beams while the women plaited bamboo into the material for walls. It was in the style of houses in Sa Na Oua, but with far more people crowded into the long one-room rectangle. In bamboo bed platforms arranged side by side along the length of one wall, husband and wife slept next to in-laws, who slept next to brothers and their wives, all separated only by mosquito netting. With no windows, the house was dark. Because there was no electricity for lights, all day the front door had to be left open to the noise and grime of the world outside.

The threshold of their house emptied onto the main road through the camp, the door framing a view of sullen traffic that flowed past all the daylight hours. The few automobiles driving by carried aid workers and government employees doing official business: collecting garbage, pumping waste, touring observers from international organizations. The new class of coyotes who were getting rich smuggling people from Laos might buzz through on motorcycles. Otherwise, the traffic passed by on foot: tens of thousands of individuals plodding from one end of this makeshift city to another in the colorless journey of daily survival. Gradually, most of the trees were cut down by new arrivals erecting new houses. Between the buildings, the naked landscape was worn hard by endless footsteps, producing dust or mud, depending on the season.

The people continued to arrive, here and at the dozens of other refugee camps across Thailand. While communists had won the wars in Laos and Vietnam, Indochina remained in turmoil. Vietnam invaded Cambodia, China invaded Vietnam. In theory, Laos was at peace, but in reality, the government continued to drive out its minority citizens with repression and violence. Refugees from the rest of Indochina flowed into Thailand by land and by sea. Even as the United Nations Refugee Agency, UNHCR, relocated these displaced people to faraway countries in earnest throughout 1979, for every refugee who left the camps, three more arrived.

From the very beginning, Thailand made it clear that these foreigners were not invited to stay. The wars of the 1960s and '70s had brought Thailand an economic boom, and the government feared that absorbing hundreds of thousands of destitute refugees would both pop the bubble and deter future investment. Furthermore, Thailand battled dissidents within its own borders, most of them communists, nearly all of them poor. The government could not risk alienating more citizens by caring for the refugees in such a way that appeared to favor them over, or even treat them as equal to, native Thai. As the government saw it, the only solution was to send these exiles back to the places they had fled or relocate them to third countries.

The primary country of resettlement was the United States, which, at least initially, acted out of responsibility for its allies in the failed wars of Vietnam, Cambodia, and Laos. By the end of 1979, roughly 250,000 people from these three countries had been relocated to American cities, with over one million more to come in the following years. As the largest group of refugees ever resettled in the United States, this influx of people changed American policy: it led to the formal framework for accepting a much greater number of refugees from around the world each year; those increased numbers in turn led to xenophobia and a resulting political backlash that continues today. Even then, as the 1970s became the 1980s, Americans' sympathy for those displaced by the wars in Southeast Asia grew thinner by the year. And yet because of continued violence and deteriorating economic conditions in the newly communist countries, the flow of desperate people did not stop. In 1980, Thailand absorbed an additional 43,768 refugees from Laos alone.

In an effort to stem the flow, Thailand instituted a policy called "humane deterrence." The government's view was that people in neighboring countries were now migrating less because of political prosecution at home and more because they saw economic opportunity in Thailand. Thai police officers took their own extrajudicial actions against refugees, sometimes robbing them once they had crossed the Mekong, other times forcing them straight back to Laos, where they could be shot in the water by Lao soldiers or marched off to reeducation camps. Officially, though, humane deterrence aimed to reduce people's incentive to come in the first place, both by preventing resettlement and by stripping the camps of any seeming benefits. Existing holding centers were closed to newcomers or simply shut down; new holding centers were built to be austere, arguably prisonlike. Human services such as education and medical care were pared back and food rations reduced to the minimum allowed by the United Nations. In Ban Vinai, restrictions forced anyone building a new dwelling to use not bamboo but corrugated tin, which ensured the interior would act like an oven in the hottest weather.

For Hmong, an additional layer of punishment was how life in the camps deprived them of their self-reliance. Officially, residents of Ban Vinai were not allowed to leave the camp. In the earlier years, some men and women made informal arrangements to work off-site, mostly as farm laborers. At no point, though, were they allowed to have their own farms: that would have taken land away from Thai farmers, and it might have encouraged the refugees to stay. While camp rations were meager, the cruelty of this prohibition was not the people's hunger; it was that since before anyone's memories began, agriculture had been the axis on which Hmong lives spun. Practically, farming designed how they spent each day. Societally, farming was the underpinning of their financial and cultural independence. Now it was gone. As if all the bones had been removed from a body, the structure of life had been taken away.

That is, unless you were female. In the absence of farming there was still water to haul, food to cook, and clothes to wash, even if they were rags. And in the moments between, in any place where one could sit, there was sewing. Grandmothers bent over their cloths and squinted. Mothers held their fabric above the heads of nursing babies. Schoolgirls sat in circles on the ground, chatting but with eyes trained on the work before them. When dark came, women and girls crowded under the orange light of gas lanterns in order to continue sewing.

In Laos, most every girl had learned to make clothes and decorate them with intricate cross-stitched designs as a matter of necessity;

skill at this essential task was a primary currency in a young woman's value as a bride. What they produced was more than mere garments. The ornate pattern on a baby carrier warned demons away from the newborn inside. The "way-finding" patterns sewn onto funeral garments helped the deceased locate the path back to the ancestors. For as long as anyone could remember, Hmong had been seminomadic farmers with a subsistence income; the elaborate textiles that girls and women created were a form of precious wealth.

In the refugee camps, the textiles took on new value. Aid workers began buying pieces of needlework, at first single pieces for themselves, then in greater quantity to sell to the world beyond. Missionaries supplied fabric and thread in the blues and beiges that were fashionable in contemporary Western home decor, and they encouraged the women to make new products that were more marketable: pillows, coasters, eyeglass cases. Thai merchants bought the needlework in bulk for resale in the tourist bazaars of Bangkok and Chiang Mai. Even before the deluge of refugees arrived in 1979, Hmong women's sewing was the foundation of a new economy being built in camps around Thailand.

As soon as Ia made it to Ban Vinai, she got in on the market. Sewing had never been her strength—even threading the needles was a chore. Here, Ia labored over the tiny stitches, knowing that the needlework was saleable only if perfect; more than once, she tore out hours' worth of work because a single mis-stitch had thrown off the design. As a newcomer to a market that had already been vertically integrated, her only option was to do assigned piecework that others assembled into finished products. Prorated for the hours spent on a single piece, the pay was a pittance.

As Ia toiled through one design after another, she saw her neighbors selling a new needlework that had been invented in the camps. In these "story cloths," traditional cross-stitching was replaced by appliqué depicting figures and landscapes that played out narratives across the fabric, top to bottom. Some showed folktales about demons and tigers; others portrayed the cycle of rice farming from planting to harvest. The most popular told the refugees' own stories: idyllic lives in the mountains bled into scenes of combat, starvation, and flight; often the blue lines of the Mekong River were introduced as a diagonal design element, across which tiny heads bobbed and cried out. Thailand itself appeared on some, represented by buses and rows of gray buildings—always at the bottom of the story, the end.

What kind of fool would spend money on these things? Ia wondered. She heard that people in the United States and France used them to decorate their homes, hanging them on the walls—and she saw that people bought them. The more personal the tales of agony and detailed the depictions of the struggle, the more buyers would pay. Ia quit the piecework and learned how to make story cloths.

In this new economy, men suddenly found they were no longer essential. Without farming, no one needed their brawn to cut down big trees to clear the fields. Without war, they weren't needed for combat. Most women in the camps had never held a pencil before, so men with some schooling could create a role for themselves by drawing the pictures their wives would sew. There were husbands who took up domestic chores so their wives could spend more time making needlework to sell, but with that came an emasculation virtually unknown in Laos. There was a bit of work in camp maintenance, also in the black market of drugs and other contraband. Otherwise, for many men, entire days passed without activity. Western observers continually reported the tragedy of Ban Vinai's mass boredom and "enforced idleness," but the hardship was much deeper than mere monotony. It was a lack of purpose. Those empty hours were filled with longing for the life they had had in Laos, and with imagining how they might reclaim it.

In 1981, General Vang Pao stepped into this void. After being airlifted out of Laos in May 1975, he had tried to restart his military command from Thailand. Months later, though, when he was exiled to the United States, the opposition leaders who were actually on the ground in Laos took control of the movement. But then came the crushing joint *Nyab Laj* attack on Phou Bia in 1978 and 1979 that drove out Ia and tens of thousands of others. With those insurgent forces now decimated—and with a colossal wave of refugees newly arriving in Thailand—Vang Pao saw his opening. Brandishing a fiery manifesto arguing for the overthrow of the puppet regime in Laos, he and other exiled Lao leaders introduced a rebel coalition. They called it *Neo Hom Pot Poi Xat Lao,* or the United Lao National Liberation Front. Most just called it Neo Hom. Outsiders called it "the resistance." By the beginning of 1981, two thousand Hmong refugees in the camps of Thailand had signed up to fight for Vang Pao.

This new battle was different from the war they remembered. Crossing the Mekong had transported them to a new world. For as long as there had been states, Hmong had been spread across maps on which other people drew the lines; for the most part, they had lived and traveled freely, rarely identifying as citizens of a certain nation. But after crossing the river, Hmong found themselves in a country that viewed them as foreigners and would not let them stay. They were enclosed by fences, captive until the officials from one nation or another told them where they could live. What they most wanted was still simply to reclaim the life they had had before the fighting ever reached them. While in theory Hmong in the camps could go back to Laos at will, the fact was that the same violence that had driven them out would be waiting upon their arrival. In this new world, they would have to fight just for the right to return safely across the border and into the nation from which they had been exiled.

But here was hope. Vang Pao was back, ready to lead his people to victory. He touted the support of the same powerful nations with which he had partnered during the war. Now, same as then, these nations saw Vang Pao as a means to their own ends. Thailand, eager to push back against the spread of communism in the region, offered Neo Hom arms and military training. Government forces allowed the resistance to operate freely along the border with Laos, in exchange for intelligence gathering. The United States no longer saw strategic value in trying to control Laos as a nation, but the Reagan administration was launching anti-communist actions across the developing world in order to undermine the Soviet Union. Using the search for POWs in Laos as administrative cover, various actors from the executive branch began funneling money to insurgents in Laos. Upon leaving Thailand in 1975, Vang Pao had sworn that in ten years' time he and his compatriots would win back Laos. Now, at least from the tedium of Ban Vinai, that began to seem possible.

———

Chou Lor was not too proud to sew. Even as his philandering resumed in the dark corners of the camp, at home he stepped into his adult role of helping to support the family. There were his elderly parents, of course, and now in addition to his and Ia's daughter there was a son. And so Chou Lor would hunch over, picking his way through the dainty designs until there was a finished square to sell.

Still, in the limited economy of the camp, it was hard not to struggle. The night before Ia went into labor with their third child, she was out until long past midnight, pilfering firewood from the surrounding hills; she gave birth before dawn. The destitution provoked her. As she watched so many young children in the camp go naked, she vowed that her children would not. What's more, her children wouldn't wake up hungry or have only rice and chiles to eat. They would have meat, at least a little bit to flavor a broth, every day. And yet no matter how much she and Chou Lor sewed, even the barest feeling of plenty remained out of reach.

Over time, shoestring businesses cropped up around camp as people tried to coax a few Thai *baht* out of the ether for themselves. Ia observed that other residents were selling cooked sticky rice. Everyone received rations of regular rice, but not sticky, making it a natural commodity. She saw her opening. In spite of official prohibitions, some residents had convinced local farmers to rent them small plots of land on which to grow food. Ia convinced her father-in-law to secure a little piece of land nearby and buy seed. She and Chou Lor did the rest: burn the land, plant the rice, hack the weeds as they sprouted.

When the crop was ripe, Ia and Chou Lor harvested it all and hauled it back to their house. It was too valuable to eat—the family stuck to the government-issue rice. Instead, each morning, Ia would cook a batch of the sticky rice and sell it: one bowlful wrapped in a banana leaf for 1 *baht* (about 5 cents in U.S. currency). It was more than she had ever sold rice for, but only because she had never sold rice before; really, it was next to nothing. When it came time to plant another crop, Ia's father-in-law decided it was not profitable enough and therefore they would not grow rice again. Ia doubled down on sewing. And watching.

There were two older women in Ban Vinai who had a lucrative business making tofu. Their big account was the camp hospital, which bought the duo's entire day's production to distribute to pregnant women as a supplement to their rations. Ia saw that the two women made a steady profit. She also saw that they argued a lot. When at last they fought so badly that one of them split, Ia wasted no time in approaching the partner who was left with the tofu-making machine and asking to join the business. The answer was: *Yes, but.* Ia became an employee, with the boss woman talking down to her as she sweated through the labor.

Chou Lor watched, too, and proposed to Ia that the machine that made this woman boss was a simple construction of cement and metal—one he could easily make. He ground down rocks to use as cement, which he fashioned into a thick-walled basin the size of an oil drum. In the center he installed a mixing blade, honed from salvaged metal. Ia dropped her boss, and she and Chou Lor began selling their own tofu to the hospital. The needlework had yielded about 12,000 Thai *baht* every few months. With the tofu, they made more than 10,000 Thai *baht* every two weeks. They continued getting the camp rations of broken rice and cooking oil but supplemented them with better food: fresh meat from a pig killed that morning, two pounds for a single day, plus vegetables to cook it with.

For the first time in her life, Ia started getting *rog,* "fat." Her scrawny body added layers, the angles gradually softening, her cheeks becoming round. But fat is more than that. Because Chou Lor's family had always been so poor, people hadn't wanted them around, assuming they were out to cadge salt, oil, and money if they could. Ia had felt their nasty looks, heard the potshots they didn't try to hide. Now her house was the one being visited by people with less, who would drop hints about what they didn't have, wished they did.

Have some of ours, Ia would tell them nobly. Clan members now asked Ia's father-in-law for help with catastrophic expenses—funerals, shaman rituals, bail for a relative in jail. When he gave them the money, everyone involved knew who had earned it. More than once, a Khang man approached Ia with compliments. *I never expected that you would be fat like this,* they would tell her. *Had I known you were going to make this kind of money, I would have married you myself.*

While Ia and Chou Lor were the force behind this income, it was understood that the money belonged to the family. Chou Lor's father, as the patriarch, decided how to spend it. For Ia to make a significant purchase, she had to get permission. If she didn't, it would be considered stealing and she could be beaten.

She did not dare ask for the thing she wanted most: her mother. Ia's father had died in 1981—a man who escaped to Thailand shortly after the death had brought Ia the news. Ia's mother remained in Laos, together with Ia's youngest brother, Tong, who had now started a family of his own. Whenever Ia received news of their lives through relatives in Ban Vinai, it pained her to hear how desperately poor they were. Daily, Ia dreamed of paying a guide the three silver bars to smuggle her mother to Thailand. But even the mere fantasy was hemmed in by reality: Her mother would not come without Tong, and he not without his wife, and she not without their son. The cost would be not just three silver bars—itself more than Ia could ask for—but four times that. Ia tucked her dream in the thatch of the roof and proceeded, carefully, to ask her father-in-law for permission to buy the next-best thing: two cassette recorders, one for herself and one to send to her mother. To Ia's relief, he agreed.

Until then, Ia had had no means of communicating with her mother other than by sending messages with the people who snuck from Thailand to Laos and back. There was a postal service of sorts, but neither Ia nor her mother knew how to read or write. Now, with the purchase of these recorders, there would be a delicate magnetic tape like an umbilical cord pulsing across the Mekong.

When Ia pressed record on the brand-new cassette deck, she tingled with excitement, this being the first time in years that she had been able to speak to her mother directly. *Hi, Mom,* she said, but that was all she could get out before the tears came. The rest of the tape was recorded through her sobs.

With each new recording she was more able to speak clearly. Always the messages were the same: descriptions of daily life and troubles, yes, but every new topic led back to the same old one, which was that Ia missed her mother terribly. When Ia's mother received the tape, she would carry her machine to the edge of the village so that she could record a reply in private. Two weeks later, a courier would appear at the Khang family doorstep in Ban Vinai, and Ia would grab the package, rip it open, and pop the cassette in the recorder. Because secreting herself would arouse suspicion, instead she would press play right in the middle of the house, where anyone could hear.

On every cassette, Ia's mother wept as she spoke. As Ia listened, her own eyes would tighten and then flood, until she was crying so much that she had to press stop and wait until she could calm herself enough to listen again. Once, describing Ia's father's funeral, her mother admitted that she had included Ia in her mourning, as if her daughter were dead. *I keep waiting for you,* her mother said. *I keep thinking that you're here, but I don't see you—I can't find you. No matter where I look, no matter how long I wait, you're never coming back.*

As soon as Ia could find the time, she would carry her own cassette player to the outskirts of camp, where the ground returned to scrub bushes and there was at least a modicum of quiet. Her mother was too poor to buy new cassettes; each time, she would record over her daughter's message and send the tape back that way. But Ia bought a new one every time, so that she could keep the recordings her mother had sent. On days when Ia missed her the most, she would play back an old cassette. What she heard was her mother, of course, but faint in the background, there was always the residual sound of Ia's own voice, softly speaking her own sorrows.

In time, the tofu business made enough money that the family could accumulate savings; they wrapped the bills in plastic and cached them in the folds of the thatch roof. When Ia sent cassettes to her mother, now she enclosed small amounts of cash for meat or new clothes—largesse that her father-in-law allowed because it made his family look good. In Laos, word spread that the scrawny girl they all remembered had gotten fat in Thailand. Ia savored knowing that they knew.

At the same time, the work required by the tofu business ground her down. Now eighteen years old, Ia rose each day before dawn, strapped her baby to her back, made a fire and cooked breakfast for the family, nursed the baby while she was eating, then strapped the baby back on and walked to fetch water. She no longer had to carry water jugs with a yoke, like when she was a child; Chou Lor had made her a two-wheeled pushcart. But because each batch of tofu required six buckets of water, more than she was allowed to tap from the camp's tanks, she had to hike to one of the many successive wells the clan had dug to supplement the camp rations. When the well site was far away, she paced herself for the long walk. When it was down by the river, she muscled the cart uphill. When she miscarried a pregnancy at six months, Ia felt sure the cause was the cart's handle, with all that deadweight, pushing the baby right out of her.

Chou Lor had his own pushcart, and on their best days he lugged his own load of water back from the well to make a second batch of tofu, doubling their profits. Their success elevated the family, and he was appointed to a council of clan leaders. These men were tasked with resolving disputes among families in their clans, but really, that was secondary work. By now Ban Vinai had become the headquarters for Vang Pao's army of guerrilla fighters. In practice, Chou Lor's new position was part of the vague and diffuse leadership of the resistance.

Chou Lor hadn't served in Vang Pao's army during the war, nor among the rebels on Phou Bia. His father had forbidden it: The man had lost all his other sons to war and disease. If he lost Chou Lor, too, there would be no one to bury him when he died, no one to feed him in the afterlife. After so many years of not participating, Chou Lor now jumped at the chance to join the civilian side of operations.

The near-daily meetings of the clan's council consisted of in-spiring words from General Vang Pao recorded onto cassettes, with reports on tactical advances and other inspiration for the struggle. After giving from their own pockets, these leaders then spread the passion to the masses, along with requests for donations that every-one knew could not be refused. In exchange for their dedication to the cause, Chou Lor and his compatriots were promised govern-ment posts in the nation they would win.

Chou Lor swelled with a new pride. He talked about going to school, and about learning how to conduct Hmong funerals and other rituals. He imagined positioning himself to move higher up in the clan leadership. Any of these things would have brought the family greater status, but for Ia, what mattered was the immediate impact: Chou Lor's work for the resistance meant he was less and less available to share the work of their household.

Increasingly, Ia found herself making tofu alone. She became pregnant again even as she still tended to an ailing toddler whose incessant cries were comforted only by riding on Ia's back. There the toddler lay, against her in a slick of sweat through the humid months, soaking her back as he peed (diapers being an unthinkable indulgence). Ia tried boiling the vat of soybeans that were the tofu's raw material, but when she leaned over, the steam burned the child and set him howling in her ear. When her father-in-law shouted to take the noisy thing away so he could smoke his opium in peace, she would leave the house without anywhere to go.

Finally, when her father-in-law was happy and high, Ia could hand him the child and work furiously to cook, smash, press, and deliver the day's batch by three o'clock, when the hospital cafeteria closed. After delivering the tofu, she returned to the long thatch house to start another fire, cook dinner for the family, and clean up. If there was a breath of time after all that, she would sit in the cold light of the lantern and stitch a design that could be sold for a few more Thai *baht*. She went to sleep knowing that the next day would be the same.

As she and Chou Lor slogged through each day, they fought. Ia was no longer silent—the years in Thailand had hardened her fear of her husband and father-in-law into rigid resentment. Ia and Chou Lor bit into each other with their words, though always just with words. Then one day, after the fourth baby was born, this changed. During a forgettable argument about a sewing needle, Chou Lor picked up the iron fire poker and struck it across Ia's head with such fury that her world went black. Ia came to on the ground, on her side, the baby she had been nursing still pressed to her breast. Her sister Ka Yang had lain like this, deathly, her own child burrowing in to nurse from the cold breast. But Ia was different. She had not killed herself.

Ia's forehead was warm and wet—blood, not just on her face but puddling in the dirt beneath her. Chou Lor was gone. Ia looked up and instead saw her father-in-law, agape at the hemorrhaging.

When Chou Lor had struck her before, back at the cave, he had been under fierce orders. This time, though, the violence had come from inside him, and that scared Ia more. She knew how it worked, had seen it too many times: a man beats his wife and gets away with it, so he beats her a second time, and a third—and then for the rest of her life. Even back in Laos it had been so common that few people, male or female, bothered to question it.

In this instant, though, Ia resolved it would never happen to her again.

Knowing no one would come to defend her this time, she rose from the floor of the dark house and walked into the light of the main street. The idle people lining the way could see the blood slick across her face and wet in her hair, but she didn't clean it off, couldn't—she needed the evidence. Her father was dead and her mother was a world away. The closest thing she had to the protection of family was her older brother Cher, who had escaped Laos and now lived in Ban Vinai. Even before she reached his doorstep, she knew what she wanted: a divorce.

Ia knew the consequences. To divorce a husband was to cut the ropes that secured a woman in this life. The man would remain in his clan, while she would be expelled. Perhaps her birth clan would pityingly arrange for her remarriage, to a widower or another undesirable partner—in any case, a downgrade in arrangement, now that she was scorned. A worse fate, though, was that she would remain unmarried. Severed from her birth clan by marriage and her husband's clan by divorce, she would no longer have ancestors. In life, she would lack their protection; at death, there would be no one to receive her in the afterlife. Even before dying, she would become a lost soul. The community would call her a curse.

And yet still, when Chou Lor came to her at her brother's home and sobbed, saying he would never hurt her again, Ia refused him. When he cried that without her he would commit suicide, Ia told him she didn't care. *If you're going to kill yourself,* she said, *go ahead. You did this to yourself.*

Two days passed, then the elders of the Khang clan showed up at Cher's home. Their objective was, always, to hold the clan together. Unspoken was their additional motivation: to retain this diligent worker who brought money and prestige to the small clan. Addressing Ia's brother, they explained that while the beating could not be undone, they would offer a deal.

In normal circumstances, when spouses separated, the children naturally remained with their father since they were part of his clan. In this case, if Ia wanted to leave, they would allow her to take her daughter, now six years old. The three sons, including the baby in her arms, would remain with the Khang clan. However, if Ia would go back to Chou Lor, they would protect her. If he harmed her again, they would grant a divorce and she could leave with all her children.

Then the clan elders turned to Ia and asked, *Could you forgive him?*

In a sense, Ia didn't need to answer. While the Hmong economy had changed, the rules had not. She wasn't going to get a better deal—this was considered generous—and really, what was her alternative? Living with her brother, she would be treated as a blight. Anything that went wrong in his home would be blamed on her. Plus, her children: the daughter who stayed with Ia would be treated as a fatherless orphan, and the sons who stayed with Chou Lor would face life with a stepmother, who was likely to treat them as orphans, too. Ia's brother told her to take the deal, go home, and do what the Khang family told her to.

When at last Ia grudgingly left her brother's house and returned to the long thatch house, baby in her arms and the gash now covered with a dark scab, Chou Lor told her he had something for her. Before the fight, they had sent off her sewing to relatives in the United States to sell; while she was gone, a payment had arrived in the mail. Chou Lor handed her a fat stack of Thai *baht,* but also a pair of earrings. He had taken a portion of the payment and paid a metalsmith to make them for her. They were meant to replace the wedding gift from her parents, those silver bars that she and Chou Lor had cashed in years before to buy medicine for their infant daughter. He explained that while the cash would surely be spent before long, times being what they were, the earrings would be something for her to keep through the years.

If it was a peace offering, Ia did not acknowledge the gesture. The money was hers to begin with, after all. But she did love the earrings, little golden hooks from which dangled a row of metal slivers that shimmered like fish scales. Never in her life had Ia owned something so valuable. She had no idea if they made her look pretty—didn't really care, didn't own a mirror. When she thrilled in putting the earrings on, it was not because she was reminded of her parents, nor because they symbolized Chou Lor's guilt. Ia loved these earrings because she had earned them herself. She would never be able to divorce the man she had backed into marrying at thirteen years old. Now, though, she had something that was completely her own—and no one could take it away. The earrings were shining emblems of her industry and ambition, right there in plain view. From then on, whenever someone looked at her, that was what they would see.

———

There are no photographs of Ia from that time. The earliest image of her that exists today was made a few years later, after she had given birth to a fourth son. She was maybe twenty-two years old. The growing economy of Ban Vinai now included a makeshift portrait studio across the sewage canal from the Khang family house. The business had just started offering color photographs, and Ia decided she would get one.

It was still expected that a daughter-in-law like her would ask her father-in-law for permission to spend money on something like a photograph, but Ia no longer troubled herself with such courtesies. Even if the men in the family might yell at her in disapproval, she knew that they would never forsake her and her income. And so she would yell back at them, saying that she had made the money herself and could spend it however she wanted. What she wanted now was a portrait of herself.

Normally, a person would dress up only for New Year's, but on this ordinary March day, Ia took the time to put on all the intricate layers of her finest traditional Hmong outfit. The skirt had scores of razor-sharp pleats, and the jacket was decorated with tiny, colorful stitches and rows of glistening coins. Tied around Ia's growing waist was a meticulously embroidered sash that reached all the way down to her ankles. It was the kind of decadent ensemble that the wealthiest parents would give a beloved daughter as a marriage gift. This one Ia had made for herself.

What's more, at a time when many women had to use rags to sew their New Year's clothing, Ia had bought every piece of this costume—fabric, thread, button, and bead—brand-new. On her ears she still wore the gold earrings with the shimmering scales, but now they were barely noticeable. Over her jacket she wore a colossal high-polish necklace of pure silver that was so heavy it hurt her back to wear it for long. On her head, a beaded hat in the shape of a cone added a foot to her total height.

As Ia walked out of her house and into the world to have her portrait made, she had a special feeling inside. *After a few kids you're going to be ugly,* Chou Lor had taunted her. *You'll look like a monkey.* Today she knew she looked undeniably great.

The portrait studio was a bamboo shack, no walls and only enough roof so that the sun wouldn't cast shadows on the subject. There was just one background: a floor-to-ceiling picture of green mountains and a rushing blue river—not Laos, but similar enough to make it appear that Ia, standing on the edge of that river, had gone home. Because the photographer gave her no more guidance than to simply stand still, she is not posed. Her hands rest at her sides, her face is blank. As her eyes stare firmly back at the camera, she easily fills the frame with just her own self; indeed, there is no room for anyone else.

By that time, in 1986, Ban Vinai had more than forty thousand residents on the official rolls, with another six, eight, maybe ten thousand "illegals," who had managed to sneak in after Thailand began turning refugees away at the Mekong. The camp was crowded as hell, a breeding ground for cholera and suicide: someone killed himself or, more often, *her*self every nine days. And still, each month, an average of 250 babies were born.

Strange fortune, then, that the other Khang relatives gradually moved out of the thatch longhouse where Ia lived, leaving just her, Chou Lor, his parents, and the children. There was plenty of room as Ia gave birth to two more sons and two more daughters. The older siblings convinced the adults to use tofu money for a television and a generator to power it—making them the only people in their section of the camp with such an extravagance. All day, the big, open living area would host throngs of kids who sat in the blue orbit of the screen; at night, their parents joined them to watch Thai movies. Never was it crowded, the house was so spacious. On occasion, the family even hosted funerals for other clans—a taboo broken, but of necessity, since nobody else had the room.

The family had enough money tucked into the roof that Ia and Chou Lor were able to quit the tofu business and its stress. Ia wanted to enroll in the camp's adult school, but she knew that English lessons would not feed her six, then seven, then eight, children. Instead, she chose to keep hustling.

The camp was more than a decade old, and money had accumulated. There were official jobs in the clinic and unofficial jobs with the resistance. As refugees resettled in wealthier countries, they sent cash back to relatives in the camps. No longer a closed system, Ban

Vinai had a jury-rigged economy that supported food stalls, barbershops, and makeshift restaurants, as well as prostitutes and drug traffickers.

In their longing for home, Hmong who had resettled in the United States constituted a satellite market. While most of the time they wore the same polyester fashions as everyone else around them in Denver or Santa Ana, an entire industry materialized to supply them with traditional Hmong clothes for the New Year celebration. People in the camps meticulously folded fabric into the persnickety pleats required for a proper skirt; they batiked and embroidered, and knit countless tiny pom-poms to adorn ornate turbans. Ia and Chou Lor got back into sewing, though this time higher up the value chain. Their product was the sash that topped any Hmong outfit. She would buy piecework cross-stitch from poorer women while he memorized popular designs for the layouts; together they assembled others' work into a finished product that they sold through relatives in the United States for vastly more than the sum of its parts.

Ia found an additional market in the silver coins from Laos that gilded the best Hmong outfits. The coins had to be heavy enough to jangle just so, which meant they had to be old, from when the money was worth something, not the tinny new specie. Being old, though, the coins were tarnished. Ia bought stacks of them from a Thai trader, then scrubbed them with foul-smelling chemicals and a wire brush until they sparkled as if they had just been born at the mint. She packed rolls of them in paper, sent them to an aunt in Fresno, and got back ten U.S. dollars—an even harder currency. It was capitalism at its purest: using money to buy money to make money. Even as they had more children and fed each one meat every day, by the time they marked twelve years in Ban Vinai, Ia and Chou Lor had $4,000 stashed in the roof.

Ban Vinai had been conceived as a stopgap solution, an administrative pause between chapters of real life. Instead, for tens of thousands of refugees it became a chapter of its own. Western observers were flummoxed as to why people stayed for so long, even as they were offered resettlement in the United States. What these observers did not understand was that people like Ia, at least, had no choice of their own. Her family was ruled by a party of one: her father-in-law—he who had lived the longest and eaten the most rice. As long as he wanted to stay in the camp, none of the family could leave.

In fact, they had received their initial clearance for resettlement as soon as they arrived at Ban Vinai, in 1979. Because Ia's father-in-law refused to go—and no one dared defy him—they gave their registration materials to a relative named Yang. Assuming Chou Lor's name and identity, that man sailed through the resettlement process. All the years that Ia and Chou Lor struggled through life in Ban Vinai, the relative and his family were building a new life in Minnesota as the Chou Lor Khangs.

What the Americans offering resettlement failed to see is that their solution did not actually address the problem that these exiled people faced. As historian Ma Vang has written, the path to citizenship in the United States was offered as rescue from the condition of statelessness. And yet national citizenship was not the ill for which Hmong sought relief. What held Chou Lor's father in place was the hope of instead returning to the world from which they had come: *yus teb yus chaw,* they called it, "our land." But it was something far beyond just land.

Since they crossed the Mekong, so much had been knocked out of balance. By the mid-1980s, nearly half the camp's population was fourteen or younger and had little or no memory of life in Laos. Because farming no longer ordained the natural order of life, fundamental elements of Hmong culture had lost their relationship to place and livelihood, existing now only as abstractions. Life as it had been was now held together only by those who could remember and took the time to care.

For older men, not the least important of these elements was the accepted hierarchy that placed them at the top of an immovable pyramid. Since the beginning of Ban Vinai, there had been horror stories about the United States: that it was populated by blood-thirsty giants; that Americans were cannibals who killed Hmong and turned them into canned meat; that, if they went there, the women would be forced to have sex with dogs. But these men had also heard stories that were more plausible and, in a sense, cause for equal alarm. How without translatable skills, these men who had always been self-sufficient farmers became financially dependent on government handouts. How without English, they became socially dependent on their grandchildren to communicate with the larger world. Should those men sign the resettlement papers and board a plane, what remained of the traditional power structure would crumble, and they would be lost in the rubble. For salvation, many looked to the same person they always had: Vang Pao.

The hope that Vang Pao's new army offered was a salve to the despair many elder men felt, and because of it they refused reset-tlement and kept their families in the camp. As their sons grew up, many of them eagerly became foot soldiers for the resistance. They lived in safe houses along the border and communicated with their fellow freedom fighters over crackly field radio connections, just as during the war. When the insurgents slipped into Laos and struck the enemy, their leaders made sure to bring cameras. Photographs were then sent back to Hmong in the United States as bona fide proof that the battle was raging and Vang Pao's promises of immi-nent victory were to be believed. Every New Year in Fresno and Minneapolis, the chorus was the same—*Next year, Laos!*—as home-sick Hmong stuffed more cash into envelopes for Vang Pao's cause.

The daily chatter about a coming victory intoxicated Chou Lor. What Ia heard was nothing more than crazy talk from a bunch of old men. As she saw it, Vang Pao was just "farting to keep the dogs warm," dealing out false promises in order to take in donations. In her mind she asserted that Hmong had never had a country of their own, and they never would. Still, when her father-in-law drew on the savings that she had earned by sewing and making tofu in order to secure his place in a newly won Laos, all she could do was watch in silence. There would be hell to pay if she said out loud what she thought: that the dream was hopeless; that the day would never come; that even if it did come, she wouldn't *want* to go back.

Ia's heart still ached to reach across the Mekong and pull her mother close, yet something in the rest of Ia had changed. She had tasted opportunity, and it was delicious. Returning to the life she had left in Laos now registered as a loss: a return to farming, to working all day just to fill a pot with rice. As long as her father-in-law was alive, she would have to bite her tongue, but the clenching only hardened her resolve not to go backward.

———

In 1985, the resistance hit what should have been a crippling mile-stone: Vang Pao's 1975 prophecy that they would win back Laos in ten years came and went without victory. And yet even as roughly fifty thousand Hmong remained in the camps without the prospect of going home, the resistance endured. Fueled by hope, it was strikingly durable. But the apparatus had one glaring weakness, and Neo Hom's leaders knew it: If the refugees left Ban Vinai and the other camps, the whole thing would fizzle out. Without the camps, there would be no base of operations, no wellspring of eager young guerrillas. Without the operations and guerrillas, there would be no ground game, which meant no evidence with which to persuade donors in the United States that their money was going to win back Laos. And without donors' money, there would be essentially nothing remaining aside from the dream itself. Left on its own, the dream would evaporate.

And so for years, Vang Pao and his henchmen fought a shadow war on resettlement itself. In public, they waged a political battle against repeated bilateral attempts to close the camps and move residents to "third countries" or repatriate them to Laos. In private, the resistance fed the rumors about cannibalism and other terrors of life in the United States, in hopes that they would scare refugees away from leaving the camps. The fear reinforced Chou Lor's father's resolve to stick it out in Ban Vinai, as one year bled into another.

In the end, the family's fate was directed by events beyond the control of anyone in the camp. In the late 1980s, a decade after they arrived, the economic experiment of communism was collapsing across the globe. As the USSR went broke, its financial patronage of the Lao People's Democratic Republic dried up. Vietnam, also starved of Soviet backing, withdrew most of the vast military presence that had fortified Laos for decades. Already, the failure of communism had so gutted the Lao economy that the cloistered nation had cautiously opened itself to capitalism in 1986. Now it scrambled for patrons.

The same nations that had opposed the Lao communists in war now presented themselves as benevolent partners. With power being reshuffled across Southeast Asia, the United States saw investing in the new Lao economy as a chess move that expanded its presence in the region as a counterweight to China. At the same time, Thailand elected a prime minister who had campaigned on the promise of breaking down Cold War barriers to trade and turning "battlefields into marketplaces"; soon after he took office, conflicts with Laos dissipated and Thai companies set about pillaging the country's virgin resources and building factories to turn the raw material into money. With each new agreement, Laos insisted on an essential condition: the insurgency, based in Thailand and endorsed by the Americans, must be cut off. And so just as at the end of the Secret War, Vang Pao's allies disappeared into thin air. Neo Hom was dropped like so much trash.

Of course, Vang Pao had not come this far to simply slink away. As the resistance saw it, the enemy's defenses had been weakened by the loss of Vietnamese soldiers and communism's economic collapse; this was the moment Vang Pao and his guerrillas had been waiting for. One month after the Berlin Wall fell in 1989, Neo Hom made its boldest move yet. From a post within Laos, they unveiled a provisional government that would operate across the nation's north. They even named a king. At the same time, guerrillas from Ban Vinai and other camps slid across the border to join forces with the insurgents already embedded there. Together they returned to some of the same French-built highways that had been strategically crucial during the war, and for a month they attacked Lao army truck convoys with surprising success. Riding on their achievement, Vang Pao rang in 1990 by issuing a proclamation calling the first general meeting of the new government to begin shaping its bureaucracy.

In Ban Vinai, Chou Lor and his cohort huddled around military radios, electrified as they listened to the communications between Vang Pao's top brass and the freedom fighters on the ground. At last, it was happening! Vang Pao himself was telling them so. As the radio sang out one promise after another, the men buzzed with plans for what had finally become a concrete future. With so much commotion, how could it not be real?

And yet no amount of bullishness or dedication could override political reality: Lao PDR was a sovereign state, even a member of the United Nations; Neo Hom was a patchwork insurgency scattered across numerous borders. In the world of states, Neo Hom had no real bargaining power. Staying true to its new trading partner, the Thai government shut down that first assembly of the Neo Hom government, publicly demonstrating that Vang Pao no longer had their backing. Vietnam offered soldiers and ran bombing raids to reinforce the Lao army's retaliation against the resistance. The United States, now working with the communist government to find its own fallen soldiers, blithely dismissed Neo Hom as a non-state actor.

As quickly as it had succeeded, the resistance was gored. What Ia had been thinking all along was truer than ever: no matter how much Vang Pao insisted that they would win back Laos, the Hmong had never had a country, and it seemed they never would.

In 1991, the U.S. State Department negotiated a deal between Thailand, Laos, and the UNHCR to close the camps and relocate the remaining fifty thousand refugees from Laos, either to third countries or back to Laos. Each party walked away satisfied: Thailand would finally rid itself of the unwanted visitors, Laos would defuse the rebels, the UN could call these refugees settled, and the United States could more readily reap the benefits of rapprochement with its old communist foe. In the camps, though, the agreement meant the worst of all outcomes. People who had bet all their chips on returning to Laos after it became safe to do so now faced the possibility of being forced back into the arms of a regime they had risked their lives to escape. Where before so many had rejected offers to resettle in the United States, now thousands jockeyed to sign the papers and get booked on a flight.

It was in this moment, six weeks after the U.S.-brokered deal was signed, that Ia's father-in-law died. He had been snared for selling opium, and in prison he quickly perished. When word reached Chou Lor that his father was gone, the family's balance of power immediately shifted. The old man could no longer hold them back from leaving Ban Vinai. As the new male head of the family, Chou Lor was now free to make his own decisions. Seduced by the resistance and its promises, he still believed that they would win back Laos and return to the life they had had before. With no one to stop him, he was excited to return to the mountains for the glorious battle. Many of his Khang relatives were going, and he pledged to join them.

In the normal order of things, that would have been that: the wife and children would have followed the father wherever he decided they should go. But Ia also felt liberated by the old man's death. Even before he died, there had been change. While Ia had not been granted the divorce she demanded eight years earlier, after she returned to Chou Lor, he had not beaten her again, even when his father told him to. Indeed, as Chou Lor learned to swallow his tongue during their conflicts, Ia's voice grew louder. Now that her father-in-law was gone, she let it be known there was no way she would return to Laos. If Chou Lor needed to, so be it. She was moving to the United States, and she was taking the children, all eight of them. And this time, her plan was not up for debate.

Fine, Chou Lor told her. *I'll find a new wife in Laos.*

But that's not what happened, and no one can say definitively why. Perhaps what changed their fate was that Chou Lor had a cousin who was already living in the United States, and when this man heard of the couple's plans to separate, he sent a cassette recording to Chou Lor excoriating him for his selfish choice. He threatened that because Ia would never be able to take care of the children by herself in America, as soon as she got off the plane he would marry her to someone else in the clan. Hearing that cleared the fog from Chou Lor's head. Later he would explain that grief over his father's death had made him want to follow his clan members back to Laos. In light of his cousin's threat, though, Chou Lor saw that he could not bear to lose his children, nor his wife of now fifteen years. He agreed to lead them to the United States.

Maybe that was it. Or maybe it was this: After their stalemate was firmly established, Ia turned to Chou Lor and offered him the facts as she saw them. She insisted she wasn't trying to persuade him; she just wanted him to understand the pros and cons so he could make a decision without regrets. Were they to return to Laos as a family, she said, they would not be able to farm, at least not yet. There in the jungle, hiding with the resistance, how would they earn the money to buy food for their family of ten? And if they couldn't support themselves, wouldn't they just slide backward into begging a livelihood off others? Wouldn't their children then disrespect them for not being able to provide? Wouldn't the clan shun them? Moving to the United States meant severing ties to Chou Lor's extended family, but it was a chance for their nuclear family to move forward instead of backward.

Ia didn't ask him to come with her—she made it clear she would be fine on her own. Instead, she paid her words out like a rope for him to grab on to, with which to bind himself to her. *Let the poverty end with us,* she said to him. *Let's give our children a better chance.*

It worked. Just as he had towed her across the Mekong when they were young, now—older, wiser—she would lead him across the Pacific Ocean.

The voyage to Fresno was not terrifying, but only because
it was so dominated by motion sickness that there was no
room left for fear. Ia began retching even before they arrived
at the airport, sickened as they rode bus after bus to get there. The
family vomited from Bangkok to Tokyo, then from Tokyo to San
Francisco, the hours grinding on with the eternity of nightmares.
When the food was gone from Ia's stomach, the endless heaving
filled her mouth with acrid bile. The smells emanating from the
meal cart were repugnant—the food itself unthinkable—but she
desperately accepted the black drink a flight attendant offered her.
Passing across her lips, it seemed like a sick joke. The liquid was
hot, bitter, acidic—coffee, though that meant nothing to her. So
little of this was familiar.

Before leaving Thailand, Ia and Chou Lor had taken a required
six-month course that prepared them for life in America: how to
use a refrigerator, how to turn on a stove, how to sign their names
in careful, blocky letters and recognize the question *How old are you?*
But there was so much the course left out. It did not tell them that
the air in Fresno would be gritty, the sky a gray dome of pollution.
Nor did it tell them that there would be nowhere to go for a walk,

that in the city forty cars were stolen each day, that soon a six-lane freeway would be built just blocks from their new home. That as forty thousand refugees like them had arrived in Fresno County, the white Americans had fled the city for housing developments on freshly cleared farmland to the north. That the streets of the southeast were now controlled by the Bloods and the Bulldogs. That the windows would have bars.

The course also did not explain that as soon as their plane touched down in the United States, the status they had achieved in Ban Vinai would be wiped away and they would start again at zero. Didn't matter that they had left the camp a family of enviable means. The savings they had propagated with such enterprise and cunning now seemed like nothing. Worse, they had no immediate means to generate new income. Within days of arriving in the United States, they signed up for public assistance.

In 1993, the average annual income in Fresno—itself paltry compared to most of California—was $12,395 per person. The family's combined welfare payments gave them roughly double that to cover all eleven people in their household. Of the $2,200 a month (in cash aid, food stamps, and housing assistance), $500 went to rent on a house at Belmont and Chestnut, another $300 to payments on a used car that a relative had sold them, another chunk to car insurance, more to electricity, water, telephone. With eight kids, the laundromat alone cost $20 a week, and that was before buying detergent. The equation simply did not work. To save $250 a month, they left the house and rented an apartment with two bedrooms: the first for Ia, Chou Lor, and the baby, the second for the other seven children, ages two to sixteen. Chou Lor's mother slept on the couch.

As a requirement of the public assistance, Chou Lor immediately enrolled in adult school: a bare-essentials education that taught remedial English and otherwise prepared "new Americans" for employment in the lowest tiers of the workforce. After roughly a year, he was deemed work-ready and placed at McDonald's. He washed dishes, cleaned the deep fryer, scrubbed the bathrooms, and mopped the floors. For the first three months, the state paid his wages. After that, the paychecks stopped, even as Chou Lor continued working five days a week and was transferred to a new location across town. He didn't understand the system well enough to know this was not right, much less to protest or ask for his back pay. Instead, assuming that working for free was the requirement so that his family of eleven could continue to receive public assistance, he just kept showing up. This went on for a year, until one day the manager called him into the office. No one had taught Chou Lor how to use the time clock, and since there was no record of his having punched in and out for his shifts, the manager accused him of having skipped work. He was fired.

After another unpaid stint, as a janitor at an elementary school, Chou Lor left the government jobs program. A Hmong man who had been in Fresno for longer tipped him off that there was work at the Foster Farms poultry processing plant. On his first shift, Chou Lor counted himself lucky to be in the room where the chickens had already been killed; a Hmong co-worker showed him how to gut and skin and cut up the bodies, how to properly arrange the parts on the yellow Styrofoam trays. Chou Lor learned how to use the time clock and was glad to reliably receive a paycheck, but the money was disappointing: $200 a week, less income tax deductions. Plus, now that he had a steady wage, the family's food stamps and cash aid were reduced. Even with him working forty hours a week, the household took in the same amount as when he had not worked at all.

Every day Chou Lor and Ia patched together a way forward, but the friction between them made the system fragile. While there was no more physical abuse, when the dam inevitably cracked, one person's rage would flood out onto the other. This was not the marriage of easy cooperation and warm cohabitation that Ia had witnessed with her parents. It was a tense partnership further strained by a financial equation that did not balance out: too little money, too many mouths to feed. And even as they tried to stop having children, still more came.

In 1996, Ia gave birth to her ninth child—in a hospital, for the first time, because they had heard it was required in order for the government to process paperwork for the baby. When the nurse arrived at Ia's bedside to footprint the newborn and complete the birth certificate, he asked what the child's name would be. They had not chosen one yet; Hmong customarily wait three days to name a child. For lack of a better solution, Ia pointed to the name on the nurse's name tag: Jim. They never gave the boy a Hmong name. Less than two years later came Lou. Then the baby of the family, Alice.

The eleven kids had to be clothed and then clothed again as the garments wore out, just as in Thailand. Here, though, everywhere each child looked there was something more—brighter, trendier, fancier—to want. Fifty-dollar tennis shoes like the ones another kid in junior high had. Soda for the walk home from school. For a while, one son refused to eat anything but Burger King Whoppers. Ia and Chou Lor could not make ends meet even for necessities, and yet Ia felt her children's cravings in her bones. As a child, she had yearned for things that were out of reach—in her case, merely a pair of real shoes to cover her bare feet, but the desire was the same. What failure to have reached America and then not be able to give her children all they dreamed of.

Ia would have joined the crew at Foster Farms, but a persistent affliction in her hip made standing on a factory line unsustainable. She spoke not even the barest English, disqualifying her from most other wage jobs. While the county's free adult school could have corrected this for her, the need for money felt too acute, too urgent to indulge in such a protracted solution. Furthermore, as she understood it, her being on an official payroll would mean that the family would no longer qualify for food stamps and housing assistance.

Ia had been sure that moving to the United States would mean she would never have to farm again. And yet within months of her arrival in Fresno, she was laboring in the fields that ringed the city limits. First it was strawberries, a fruit she had never seen before, then cherry tomatoes, whose plants harbored ghastly green caterpillars whose pulsating bodies were as long as her fingers. Always it was all day bent over, fingers aching from picking someone else's crop of a thousand tiny fruits. She learned to be delicate with the berries, to stomp on the caterpillars without losing pace. The kids stayed at home with her mother-in-law, and at the end of the day she brought home forty, fifty in cash. She preferred to see it this way: two days and she had $100, those three digits something she could hang on to. If there was a path out of being so miserably poor, this was a step.

———

Ia had come to Fresno as part of the largest wave of refugees in U.S. history: 1.28 million people, displaced from mainland Southeast Asia in the aftermath of the wars that ended in 1975. Of those, 880,000 came from Vietnam, 150,000 from Cambodia, and 250,000 from Laos. Of the latter, roughly 140,000 were Hmong.

The federal government scattered the Hmong into cities across the country in hopes that their dispersal would accelerate assimilation. What happened instead is not surprising: mind-bending cultural differences, paralyzing language barriers, searing racism, unwinnable financial struggles, all of which led to a perilous sense of isolation. Instead of melting into the crowd in Providence or Denver, the majority of these new immigrants responded by moving again—to be together.

In 1977, Fresno had one Hmong family. Five years later, twelve thousand Hmong lived there. This small city had long been the industrial center of the dry valley that runs four hundred fifty miles down the middle of California; soon it became the center of Hmong America, too. By the time Ia arrived in late 1993, thirty-five thousand Hmong lived in Fresno County, making up 5 percent of the total population.

While each family had its own set of reasons for coming, there was a unifying theme: Fresno was the unofficial capital of the San Joaquin Valley, which was renowned for having some of the most productive agricultural land in the country. Many Hmong believed that moving there would enable them to farm again. In this way, they were part of a long tradition of immigrants drawn to the valley for its ag economy. Today kids in the Fresno County school system speak more than fifty languages other than English at home. When their parents and grandparents address them in Portuguese, Punjabi, Mixtec, and Ilocano, their words are often rooted in a rural past far away.

But agriculture in the San Joaquin Valley is the polar opposite of the subsistence farming most Hmong practiced in Laos. From the very start it has been profit-oriented and capital-intensive: buy land, buy inputs, buy machinery. Unless new immigrants arrive with loads of cash, most can join the system only as poorly paid laborers who pick the fruit and process the chickens on a factory line. Some enterprising Hmong did manage to start and sustain their own farms in the early years. As necessarily commercial enterprises, though, the farms bore little resemblance to those their proprietors had had in Laos. These farmers grew mostly specialty vegetables for a Pan-Asian clientele; rice, once their primary crop, was now bought at the store even by the farmers themselves.

And they were the fortunate ones. Vastly more did not have the chance to farm at all. Instead, Ia and most of the other 120,000 Hmong who had resettled in the United States by the end of 1993 were dropped into an economic system in which there was little place for them except at the bottom. Some adapted, rose through the system, and thrived; most did not. The year Ia arrived, eighteen years after the first Hmong came to North America, more than 60 percent of all Hmong in the United States lived below the poverty level. In Fresno, which had the largest population nationwide, 90 percent were on welfare.

Poverty was not the only blight they had to endure. Multiple studies showed that Hmong Americans had starkly higher rates of mental illness than the average American, greater even than other Southeast Asian refugees. Depression was rampant. So were the fall-out behaviors of domestic violence and substance abuse. Naturally, the afflictions fed off each other: poverty deepened the trenches from which the heavy heart had to climb, and the weight of so much psychic strain made it harder to ascend financially.

From the beginning, Vang Pao positioned himself as the light that would help Hmong prosper in this darkness. Through a net-work of nonprofit organizations, he offered material and social support to newly arrived Hmong. He organized a national council of Hmong leaders that could act as a sort of government for Hmong affairs. At the same time, his organization Lao Veterans of America brought delegations of Hmong veterans to Washington, DC, and hired a lobbyist to advocate for their interests. Among other things, the group pushed legislation that allowed Vang Pao's former soldiers and their wives to bypass the U.S. citizenship test's requirement that applicants speak English and to instead take the test aided by interpreters. "The contributions that Gen. Vang Pao has made to the Hmong and Laotian people of California have been invaluable," Representative George Radanovich proclaimed on the floor of the U.S. House in 1996. "I am pleased to have him as a constituent in California's Central Valley."

Even as Vang Pao facilitated life in the United States, though, he never wavered in his ultimate goal: winning back Laos. His battle cries thrilled those for whom moving to the United States had only served to complete the sense of displacement that began in Thai-land. Men who had been leaders in Laos found themselves relying on their children to communicate with authorities. Because they lacked English language skills, they were expected to work entry-level jobs that were supervised by others—even, unthinkably, by women. Elder Hmong women, meanwhile, largely stayed home to watch their grandchildren while their own children went to work.

Living in apartments and small houses spread across Fresno or another city, they were often separated from everyone they knew except for the people they lived with. When they left their homes, they faced relentless racism.

Furthermore, both old and young watched as the fundamentals of their culture eroded further. Hmong religion does not center on a church or single leader. Instead, it is composed of rituals that rely on the participation of many clan members: to play formal roles, but also to more generally reinforce the sense that the group remains unified. In the United States, people showed up for these gatherings less and less often. Increasingly, young people could not carry on the traditions because they had failed to learn the rituals in the first place. Those who cared watched in despair. In light of this, the desire to return to Laos, to *yus teb yus chaw*—our land—took on new fervor.

As in the refugee camps, Vang Pao and his cadre were there at every turn to stoke this longing and turn it into donations to his coalition of rebels, Neo Hom. Contributors were given stamped certificates promising one thing or another after the country they had been forced to leave was reclaimed: free airfare to return to Laos, a house and a new car once they got there, double their money back. Most famously, Neo Hom sold positions in the government that would be installed after victory was won. To secure a position, men needed only to pay a fee and then make a monthly contribution. To be a village headman cost $250 up front plus $25 a month. To be a cabinet minister was $5,000 plus $500 monthly. Becoming a general in the army was possible, too, with a price tag starting at $5,000 for the third-tier rank of brigadier. It's hard to calculate just how much Neo Hom netted from this apparatus over the two decades it was in place, but Shoua Yang, a researcher in Illinois, has offered some sense of the scale. In 2001, seven hundred army general positions were sold, bringing in an estimated $3.5 million. Two years later, all eighteen national ministerial positions had been filled, which would

net more than $100,000 annually from monthly dues alone. If any-
one defaulted on the payments, there was a wait list to fill his place
in the cabinet.

By the time Ia and Chou Lor arrived in Fresno in 1993, Neo
Hom's last-gasp offensive into Laos had been quashed. Vang Pao had
been banned from Thailand, and the closing of all official refugee
camps had mostly eliminated his insurgents on the ground. There
were still rebels around Phou Bia and elsewhere in the country, but
they were loyal to leaders who had risen up in the general's absence. Meanwhile, Laos had reestablished diplomatic relations with
the United States, which meant the American government was no
longer going to back up Vang Pao. And yet even as Neo Hom's fight
for Laos might have appeared to be over, Vang Pao's people continued to ask for money.

Vang Pao himself never made the appeal overtly—he only ever
requested people's "support." But clan leaders would show up at
Ia and Chou Lor's door saying that because the general was their
father, they were obligated to donate to his cause; that even if the
family's funds consisted of just one minimum wage paycheck from
the chicken plant, they should still give at least $100. Ia suspected
the money went straight into their pockets, and still she felt she and
Chou Lor had no choice but to hand it over.

There isn't a single reason that, when Vang Pao's henchmen came
knocking, people did not just turn them away. The strategy of having clan leaders asking clan members for money certainly drew on
traditional hierarchies that Hmong were reluctant to defy. And some
people were plain scared. As early as 1985, the FBI had investigated
one of Vang Pao's nonprofit organizations for demanding money from
newly arrived refugees and telling them that if they did not continue
to donate, their relatives in Laos would be harmed. One high-profile
leader who had opposed Vang Pao had received death threats. In fear,
he built an eight-foot-high fence around his entire house.

Strange, then, that probably the larger reason that people continued to give to Vang Pao's collectors was that they still believed in the general himself. Or at least they wanted to. For so many, there was still an aching desire to return to the life they remembered living long ago—before the war, before Thailand, before welfare checks and lonely apartments. Those who continued to believe that Vang Pao was the last and best chance they had of returning to *yus teb yus chaw* in Laos looked past his inconsistencies, or didn't see them in the first place. Membership in Neo Hom, once essentially mandatory for Hmong in the United States, did quietly drop to roughly 30 percent of the community by 2006. And yet that still meant roughly fifty thousand people. Even after ten, then twenty, then thirty years without victory, there was no other person who came close to eliciting the devotion from Hmong people that Vang Pao did. That remains true today.

And so for many Hmong it was earth-shattering when, on June 4, 2007, the FBI arrested Vang Pao and nine of his associates. They had been caught in a sting operation, which found the group ready to pay an undercover agent nearly $10 million for antiaircraft missiles, AK-47s, land mines, and other military-grade weapons. According to the prosecution, they planned to deliver the supplies to guerrillas in Laos, who would blow up government buildings in Vientiane and take the nation back in a violent coup. Whereas four decades earlier, the U.S. government had given Vang Pao and his army comparable weapons for free, now it charged them with terrorism. If convicted, Vang Pao would spend the rest of his life in prison.

On the surface, it could have appeared that Vang Pao was truly guilty. Around 2004, he had fallen out of favor among some Hmong Americans, veterans especially. After years of protesting Laos's human rights abuses against Hmong still in the country, he seemed to abandon their cause and instead voiced support for the establishment of Normal Trade Relations between the United States and Laos—even meeting with Vietnamese government officials in the process. A sensational attack on Laos would signal a return to his original convictions and, likely, win him redemption from those who had departed the flock. But that is not the prevailing theory of what happened. Given Vang Pao's history, many believe the whole thing—talk of attack plans, photos of him appraising weapons—was just PR to raise more money for a war that would never happen. Indeed, during bail hearings in Sacramento, Vang Pao's lawyers repeatedly argued that the FBI's accusations were overblown. Their case was simple: even if Vang Pao and his crew had purchased the weapons, their plan to use them was simply not viable. "The notion of the Hmong people taking over the government of Laos," the defense told the courtroom, "is a fantasy." Vang Pao, dressed in an orange jumpsuit, listened in silence as an interpreter relayed the proceedings to him.

Outside the courthouse, more than two thousand of Vang Pao's supporters protested. For weeks there had been similar rallies, not just in Sacramento but around courthouses and capitol buildings across the country. Holding portraits of Vang Pao and waving American flags, the protesters wailed as if they were attending the man's funeral. FREE OUR BELOVED FATHER read a sign in Sacramento. HMONG ARE NOT TERRORISTS read another in Madison, Wisconsin. To raise money for Vang Pao's legal defense fund, the community was asked to make cash contributions.

———

Among the military elite who had first immigrated to the United States after Vang Pao's arrival in 1975 was Kue Chaw, who had worked as a radio operator for the CIA. The Americans had given him the code name Bison, for his burly build, but he had been in the military since he was so light that the parachute carrying him would lazily float to the ground. He fought for the French at Dien Bien Phu in 1954 and continued against the communists until the day the war ended for the Hmong and he was ushered onto a jam-packed C-130 transport plane bound for Thailand. One of the lucky few.

In March 1976, Chaw and his family of twelve arrived in Philadelphia. Grimy snow lay on the ground. Police sirens wailed through the night. Neighbors egged the doors and windows. Shivering with a chill he had never known, Chaw ached for the land he had left. And yet for him the war was over. Within the din of the United States, he would find precious peace for the first time, and for that he saw this place, not Laos, as the promised land. He renounced Vang Pao's insurgency as no more than the dreams of angry men. As the leader of his own smaller clan, his goal would be to make a new life in America.

For several years, he and his wife tried to make Philadelphia work, growing herbs in hanging planters outside their too-small apartment, just to be able to flavor their broth with a trace of familiar flavor. The heartache was too much.

In the summer of 1980, Chaw's American sponsor gave him a map of the United States and pointed out the places with milder winters. Chaw's mother-in-law made a down payment on a '77 Chevy Caprice. He rounded up a carful of men who knew how to drive, got the rest of his circle to donate gas money, and set off on a road trip in search of a place to set down roots. They bounced from Minnesota to Oregon to Tennessee and, finally, to North Carolina. It happened on the Blue Ridge Parkway: He stopped to fill up the tank, walked out behind the gas station, and found himself surrounded by trees. He just kept walking deeper into the green. A light rain began to kiss his skin and the smell of woodsmoke filled his head. He thought, *This is it.*

Back in Philadelphia, Chaw convinced others to join him in part by explaining that they could actually grow things in North Carolina. By fall, he led the first wave to McDowell County, in the western mountains. Locals insisted that they couldn't grow rice there because no one ever had, but Chaw still sent word to Laos asking his sister Phoua to mail him seed. When her package failed to arrive—intercepted by customs, he assumed—Chaw sent back instructions for how to conceal the grains. At last they arrived: this time just twelve seeds, each one tucked into a slit in the packaging itself.

When spring peeked out from behind winter, Chaw and his wife prepared the ground in the backyard, where they could monitor the plants daily. On March 1 they planted two seeds, on March 15 another two, and so on, at two-week intervals. The first sprouts were thrilling, and the couple buzzed as their plants grew thickly through the summer, some as tall as Chaw himself.

The reckoning came in autumn. Some plants produced bushy masses but no flowers. Others produced flowers but proved barren. Only the two planted on April 15—one purple rice, one yellow—managed to produce seed. That was enough. Chaw asked to rent an acre from his neighbor, and on April 15, 1982, he and his wife used the seeds from those two successful plants to start their first small crop. They called the purple rice *nplej tshav*—"blood rice," the go-to name for any variety that color. The yellow rice didn't have a name, so they called it *nplej Phoua,* after his sister.

Chaw and his wife kept their children out of the rice field. His vision for a Hmong community in North Carolina had never included returning to farming as a livelihood. The whole point of living here was to reap the opportunity America offered, which meant the children should spend their time studying. Chaw started an organization that attracted Hmong to North Carolina and supported them in finding employment and, through that, self-sufficiency without government welfare.

Busy with his advocacy, Chaw left the rice field to his wife to tend the second year. But how much work it was for one person! And from so many days spent in the sun, her light skin began to turn dark. It wasn't worth the sacrifice. After the second year, they ceased farming rice.

In the meantime, though, other Hmong had asked for seed. Chaw gave it away freely. Crops of *nplej Phoua* and *nplej tshav* grew, and in turn their offspring was shared. More seed was sent from

Laos to the United States, and from North Carolina to Georgia and Arkansas, Oklahoma and Tennessee. Over time, wherever the summers were long enough and a Hmong person could find a scrap of land not far from where she lived, the green shoots materialized: in big backyards, in community gardens, on marshy land too soggy for a regular crop. By the time Ia arrived in the United States, Hmong rice had jumped the Continental Divide. A few women had even begun figuring out how to coax a crop from the rich, dry soil of the near desert in Fresno.

———

Ia was not cut out to be someone else's farm laborer. She didn't mind the work itself—it was piecework, and her innate hunger for money fueled her to pick briskly up one row and down the next. What broke her was the disrespect. Some farmers didn't even offer water to drink. After one particularly enraging day of being told to haul heavy buckets of tomatoes from one end of a field to another and then, because of the manager's mistake, back again, she blew up at her employer in a tirade about decency and left the field, vowing never to hire herself out again.

That fall, she enrolled in adult school. No social studies or great books—this was education tailored to get non-English-speaking students speaking enough of the language to enter the blue-collar workforce. As a result of federal and then state welfare reforms, Ia was told she was required to attend school in order to continue receiving public assistance. She welcomed the mandate. At last she would be in class, learn some English, perhaps even advance into employment that held more dignity than picking other people's fruit.

It was 1997 and her tenth child, Lou, was five months old. He refused the bottle, so that first night of adult school she tucked him under her coat and took a seat in the classroom with him concealed against her breast. Inevitably, he cried out. The teacher stopped the lesson and turned to face the pupils, bewildered. When the woman asked what the noise was, Ia sheepishly unzipped her coat to reveal the infant, nursing. The teacher escorted her out of the classroom apologetically, promising that she would explain Ia's situation to the caseworker and have her excused from school. Ia, without the English to object or explain or cry out in defeat, said nothing. It was her first and last day of school ever.

The following spring, real opportunity came. An auntie named Chang asked Ia if she wanted to grow rice on some land that her brother was renting out. Ia immediately replied yes, even though it made no sense. In Fresno, rice was cheap and plentiful—Ia bought it in fifty-pound bags and ate it twelve months of the year. She didn't intend to sell her crop, and yet growing it for her own consumption would never be cost-effective. Indeed, in order to finance it, she would have to swallow her pride and spend weeks picking beans for someone else. Here, though, numbers went out the window. What enticed her was the rice itself. Growing her own meant that for the first time since Laos she would have *mov nplej tshiab*, something no amount of money could buy.

Traditionally, *mov nplej tshiab* refers to the first serving of rice eaten from a new crop. The name, roughly pronounced "mon blay chia," means essentially "fresh rice." But so much is lost in translation. In a country where staple foods never come just picked from a field, where calories are abundant regardless of the season, the idea of rice being *fresh* has little significance. In Laos, though, every year Ia's family and so many others watched carefully as their stores of rice dwindled over the winter and spring. In the best years, it lasted all the way until the new crop came in. In most years, though, sometime in summer they faced the hungry season: when their rice had run out and they were reduced to filling their bellies with cassava and corn, foods normally reserved for livestock.

To hasten the end of those hollow days, they would make the new rice crop accessible just a little bit sooner by picking some of it still green. The grains would be full but not yet fully developed, much of the sugar inside still waiting to be converted into starch. To make this emergency ration palatable, they would toast it over a fire. What happened next was like a divine gift. As the green rice browned, it would release a blanket of aromas, first earthy, then sweet and buttery. Next, cooked in water, the rice released a new palette, nutty and warm.

It was the alchemy of necessity: all their wanting transformed into splendor. Ia, as a child, savored the one meal of *mov nplej tshiab* she ate each year. Everyone did.

Before anyone could eat the *mov nplej tshiab,* a separate meal was prepared. A chicken was killed, if there was one to be had. Tiny cups were filled with rice wine. A mound of fresh rice was roasted until it popped open and the fragrance inside exploded out, as if ringing a bell to the spirit world. The male head of the household would call to the spirits of the deceased, that line of men and women who had led the family before him, to come satisfy their own hunger. In exchange, the living requested protection and guidance through to the next harvest. *Bless us through the coming year,* the man before the altar would say, *so that we can have another prosperous season and feed you like this once again.* It was an infinite exchange, going backward to when the deceased themselves offered rice to their forefathers, going forward to when this man leading this family would be fed in the afterlife by his sons and their sons.

By this point in the day the children would be tugging on their mothers' legs, impatient for the rice whose smell had by now filled the dark home and wafted through its thatch walls into the world outside. Men would eat first, then women and children. After perhaps months of living off corn mush, the *mov nplej tshiab* gave them sustenance. With its inimitable toasted flavor, it gave them succulence. And it also gave them something beyond food. As the fresh rice passed between the lips of the living, it was confirmation that they had made it, that they would last another year. It was at once a celebration of renewal and proof of sheer survival.

By the time Auntie Chang approached Ia with an offer to farm, it had been years since Ia had lacked rice. But she had not had *mov nplej tshiab* for decades—since before they arrived in Fresno, since before all these children and all these years devoted to making sure they had clothes and meat, at least a little bit, every day. Ia had not had *mov nplej tshiab* since she was a child herself, since before they fled Sa Na Oua during the rainy season of 1978, leaving their rice crop behind them in the field. So when Auntie Chang asked if she would like to grow rice out in the dull fields of Sanger, southeast of the city, Ia was surprised and confused—didn't even know rice could be grown there—but she said yes without another thought.

————

Because Ia couldn't afford the whole farm herself, she split it up with some other women. Each fifty-yard row cost $10 to rent for the season. The other women took five rows apiece; Ia took ten. In April they planted seed given to them by Auntie Chang, and nearly every day clear into September they met at the farm to work their crops. They all knew how to grow rice, but none knew exactly how to grow rice *here.* They compared strategies and eyed one another's plants as they grew. Energized by the unspoken competition, Ia weeded her rows voraciously.

When the rice finally matured, the women sweated through milling it the way they had in Laos, rigging a traditional wooden mortar out of railroad ties and part of an old telephone pole. The final product cooked out to be soggy and somewhat bland. Disappointing, but for Ia it didn't matter. The reward had already come, spread over months of simply being at the farm, together with the other women, instead of locked away in a cramped apartment with too many children and too little money. On their plots of rice the women had belonging, connection, ownership. They had purpose.

Ia had also found a private joy. When she was at her rice crop, everywhere she looked, she was reminded of her parents. Of course she thought of them off the farm, had done so every day since they had lost each other two decades before. When Ia left Ban Vinai, she had packed into her bag every one of the cassettes her mother had sent her over the years; here in Fresno, they continued to mail tapes back and forth across the Pacific. When something went wrong in her life, Ia could cry into the recorder and know that her mother's comforting words would come back to her in two weeks' time.

But the way she reached her parents through the farm was different. The rice was a medium for memory, a spiritual bridge on which her heart could walk across all that longing and return to when she was with them both in person. It happened when the first green shoots poked through the soil, then when the leaves grew thick and wind rushed through them. When the plants miraculously flowered and then filled out the stomach of each little grain, the past that felt so far away came surging back. Ia could hear her mother and father, voices trilling with excitement. *The rice is almost ready!* they would say. *Come with us! Let's go!* At the farm, she could touch them again—almost. And there was the bittersweetness: the rice brought her closer to them, while at the same time clarifying just how far away each of them really was.

The second year, Ia doubled her planting to twenty rows. Again, the rice was mediocre. But when Auntie Chang's brother told the women they would have to give up their land, Ia didn't consider giving up growing rice. Instead, she turned this development into an opportunity to do more. She found a farm southwest of the city whose retired-farmer owner leased out thirty acres to a Hmong man, who in turn subleased the land in bits and pieces to relatives. While Ia was not a relative, she was still the same person who had talked her parents into letting her grow opium at age eleven. Now she talked her way into three acres of prime land, a fivefold increase from her plot with Auntie Chang.

The new, larger plot suited Ia's natural predilection for more—doing, getting, earning, dreaming bigger, higher, better, *more.*

At the same time, though, it forced her into uncharted territory: out of the comfort of farming with friends, and into the capital-intensive agricultural economy of the San Joaquin Valley.

There's a Hmong wisecrack about the United States: *If this is "the land of the free," how come nothing here is free?* In Laos, farmland was available to anyone willing to cut down the trees and burn away the brush; water fell from the sky. Fresno's abundance works from a different equation. The valley has some of the world's most fertile farmland, its soil composed of eons' worth of sediment eroded down from the mountain ranges flanking it on the west and east. But rainfall is scant. Once upon a time, there were mighty rivers that flowed off those mountains into the valley. When Europeans arrived, California as a whole supported the largest concentration and diversity of indigenous people in North America, and more than half were in the San Joaquin Valley and adjacent Sacramento Valley. But that past has long since been overwritten by more powerful people, who, beginning in the twentieth century, used dams and canals to tame the rivers to flow on command.

Today, to do anything more than graze cattle here, agriculture requires the capital investment to provide a transfusion of water: pumping it up from the aquifers, or channeling down from the reservoirs, then out to the farms and across the fields. Because of this, modern agriculture in the San Joaquin Valley has always been an inherently, inescapably commercial endeavor. Subsistence farming, which most Hmong practiced in Laos, never existed here. Indeed, as water sources have become oversubscribed during the past few decades, farming has required ever more monetary input, which in turn has necessitated an ever greater output to allow any business to operate in the black.

Ia was ready to play the game. When she got the three acres southwest of the city, she split them evenly: half rice, half Asian-style long beans. There is no love in beans. The only reason anyone grows this sadistic crop is for money. The vines start out innocently enough in the cool of spring, climbing the six-foot-high trellis and then gradually twining back onto themselves and blooming with bulbous purple flowers. When the triple digits hit, though, the plants burst with growth, adding twelve inches of vine in a day and spurting out beans like a Hydra. Pick today, and the row will be flush again tomorrow. The hotter it gets, the more there will be. During the summer weeks, when the county health department warns people to stay indoors, the long bean farmer instead tapes her thumb with an aluminum blade like a medieval fake nail, covers her body in layers of clothing, and trudges to a field that's humid and slippery with irrigation. Sweating up one row and itching down the next, she reaches and crouches and digs through the sticky leaves to sever every last bean with that tiny knife on her thumb. The buyer pays whatever he or she has decided the price is. In the flood of mid-August, a box might bring just ten measly dollars. But if it's early or late enough in the season and the market is tight, the price can be as much as $30 or $40 a box.

Starting that first year, the long beans underwrote the farm. Bean money paid the rent on the land and the monthly power bills for pumping irrigation water. In time, beans would also pay for new shoes and Whoppers and soda for the walk home from school. That first year, though, paying for the farm was enough. The glory of the equation came in mid-September, when Ia watched as five times as much rice ripened before her eyes, stretching out like a yellow sea. She could feel her mother and father beside her as the weight of all those plump grains pulled their stalks down into graceful curves, each one a rainbow with a pot of golden rice at the end.

Most other farmers with crops this big harvested with a tool like a scythe, clearing each row all at once for the sake of efficiency. Ia couldn't bear to do so. Not every plant ripened at the same time, and harvesting en masse would mean sacrificing those that were not yet mature. Instead, she used a little knife that allowed her to cut one stalk at a time. Patiently, with the help of her husband and older children, she harvested her way across the field once, then a second time. Later, in October, she made a final pass, this time using just her fingers to strip the latest-ripening seeds from the stalks, careful to get every last one.

Ia and her family toasted the first cutting, offered it to the ancestors, then tried it themselves. Rather than soggy and bland, this rice was ambrosial. Maybe there was something about the land, or perhaps it was the new seed she had gotten from a different relative, or perhaps both in combination. Whatever the reason, Ia finally had *mov nplej tshiab* as it was meant to be. And a lot of it. She wasn't one to brag exactly, but she was one to talk. Word got out. Before long, people were asking to buy her rice. Ia invited them in. While the profit couldn't compare with that of long beans, in the moment that the bills hit her hands, it felt like a jackpot: one hundred cash for a five-gallon bucket, sometimes two or three going out the door at once.

Now people lined up to buy Ia's rice at a price five times what they paid for the best rice at Asia Supermarket. In a sense, it was silly even to compare the two. Store rice was sheer calories. Ia's *mov nplej tshiab* was a miracle. It was a portal through which people could touch their own memories, from before the public assistance programs, the refugee camps, and the wartime rice rations. Tasting *mov nplej tshiab* transported them backward to a life of plenty. Even their own children couldn't grasp how such a bare-bones existence as they had lived in Laos could be called abundant. Wasn't *mov nplej tshiab* itself conceived as a response to the scarcity of the hungry season? But fortune can be measured by more than one metric. The life to which this rice returned them was rich in its independence and self-sufficiency; it was bountiful in familiarity, stability, knowing. It was a time of infinite belonging. Ia's rice was delicious, but what drew in customers was that the rice stood for something else—something priceless, because it was irretrievably lost.

Ia, as the person who could provide that transcendence, came to be desired as well. The second year at her new farm she had more buyers than buckets to sell. Same the next year. Her natural response was to grow more. Anytime someone within the larger farm gave up her land, Ia negotiated to take it over. When the farmer with the biggest holding got cancer, Ia offered to "caretake" it until the woman was well. Piece by piece, Ia went from three to nine acres—a daunting amount for someone to cultivate by hand, alone. And yet on the borders of her allotted land she planted even more: cucumbers, sweet potatoes, watermelon, squash, their leaves rambling into the paths and driveways to expand both her bounty and her claim. She learned to drive and bought a minivan, in part so she could pick her kids up after school and bring them to the farm to help. She planted more and more rice and more and more long beans. She made more and more money. She got fat for real, this time with American dollars. And this time to stay.

In 2016, after a particularly good year on the farm, Ia and her family made a down payment on a house. Ia's first choice was to move out of Fresno proper and to the countryside, where she would have enough land to raise animals. Instead, they ended up on the edge of the sprawling city, in a development of starter homes called Creekside Ranch.

They forked over the money after the rice was done in October. By the end of November, the empty lot they chose had been transformed into a home just like the one on the billboard advertising the development: two-car garage, beige all-weather siding, patch of green lawn in front. In the first week of December—exactly twenty-three years since the family emigrated from Thailand—Ia moved into the house with her husband, five of her sons, two of her daughters, one of her daughters-in-law, and her mother-in-law. Alice, Ia's precious youngest daughter, was in eighth grade.

When they first came to Fresno, in 1993, the land that has become Creekside Ranch was a citrus orchard. Indeed, even when they moved into their house in 2016, across the street was still just bare, bulldozed dirt, with a view beyond to a scrubby pasture. Now, in July 2017, the house on the corner has just received its own beige siding and the block is complete. Tucked behind brown walls that keep out the noise of traffic on the thoroughfare, the pleasant, nondescript neighborhood could be anywhere from Iowa to Idaho.

Inside Ia's house it looks as if the family has always lived here, with a pile of shoes by the doorway and beauty products crammed onto the bathroom shelves. On the granite kitchen island are two rice cookers and a three-tiered wire basket crammed with keys and mail and rolled-up socks—a household lost and found for the eleven people who live here. Smooth across the wall above the dining table is a decorative sticker in the shape of a tree, with cursive writing across the branches. It reads, "Our family is like the branches of a tree. We may grow in different directions, yet our roots remain as one."

On the other side of the combination kitchen–dining room–living room is a forty-eight-inch TV, and behind it a gallery of framed pictures. The largest one is a poster showing General Vang Pao soaring high above the military base where his final departure from Laos took place. Warplanes surround him, but they are dwarfed by the winged horse that he rides, flying up, out, away into the blue sky.

Beside the general is a photograph of Chou Lor, as well as a snapshot of his father in Ban Vinai. Most of the rest of the pictures are portraits made in Hmong photo studios showing Ia alone: Ia in a black-and-blue Hmong dress, laid over with a heavy gold dowry necklace. Ia like a priestess in a green silk Lao-style sarong, standing before an altar adorned with golden foxes. Ia holding a parasol against a turquoise sky, smiling gaily amid a cloud of butterflies.

There is just one photograph of Chou Lor and Ia together. In it, each wears a traditional Hmong costume with all its complicated layers. Positioned stiffly against a background of flowers, the two of them look hot and uncomfortable, the way children often do when forced to stand before a camera when they would rather be somewhere else. As posed as the image is, there is a sad truth to it: over time, Ia and Chou Lor's relationship has hardened into a mostly cold coexistence.

Concealed under the turban Ia wears in the photo is a scar on her head, from when Chou Lor whipped her with the iron fire poker in Ban Vinai. Three decades on, that beating and the one that preceded it remain raw in her mind. When she and Chou Lor argue, Ia will summon the past in order to condemn him again: for not stepping in when Ia was accused of stealing and for not refusing when his father told him to beat her for it; for beating her of his own volition the second time, in Thailand. Even when they are not fighting, the memories motivate her to put distance between herself and him. Today, when Ia tells stories of her past to others, it is always "I," never "we." Years have passed since the two of them shared a bed.

In a certain sense, Ia's real home is the farm. During the growing season, she returns to the family's house mostly just to sleep at night; each day before dawn, she is on her way back to the farm. "The farm." It doesn't have a fanciful name like Creekside Ranch. It's outside city limits, in an area that hasn't been subdivided yet. Mostly the landscape there appears to be devoid of humans, colonized instead by razor-straight lines of grapevines and dark, lonely groves of fruit and nut trees. Guarding the access roads are gates with heavy locks and NO TRESPASSING signs.

But at the farm where Ia grows, as at so many Hmong farms, the land is busy with people who have rented as much land as they can get, and planted as much as they can on that land. Vines of melon and squash blanket the ground while long beans and bitter melon and sweet peas grow skyward up trellises. There are tight rows of sticky corn and bushy rows of lemongrass and a dozen kinds of leafy vegetables with no English name. Underground, there are jicama and sweet potatoes, taro and green onions.

In the midst of the plantings, there is almost always a simple shelter, echoing the temporary houses that Hmong farmers in Laos would build at their rice fields and live in during much of the season. Ia's shelter is double the size of most, and has an addition on the back end, but still it is nothing fancy. In Laos the house would be fashioned from bamboo and thatch cleared from the forest before the land was burned. Here salvaged posts hold up a roof of secondhand plywood sheets, which are in turn held down by iron roasting pans and odd-cut wood thrown on top. Where there are solid walls, they are merely more plywood tacked to the posts or suspended from the rafters with twine. It is hardly raintight, but then it hardly ever rains here.

Ia calls this building a house, but the only furniture is a lunch table of sturdy-enough construction and a pair of all-purpose platforms that serve the need of the moment, whether it's a place to stack boxes of long beans or nap after lunch. There is also an earthen hearth, built right up from the thirsty clay ground that comprises the floor. All of it—shed and contents—has been built by Chou Lor over the course of two decades. And all of it is covered in an unmitigated accumulation of stuff: blankets and buckets, plastic plates and sunglasses, old radios and broken hoes. On the lunch table sit baggies of chicken bouillon and clumps of dried-up rice, sticky seeds saved from an especially good cantaloupe and the heavy cow bones given to Ia after her last shaman ritual. Chou Lor makes sure to hang up fifty-gallon bags for both trash and recyclables, but most often they are so full it is hard to get more in.

Even when the trash bags are empty and beckoning, Ia often doesn't bother to use them. At times it seems she simply has too many ambitions in motion to take time out for the menial work of cleaning. Or maybe her messiness is an old habit: in Laos, the pork knuckles thrown on the dusty ground after lunch would disappear in the mouths of hunting dogs, the watermelon rinds would be stripped by rangy chickens and loose pigs. Here, though, the only animals are the rats hiding in the cracks. The bones and skins that Ia drops at her feet just desiccate along with the paper bags, bean pods, and flip-flops—everything slowly ground down into the dull dust that seems to make up the earth here. By the west entrance, a broom with frayed bristles lies in the dirt, perhaps conquered by the Sisyphean nature of its task.

———

This morning, Foster Farms hosted an event to honor employees who had worked at the Fresno chicken processing plant for twenty years or more. Ia and Chou Lor got as dressed up as they ever do, with sandals instead of flip-flops. He put on slacks instead of work pants, while Ia wore the same thing she always does: stretchy black pants, a black V-necked shirt decorated with a colorful design, a safety pin affixed to the neckline, just in case she needs one. At the factory, the Foster Farms representatives laid out doughnuts, orange juice, and bacon. The managers made speeches in English and presented certificates of appreciation. There was no pay raise given but gifts were distributed, if somewhat haphazardly: One woman received a ring, one man received his-and-hers watches. Chou Lor, in honor of his twenty years on the graveyard shift, was given four pieces of luggage.

By the time Ia and Chou Lor arrive at the farm it is ten o'clock in the morning and already 90 degrees—well on its way to being the seventeenth day in a row of triple digits. People in Fresno get used to this kind of heat, or at least ration their alarm. It is still only mid-July, after all, meaning the misery of August has not even begun. When the temperatures scorch, the Fresno County health department just issues a heat advisory and urges residents to stay indoors.

The farm has no indoors. It is true that to duck into the shed's shade after weeding in 107-degree heat feels like rapture, but indoors it is not. The thing to do in this weather is arrive before dawn and knock out a day's work before the truly punishing temperatures begin. But crops do not care how hot a person is: the work must still be done. That today's cooler hours were lost to the Foster Farms reception means only that Ia and Chou Lor will start weeding in the rising heat. Chou Lor strips off his shiny dress shirt and pauses in his undershirt, the ribbing stretched over his American-size gut. His gaze is dull; the circles under his eyes seem to have become permanent after so many years of working through the night. He covers himself with a long-soiled work shirt and marches to the field.

Ia lingers on the bench, staring from the shade of the shed toward the labor that calls her. Without leaning over, she wearily bends her left knee and twists the foot up behind her, tugs on a gray tube sock. Right foot, same. A mauve cardigan with dull beads lies in the dirt at her feet, where she dropped it at the end of yesterday; she groans down to pick it up. Slides one arm in. Slides in the other. Stretches the two sides to meet over her round belly and fastens them with a safety pin. Scarf over hair. Hat over scarf. Hat flaps knotted under her chin. Sigh. When she is all covered and there is nothing left to do, she pushes herself up and out into the blistering light.

The reality is that Fresno is a terrible place to farm rice. The plant itself is spectacularly adaptable; since domestication, humans have coaxed rice to grow in nearly every valley, hillside, and plain from Pakistan to Indonesia to Japan. In some riparian lands, rice has been conditioned to contend with seasonal floods, on underwater stalks that get up to sixteen feet tall. Elsewhere, including in Laos, rice is planted on dry land, fed only by rain. This is the provenance of Ia's rice, of course, but "dry" is a relative term. Sa Na Oua would get fifty or more inches of rain every year. Fresno averages less than twelve, and in most years not a drop of it falls when the rice is actually in the ground.

Maybe rice could have made sense here in Fresno when the rivers running off the Sierra still flowed down to the valley and roped their way across the flats all the way up to the Delta. The Yokut and the rest of the people native to the San Joaquin Valley never developed agriculture, likely because they didn't need to: the wild provided so much food that they weren't hungry for more. But back then, with enough cheap labor to do the work of coercing the water out of the rivers and wetlands, someone could have grown rice here in a way that seemed half natural—maybe. Not now, with the mighty rivers corralled behind walls of concrete, and the valley floor a man-made semidesert. Every drop of water that Ia's rice plants receive is pumped up from one hundred feet below the field.

And that's shallow, by valley standards. During the six-year drought that the state cautiously pronounced as over in March 2016, farmers were drilling new wells twelve hundred feet deep—the dwindling groundwater a milkshake, they would say, that only he with the longest straw gets to drink. Even after the drought was supposedly finished, shallow pumps like the one here would suddenly spit up air or sand instead of water, the milkshake having dropped out of reach.

Left to survive on their own, Ia's rice plants would die within days—indeed, would never sprout in the first place. She floods them two or three times a week, but of course right there beside them in the troughs are the flinty weeds that grow like mad with the luxury of irrigation. In the early years, she could burn all the weeds to the ground before planting to give the rice a head start. Since air quality regulations put an end to that, now she and other farmers scorch their fields with Roundup each spring instead. Seems almost for naught, really, since by midsummer the competition is as tall as or taller than the juvenile rice plants. Every day in July, she and Chou Lor bushwhack into the itchy jungle of the field and wrangle the weeds into submission.

With each of them working alone down one row and up the next, the morning and then the afternoon passes in bent-over, slow-moving silence. At four, Chou Lor heads home to eat and sleep some before clocking in for his midnight shift at Foster Farms. Ia grants herself a nap, maybe fifteen minutes, then she weeds some more, but not much. Enough handwork. Standing on a rickety table across the shed is her backpack herbicide sprayer, a translucent plastic box the size of a very full grocery bag marked with an American flag logo. She unscrews the red cap that reads ACHTUNG. From a jug covered in fine print she pours green liquid into a laundry soap measuring cup, then pours that into the hole.

What herbicide she uses depends on what she can get her hands on. California requires a license to buy and apply most pesticides, and because Ia doesn't speak English or read in any language, she can't take the test. Chou Lor can buy Roundup from the store, but for stronger stuff they rely on a guy who sells opened jugs out of the back of his pickup and describes the contents in Spanish, another language Ia doesn't speak. Otherwise they get the chemicals from friends, who themselves buy through family members in Oklahoma or Arkansas, where the regulations are looser. The kind that actually works is hard to come by since it was banned altogether in California. Most of the time, Ia ends up with a spray that is better for amphibians but worse for her, as it knocks the weeds back but doesn't kill them.

Ia dumps a second cup of green liquid into the hole, then fills the sprayer with jug after jug of water, the table underneath shifting and cockeyed under its weight. She turns her rear to the backpack, wriggles the straps over her shoulders, and heaves on the load. Once this beast is on her, the goal is to empty it as quickly as possible. Ia lumbers into the field and starts spraying the river of weeds that was stomped down all morning. Underneath them lies a ghostly layer of leaves that are green at the base—weeds they sprayed in June, starting to regrow.

This is Ia's day and her week and her triple-digit summer: hoe, spray, water the rice to keep it alive for a few more days, repeat. As the orange sun is replaced by the orange sodium lights in the farmyard next door, the temperature returns to 90 degrees—cooler, but not cool. When it's too dark to see, Ia lowers the backpack to the ground in the middle of the row, marking her place for tomorrow. She drags herself to the shed, where one of her sons waits by the blue glow of his phone screen. He drives her home in his SUV. Nine hours later, against the dirty smudge of sunrise, a different son driving a different SUV returns her to the farm, and she begins the cycle again. One would think, even wish, she would have quit years ago, and yet she does not. What others can't see is that the farm is more than the sum of its sweaty, sticky, achy parts. What keeps Ia working day after day is a higher purpose, one that could be called divine.

———

Around the time that Ia got the land at this farm, in January 2000, other things began to shift in her life—things slow and momentous, like tectonic plates redrawing the shape of the Earth. It began with the family's annual New Year's *hu plig*. This is the ritual in which the spirits that guard a family are called in and honored, then asked to renew their protection for the coming year. In Thailand, Chou Lor's father had always performed the ritual. When the family arrived in Fresno without him, someone had to take his place.

It was expected that Chou Lor, as the man of the house, would do it. He did try, several years in a row. An aunt in Santa Ana even recorded what he should say onto a tape so he could memorize it. Done well, the words would flow like verse, colored by the speaker's charisma. But Chou Lor had neither the memory to learn the speech nor the confidence to execute it well. During those first years of his quiet, stilted offerings—the years of farm labor and working for free at McDonald's—the family's fortune only limped forward.

The same year that Ia started her farm, she began listening to the aunt's cassette herself. For Ia, confidence was no issue. And the performance of it—the music—came naturally. Her father had been gifted in matters of the spirit. While he hadn't been a shaman, he had been able to heal the sick by calling their souls back to their bodies. At the clan's funerals, it was he who sang the hallowed songs to guide the dead to the land of the ancestors. And every New Year, his masterly *hu plig* brought the family another year of prosperity. Ia's father had taught these skills to his sons, not to his daughter. But he did enlist Ia as his helper in the rituals, and from the shadows she listened intently.

After too many lackluster years in Fresno, Ia finally told Chou Lor to step aside. Channeling her father's voice, she took over doing the *hu plig* herself. The very first year she performed the ritual, she saw that things started breaking their way. Their fortunes turned a corner. What came next would, with hindsight, seem almost pre-dictable—obvious to anyone who had been paying attention, since it began decades earlier.

When Ia was a child, after some years of simply listening to her father communicate with the spirit world, she began to make con-tact herself. At maybe eight years old, she and an older friend tried performing a ritual called *neej poj qhe*. Sitting by the fire ring, the other girl donned a black fabric scrap as a veil and practiced a simple rite that culminated with throwing a handful of rice into the flames. Nothing happened. When Ia did the same, her body began to shake and her mouth opened. An unknown force gave her its voice, and she began to chant in a language she did not know.

The second time, a few nights later, the chanting seemed to open a door in the darkness behind the veil. Before her was a nar-row path leading into a bright world inhabited by the dead, and unseen voices guided her forward. She was told to gaze downward, lest the lost souls lining the path have a chance to make eye contact and steal her breath. Feeling protected by these invisible escorts, Ia proceeded deep into the underworld to silently look upon the loved ones who had passed away, grandparents she had never known.

From then on, every few nights, the force rose up and drew Ia into a trance. The first time, Ia's mother had shrugged it off as the games of foolish children. But as the force appeared with more reg-ularity, her parents grew concerned. At times Ia, among the dead, saw the spirits of the living, whose presence foretold their earthly deaths. One night she saw a family member in the underworld; two days later the woman was dead.

Her father decided this was enough. Ia was too young, unable to understand what she was seeing and unprepared to protect her-self. But even as Ia's parents demanded that she stop, the chants would stream out of her. As night fell, the force would well in her chest and explode out as tears. Ia herself wasn't sad, and yet she felt her chest constricted by emotion. Her father enlisted a shaman to sever her connection to the spirit world. It worked, at least for a while.

Roughly a decade later, when Ia was getting fat off tofu money in Ban Vinai, came the next chapter. Asleep in the Khang clan's longhouse, she began to have strange, exhilarating dreams: She would be climbing a steep, rocky mountain. The footing unsure, she would seize a vine and pull herself up the scree, hand over hand. The vine would snap with her weight. She would tumble down, down, down—but just as she would be about to hit the ground and die, she would soar up, flying. The dream came one night after another, and in time it morphed: now there was no falling, just flight, breezy and free.

She told her father-in-law about the dreams. *Oh really?* he would say. Beyond that, he would merely chuckle. He knew what they meant, but didn't tell her—to him, she was still just a girl.

Two more decades passed. In Fresno, in the mid-1990s, the force resurfaced. Now in Ia's hands, it was a tingling discomfort that arrived as night fell but cleared at daybreak. Over time, the sensation grew so intense that when it came she could be holding a knife and not register the tool's weight between her fingers. She could not sit still, felt as though something were crawling up her arms. She sought help from medical doctors and Hmong healers alike, to no avail. Without diagnosis or relief, Ia endured the affliction for eight years.

Then, some time after she started farming and began performing the New Year's *hu plig,* a new dream came to her: She was in Sa Na Oua, walking to her parents' house. The path was barely wider than she, hemmed in by thick bamboo that obscured the view of what lay ahead. She was scared. Ghosts appeared before her, malevolent, but in the same moment she felt the presence of invisible guides flanking her, whispering words of protection. They instructed her to call out a supernatural battle cry, invoking the god of thunder to strike down the ghosts, and as her voice boomed forward she jolted awake in her bed, screaming out those mythic words into the real dark. It was not a nightmare. There, on a mattress on the floor in Fresno, Ia felt lighter. Her fears were gone. Shortly thereafter, a shaman determined what anyone, in retrospect, could have guessed: the spirit was summoning her.

This is how it always happens. The original shaman of mythic time, Siv Yis, was a magical being who was sent to the Hmong to protect them from sickness and other earthly afflictions. Eventually, he returned to the divine realm, but before going he promised to continue to protect Hmong by imparting his abilities to certain people. Today his powers live on as supernatural guides that help shamans travel to the spirit world and negotiate healing for the rest of the living. The powers announce themselves in the form of an incurable illness; when the afflicted person accepts his or her calling to become a shaman, the symptoms resolve at last.

Many people resist the message, for while it is an honor, it is also a burden. People are chosen by the shaman spirits for their kindness and purity, and once they become shamans, their duty is to help anyone who asks, without remuneration. Performing even the simplest shamanic ceremonies requires hours of demanding, potentially dangerous physical work, which is bookended with hours of ritual and feasting. With so many around them suffering, shamans often find that their time ceases to be their own.

When Ia was a child, her mother was chosen. The call manifested in a stomach illness that knotted the woman's innards into a mass, which gradually grew hard to the touch. At times her body would shake, as if she were having a seizure. Desperate for relief, she wished to embrace her fate, but Ia's father wouldn't allow it. Times were lean as it was, and if she became a shaman, the countless hours she would spend healing others were hours she wouldn't be able to contribute to their livelihood. Also: her mother was female. Back then, many people thought it was improper for a woman to become a shaman; those women who did were believed to be less powerful than their male counterparts. Anyway, even if Ia's father had consented, Sa Na Oua had no female shamans to instruct her, and it would be unseemly for a male shaman to teach a woman. Ia's father decided that the spirit calling Ia's mother would be ignored; the pain gripping her simply had to be endured.

When Ia learned that she had been chosen, she complied without hesitation. Immediately she commenced the ritual process of pairing with a shaman teacher to instruct her in the art. She found her master in an elderly woman, roughly the age of her mother, and received her education diligently.

Hmong shamans attend to illnesses both physical and mental. In a sense, all afflictions are approached from the same foundational understanding: every person has multiple souls, and illness usually results from one of those souls being lost from the body—most often having been scared off, lured away, or stolen. The shaman's main work is journeying to the spirit world to locate the soul and negotiate for its return. Sometimes this entails mere diplomacy and the offering of an animal's soul in trade. There are also times when a shaman must lead her spirit army into battle with demons and other unruly denizens of the supernatural realm. Not until she faces the spirits does she know whether to employ gentle persuasion, cunning investigation, or sheer muscle. Ia relished it all.

The master taught a hybrid of traditional Hmong shamanism and Chinese mysticism, with elements of Thai Buddhism as well. While some more orthodox Hmong shamans dismiss this nonconventional approach, Ia embraced the richness. She dedicated herself to the ceremonial care of her spirit army and her shamanic tools. To house them she constructed an elaborate sanctuary. A traditional Hmong shaman's altar is sanctified but simple, a small shelf with necessary items—water and a bowl of rice to feed the spirit guides, incense—plus just enough gold paper to line the edges and distinguish it from ordinary life. Ia's altar reached to the ceiling and was bright like Las Vegas. Nearly every square inch was festooned with metallic flowers and pearly beads, statues of wise women and men, gods and goddesses, and an evolving menagerie of glossy animal figurines—bears and swans, hummingbirds and dragons—all of it glittering under a decorative light that switched from green to blue to purple and back again, twenty-four hours a day.

The bling was Ia's zeal manifested. As she treated members of the community, her reputation spread. Weekends filled up with performing rituals, first in Fresno and then in Sacramento and Stockton, requested by phone from Minnesota and beyond. And that was only where her new life began. As Ia understood it, being a shaman was evidence of a divine assignment that extended to her entire existence.

Just like everyone she knew, Ia had had her story written by the celestial parents before she was born. They determined whom she would marry and whether she would be rich or poor, and they also determined her overarching spiritual occupation. Some people were chosen as leaders, others as workers. For Ia, being chosen as a shaman showed her that she was assigned to be a healer, and her purpose in life was to help others. People began to seek her out for things beyond the strict purview of a shaman, asking for counsel on everything from traditional etiquette for modern weddings to navigating trouble with the police. Each time, Ia turned toward, not away, giving the needy person whatever wisdom, guidance, and support she could. At times, she would borrow money so that she could give it to someone who had asked for a loan.

It followed that Ia came to see herself in a new light. Before, she had inwardly felt bitter about her lot. Working like a dog to provide for her family every day since she was fifteen years old, Ia had thought her earthly destiny was to merely pay off spiritual debts from a past life. Now, at age forty, Ia saw that she had been *chosen* to provide, not just for her children but as a sort of mother to all. From then on, everything in her life would serve that purpose.

It was an all-encompassing assignment, one that would never

be complete because Ia could always be doing more. But because the work was divinely mandated—because it was *meant to be*—Ia felt she would no longer labor alone. In any endeavor that served her purpose of helping others, she trusted that to complete the task she would be provided with the support needed, be that physical strength, human helpers, added self-confidence, or just sheer luck.

This included the farm. From outward appearances, nothing had changed. Ia's rice did not now magically grow unassisted—it was as much work as ever. Still, between 2005 and 2017, she expanded the farm, and with each new acre she patched on a layer of invention and make-do to the improvised system that brought the plants from seed to harvest each year. Finding the words to buy pesticides out of the back of some Spanish-speaking man's truck. Learning to drive enough to get her kids to the farm after school. After her minivan was totaled and her learner's permit expired, finding a way to still get at least herself to the farm every day. The system was rickety—it still is.

What held it together was the essential glue of her certainty that this whole thing was meant to be; indeed, that if she tried to veer from this path, divine hands would steer her back. That faith is what fueled her through day after day, year after year, of crippling farm labor, including the wretched work of weeding in triple-digit heat. When the shadows had left the field for the night and Ia was still plodding forward with a leaden backpack of weed killer, that belief in her destiny was what lit the way.

After lugging the herbicide backpack for days straight in July, Ia had such intense pain in her back that she was reduced to crawling from one room to another at home. For relief she lay down in bed and massaged her hips, only to discover mysterious lumps under the skin. Now, in August, what has become a constant, numbing pain in her hips has been joined by a swelling on her right ankle that shouts angrily each time she bears down. Increasingly, meals have been followed by intense pain in her stomach. As days turn into weeks and the stomachaches continue, she recognizes that it must be something more than indigestion.

A voice inside her worries it is cancer, and yet she does not go to the doctor—her consortium of medical providers does not inspire trust in her. Part of a federally funded program called PACE (Program of All-Inclusive Care for the Elderly), the consortium is a corporation that acts as a senior care bundler, providing or at least coordinating all their members' needs, from dentistry to counseling to in-home care. Ia finds that when she is scheduled to see a doctor because of issues in one part of her body, she sometimes inexplicably receives treatment for another instead. Other times she is told that her appointment has been canceled and she is simply turned away. When she does get examined, the providers offer her vague explanations through an interpreter and then usually hand her a prescription for a new bottle of pills that, more often than not, she never takes.

In August, instead of going to the doctor about her stomach, Ia just continues working. The woman who farms the neighboring plot has gone to the "Green Mountain"—meaning up north to grow marijuana, along with seemingly half the Hmong in Fresno. Until the woman returns, Ia is subletting her two acres, which puts her at four acres of rice—more than three football fields, and the biggest crop of her life. Until that rice starts yielding cash, though, everything on the farm and beyond relies on the money from her five acres of long beans.

Earlier in the season, the stress was that the long beans were doing poorly. By June, when still the vines had not begun to flower, Ia feared she would have no crop at all. Standing at the edge of the field, she broke into tears and called to her parents in the spirit world. *Mom and Dad, I need you,* she cried out. *What am I going to do if the beans don't grow? Please, come and help me!* The next day the vines burst into bloom.

Now the continuous heat has brought them on in a rage, and because of them she and Chou Lor must quit weeding the rice before it is done. Once the beans start producing, if left for even a few days, they will grow too big, dry out, and threaten to stop making more. So the two of them and at least one of their kids spend all day, every day, picking. The beans' prolific habit, wretched as it might seem to some, is the very reason that Ia chose them: this time of year, they are money growing on vines. The best seasons are remembered as those when so many beans were picked that underneath the blades taped onto everyone's fingers, the thumbnails finally rotted and fell off.

But between the work and the heat and the stress they bring, Ia's stomach only burns more. Seeking relief, she tries a brown powder from the herb seller at the flea market, one heaping scoop dumped into her water bottle. The next week she tries a white powder, spooned straight into her dry mouth. Her oldest daughter, who lives in Oklahoma, sends Chinese medicine from Tulsa. For Ia's hips and foot there are baggies of pills from the Hmong grocery store, baggies of pills from a Thai healer, a cream her aunt gave her, as well as Icy Hot and Tiger Balm from Walgreens. The doctor, when eventually consulted, suggests Tylenol. They all work, at first. Then the pain comes back.

In times past, Ia would have cried her suffering into the cassette recorder and put the tape in the mail to her mother. Now, though, her mother is six years dead. Ia kept every recording her mother ever sent, so that she could listen to them during crises like this. But over time the magnetic strips degraded, sticking to themselves until each one became an unrecoverable snarl. Just a single tape remains, the last recording her mother made before she died. When Ia listens to it, the music of that familiar voice is a balm. Still, the pain always returns.

Normally, this time of year is when the months of toil begin to pay dividends of joy. Weeds shrink away into the shadow of rice plants that have grown tall and thick. As the breeze washes through a field, the lissome green leaves sway and whisper a papery music. Dragonflies arrive to loop and swing and ride one another above the crop, heralding the imminent blooming—just as they did in Laos when Ia was a child. From each plant's thicket of leaves there shoots up a straight, tight wand of buds that stands taller than Ia herself. Soon, on each stalk, hundreds of tiny flowers open and release a sweet, gossamer fragrance. The scent of one alone would be undetectable, but in olfactory concert they are miraculous.

This year, though, as Ia struggles, so does the rice. When days are hot, the plant needs the cool of night to enable the delicate chemistry of pollination: at the right temperature, pollen grains swell with moisture and break open the flower's anther, raining down to fertilize a microscopic green egg whose insides will then grow into a grain of rice. But these temperatures are wrong. August gives way to

September and the heat never breaks—many nights don't dip below 80 degrees, and there is no morning dew at all. She has planted a dozen different kinds of seed, and as the earliest-maturing types shed their flowers, their collective shape portends an anemic harvest. Instead of bowing over with the weight of filling grains, too many stalks stay standing straight up, stiff and barren. In the breeze, their mostly empty seedcases shiver.

Ia sees them, their unwelcome omen only pumping up her stress. On certain days, though, when one medicine or another has kicked in, she also sees past them. At those times, her gaze falls on the solitary plants that managed to endure the heat and still swell the pollen, burst the anthers, fertilize the eggs, and grow them into bouquets of grain. There in the forest of sterile stems, these survivors instead arc down, heavy and golden and starkly alone. One day, Ia ventures into the field to gather them, one by one, and assemble them into a skinny sheaf. She has her tallest son wedge the ends between two crusty boards in the ceiling of the shed so the bundle can hang out of the way, untouched. Bright against the cobwebs, the bouquet dangles over the walkway like mistletoe.

———

Chou Lor is a shaman, too. Of lesser standing, it must be said, but still, Ia hoped that he would respond to her illness by making a spiritual investigation into the cause. He did not.

Their second daughter, Song, is also a shaman. While she is just starting out, she possesses enough knowledge to make an inquiry herself. When at last she does, though, her conclusion is unsatisfying to Ia.

Desperate in her pain, Ia finally kneels before her own altar. Speaking now as a shaman, she addresses a ceramic queen in white robes who is draped with a string of brassy Mardi Gras beads. *Mrs. Chou Lor Khang is in such pain. She has taken all this medication and yet found no relief. Why this suffering? Where does it come from?*

Ia, in her heart, receives a resounding answer. It is Chia Yang, Chou Lor's uncle. Decades earlier, in Laos, this man was killed by a land mine. He had two sons, but both are dead, meaning no longer does anyone living feed him in the spirit world. The issue is simple: he is hungry. Making Ia suffer is his way of asking for help. There at the altar, Ia the shaman makes him a deal. If he ceases tormenting Mrs. Chou Lor Khang, she promises to give him what he needs through an offering of food and spirit money.

Ia's relief is immediate. The days that follow are exultant. Blessedly cooler, as well. Ia picks box after box of beans with a smile on her face, breaking the radiance only to crab at Chou Lor for not having done the spiritual inquiry himself. He absorbs her hostility, pushing back only slightly before turning away in silence. Their daughter Alice, who has been conscripted to help pick the deluge of beans, keeps her earbuds in and turns up the volume on her K-pop.

The rice continues to ripen, plant by plant, and by mid-September there is enough to make the first *mov nplej tshiab* and prepare an offering to the ancestors. Unlike the New Year's *hu plig*, this ritual must be performed by a man — the exchange is strictly between the living head of the household and his forebears in the Khang clan. Chou Lor plays his assigned role with diligence but little more. For each ancestor, he burns a handful of spirit money and repeats the same flat appeal: "Please accept the offering I'm making to you." He stares at the flames in his far-off way. He fiddles with the lighter. When it comes time for him to offer rice wine, Ia, who does not drink alcohol, delivers him three Styrofoam cups of Pepsi. Beyond that, there is nothing for her to do but watch from the sofa and correct him in her mind.

Still, within days of the offering, their fortunes brighten yet again. The heartache of the late-August heat wave that left so many of the early-flowering plants sterile is replaced by the warm glow of twenty rows of perfect rice, all those fat grains click-clacking in the wind. The rest of the crop appears to be lining up faithfully, moving from green to yellow to gold in a shifting tapestry that will bring one type to maturity after another. By the fourth week of September, the ripe plants have thickened into an unbroken mass stretching from one end of the farm to the other.

From within the field, Ia can no longer see the road. The plants are so tall and thick they block out the larger landscape, creating a separate world that is just rice and sky. Ia disappears into the leaves' embrace. She abandons the long beans. The specter of cancer fades from her mind. When her ankle howls in pain, she simply accommodates it with a wooden limp and a leaning stance. There is no time for pain or worrying. Right now there is only this rice and the urgent, cathartic duty of harvesting it.

———

After the crop is cut in the field, it is beaten off the stalk, and the chaff is winnowed out. Then the grains are roasted. This last step is, in a sense, what defines *mov nplej tshiab*—in earlier times, it was the thing that turned green rice into a delicacy. These days, some farmers secretly roast only half their crop and mix it with raw rice, which has led to generalized mistrust of the quality of local *mov nplej tshiab*. When customers call to suss out if Ia does the same, she takes umbrage. Her product is only the highest quality.

Farmers skimp on this step because it's a lot of effort, especially after all the work of getting the grain out of the field. Traditionally, each family would roast only enough for one meal. At Ia's farm, they roast nearly every day for six weeks straight. In truth, "they" is really Jimmy, the sixth of her seven sons. He is by far the tallest member of the family and supersized all around: arms like calves, calves like thighs. Sometimes, when his back itches, he scratches it with a rake. Like Ia, he wears the same uniform every day. For him, it is baggy athletic shorts and a T-shirt showing the Hulk or another comic book hero, posed as if to explode off the fabric and spring from his chest.

While anyone less robust would be ground down to a nub by the work of roasting the rice, Jimmy chooses it. As soon as he arrives in the morning, he arranges an armful of old fence posts so their ends lie in the handmade clay hearth in the center of the shed. He douses them with lighter fluid and sparks the day's fire, whose flames lick up through the circular opening on top of the hearth. Over the fire he sets down a wok the size of a car tire, pours a jug of water in its basin, then dumps in a five-gallon bucket of rice. With a hoe as his spatula, he rakes the heavy mass continuously, stopping only to push the burnt fence posts deeper into the fire.

Just a few minutes into roasting, the fragrance is born. It begins as wet pumpkin, loose and fleshy, then becomes a sweetness just at the edge of burning, like chestnuts in a street cart. When at last the magic arrives, it hits out of the blue, the brain suddenly recognizing that the invisible molecules have coalesced into something more whole, as if the soft aroma could now be held in a person's hands. Some say it smells like heavenly popcorn or perfect toast. Caramel comes to mind, but this is not mere sugar. Jimmy calls it fatty. Really, no one has the exact words; there are only attempts to describe it. Wafting out of the shed, the scent overpowers even the smoke from the hearth's all-day fire.

People start to appear. On Sunday afternoons especially, there are caravans of minivans and SUVs. People pile out the doors, and right there in the driveway they change their clothes, trading ordinary city outfits for the elaborate puzzle of pleated skirts and fitted jackets and long sashes that their Hmong ancestors once wore every day. Posing with the rice, they click off scores of photos. The best among them sing to the rice while the rest film videos with their phones. Some hire professional photographers, who arrive at the golden hours late in the day and use long, heavy lenses to capture the right glow. Other farmers charge $250 for a photo shoot in their rice fields, but Ia can't bring herself to do so. While some of the groups at least ask her for permission, just as often she learns that they were there only because her kids have seen the pictures posted on Facebook.

The first person who comes to actually work is Youa, the woman who loaned her land to Ia this year because she decided to grow pot up at the Green Mountain. After that plan fell through in the spring, Youa spent months with nowhere to go but her living room, nothing to do but babysit her grandkids. Watch YouTube. Gain weight. Get sick. Lose teeth. When Youa visited the farm and saw Ia's crop, smelled that smell, the next day she returned, suited up in her thick work clothes, and spent the day cutting rice—trading her labor for *mov nplej tshiab.*

Youa's mother-in-law, a skeletal woman said to be more than one hundred years old, is too frail to stand in the sun and harvest. Still, she comes out to the farm to thresh the grain off bundles of harvested rice in the back shed. Next, a gray-haired aunt whom Jimmy refers to as an "OG grandma" calls from Minnesota, asking Ia to perform a shaman ceremony for her. Ia tells her to instead come help with the harvest, and by week's end the woman is working at the farm and sleeping on Ia's couch.

One day, while Youa's mother-in-law is threshing rice in the shed, a relative calls her, looking for comfort. Through tears, the caller says she is sad about her husband's recent death. Without stopping her work, Youa's mother-in-law replies, *I'm sad about losing my husband, too. Come out to the farm.*

This woman, Pao Houa, had to get her children's permission, since she didn't drive and needed them to transport her. Her children all thought it was a bad idea, her being out in the glaring sun, doing manual labor—she was already so fragile from her ceaseless crying. In the end, they consented, only because she had barely left the house since her husband's death in March and this was the first time she wanted to go anywhere.

The first morning, her daughter Linda drove her to the farm. When they pulled up, Pao Houa leapt out of the car, closed her eyes, and breathed down into the bottom of her chest. *Do you smell that, daughter? That's the smell of rice!* Her voice revved up and spilled over with memories of Laos, of her childhood, how the last time she harvested, forty-six years earlier, the harvest knife had to be made in an extra small size to fit her tiny hand. She excitedly shoved a harvest knife in her daughter's hand so she could try it, beckoning her to the field. Stunned, Linda agreed that her mother could stay the day, on one condition: no crying. Pao Houa smiled her agreement.

A week in, the soft face that for so many months was muddied with tears had a new light. Daily, Pao Houa's children encourage their mother to go to the farm. Today she arrives in borrowed men's clothes: a heavy blue overshirt and huge windbreaker pants whose extra length is stuffed into galumphing Timberland-look-alike boots. Over this is a valentine-red apron trimmed in lace, where she stores her knife and a clump of rubber bands for bundling the rice.

Pao Houa has proven to be an ace in the field, and by late morning she is several yards down the field from her co-worker. The clearing she has made by harvesting is surrounded by taller, uncut rice, putting her in a private chamber. There alone, she begins singing. Her voice is clear and high, like birdsong.

"Since you've left this orphan behind,
How I have missed you."

The breeze rustles the rice.

"Death has left me behind to yearn,
So now I'll sing with the birds and the insects."

Her melody melts into quiet weeping.

Sorrow cannot be approached head-on. If Pao Houa were to call out to her deceased husband directly, she would open the door to the spirit world and immediately become vulnerable. Opportu-

nistic spirits could prey on her. Even her husband, coming to relieve Pao Houa's anguished cries, might reach across worlds and pull
her soul close to his; this would cause her living body illness, even
death.

For this reason, grief must be addressed obliquely: rendered into
these misty lyrics, cast into the air. For generations this is how it has
been done, Hmong women singing their troubles to the natural
world before them. In theory, Pao Houa could sing in her backyard,
but the comfort would likely be sheared away by the dissonance
of the traffic noise or the non-Hmong neighbors over the fence,
wondering aloud at the peculiar song. Here at Ia's farm, though, the
rice plants are a sanctuary. They enclose Pao Houa, blocking out
everything but the sky. They stand as an audience, tireless in their
sympathy. In the safety of this temporary bower, Pao Houa sings her
heart to the rice.

The woman behind her in the next row coos a few words of soft
acknowledgment. At first Pao Houa says nothing, focusing on the
rice before her as tears roll down her face. There is a breath of wind.
Then, morsel by morsel, Pao Houa speaks her pain to this woman in
the next row, this woman whom she has never met before. Through
the veil of rice, the woman hands her back morsels of comfort.
The woman does not know Pao Houa's particular heartache; her
own husband is alive, waiting for her at home. But she does know
a shared loss that is perhaps more important—every woman here
does. Altogether, the morsels this woman offers to Pao Houa com-
prise a larger sentiment: *You are not alone.*

Gradually, the two let go of words. A breeze sweeps across the
field and the rice gives it shape, beating against itself with tremulous
life. When the wind passes, in the stillness left behind there is soft
weeping, now from both Pao Houa and this woman beside her. The
two of them keep staring inward, at the rice that they never stop
cutting. Eventually, the feelings are metabolized. Five minutes later
they are red-eyed but quiet. Another five minutes and the woman

beside Pao Houa tells a little joke. Pao Houa responds with a sniffle, then a joke of her own.

When it is time for lunch, Pao Houa stashes her knife in the pouch of her apron and heads toward the shed. The row is so thick with leaves she cannot see her feet in the big, borrowed boots, and after only a few steps she trips wildly, letting out a shriek as she disappears from sight. "What happened?" the other woman calls out, searching for her. "Are you okay?" Pao Houa, sprawled across a bed of flattened rice plants, lies on her back and just laughs, looking up at the sky.

In the shed, Ia is already seated at the lunch table along with the OG grandma and Youa. Giggling as she enters, Pao Houa tells Ia how she fell in the rice and left a spot that looked as if deer had bedded down for the night. Youa chimes in that she also fell this morning, couldn't get up. Laughing harder, Pao Houa admits she fell more than once.

"Don't tell your kids!" Ia says, chortling. "If they find out, they won't let you come back."

Pao Houa smiles, suddenly devious. "Well, then I'll wake up before them and sneak out of the house!"

During harvest there is no time for cooking, so lunch is a mound of *mov nplej tshiab* the size of a throw pillow and Lao deli food served from Styrofoam take-out boxes. Enough trash is swept off the table to make room to eat. But Ia can't stand such a loveless banquet. As they are about to dig in, she disappears into the field and returns with three profusely ripe Hmong cucumbers. The women automatically commence slicing them in half and scraping their day-glo-orange innards into a wide bowl, their arms crisscrossing as they reach across the table, voices laid one on top of the other.

A woman with deep lines in her face sits apart. Her name is Mai Der. Leaning back on a post, she tells the others she is exhausted. Ia has sublet her a little patch of land, and she, too, is growing rice, though not well. Her husband died last winter and the work has proven to be more than she can manage alone. Each day she pings madly between harvesting her rice in the field and threshing it off the stalk into grain, which she does in a pitiful tent of tarps and fence posts pitched along the driveway. Already it is evident Mai Der will have to give up growing rice after this season. For now she scrambles to collect what return she can from this year's struggle, by getting the rice out of the field before the birds eat it all.

She envies Ia's crop, so tall and lush. Mai Der tells the women that with no husband, she had no one to buy fertilizer for her. What's more, her hands were too arthritic to operate the herbicide sprayer. Her crop is pitiful, and the mere sight of it brings her to tears.

"If you do it again next year," one woman offers, "I'll come help you."

Mai Der smiles and sighs. "My kids are always complaining about having to bring me here," she says tiredly. Because she lives half an hour away and does not drive, every day she must beg one of her children to drop her here on the way to work. At night she is often the last person on the farm, waiting for her ride home in the dark.

Ia steps in. "Next year, come help me harvest mine instead. I'll pay you double!"

"Enh, harvesting just makes you think about your old life and what that used to be," Mai Der says sadly. She props her head up with her hand. "I think I'd rather just sleep."

The bowl in the middle of the table is now full of slithery ribbons of cucumber topped with melting ice cubes from the cooler. Ia gives them a long pour from a pink box of sugar and stirs the sweet into the sour of the soupy fruit. It is a long-ago taste, nothing that can quite be re-created from the store. From all directions hands reach in to spoon it over their bowls of rice. Pao Houa takes a bite of hers and swoons.

Ia, beaming, turns to her with approval. "This is why we told you to come to the farm. So you wouldn't cry as much!"

"I already cried twice today," Pao Houa says, laughing through her nose. "Just talking about it, I feel like I'm going to cry again!"

"Why did you cry?" Ia asks.

"Since my husband is gone, I don't have anybody to talk to anymore."

"Well, then, from now on you stick with me," Ia says. Shakes her spoon at Pao Houa and gives a solemn nod. "I won't let you cry."

The not crying is not the point, of course. What Ia really offers to Pao Houa is the sticking with. After lunch, the two of them work side by side for the rest of the day.

Anyone can see that Ia should not be in the field at all: she should be resting the disaster that is her body. Each day her foot screams in pain until it tires out, like a baby, into disquieting numbness. Her stomach has relapsed, and with even a small meal it smolders and aches. And yet she keeps on harvesting alongside Youa, Pao Houa—whoever her companion of the moment is. She can't stand to miss a minute of this. In a life devoted to helping others, this is the grand dessert. As Ia offers these women this makeshift community, she gives herself the same gift. In their company, she can safely reach back and touch all her own memories, her own feelings, knowing that the women will be there to catch her, too.

"This is the happiest I am all year." She says it over and over again.

————

All day and into night, Ia's phone rings. "What is it?" she answers. But she already knows. All those years when Ia lived at the refugee camp in Thailand, it felt as though she had no family at all. These days, women appear from out of nowhere, sweetly addressing her as "aunt" or "mother-in-law," sometimes even "grandmother." They want one thing: rice.

The best stuff at Asia Supermarket is from Thailand, sold under the brand Hmong Lady. The fronts of the fifty-pound bags are like posters, printed edge to edge with a photograph of deep green paddy fields backed by forested mountains. In the foreground is a superimposed image of a young woman in a pristine turban and elaborate traditional costume, laid over with a breastplate of glittering coins. Her manicured hands hold a sheaf of rice and a sickle; her mouth performs a dutiful smile.

The rest of the year, Hmong Lady rice is fine. In September and October, though, what people want, what they ring Ia's phone off the hook for, is her rice. Seeds that were smuggled out of Laos and planted in this new soil. Harvested by hand and roasted over a fire, just as they remember. When women in Fresno load Ia's rice into their cookers and the caramel aroma slowly fills the whole house, they can ride back to Laos on the smell alone. As early as August they begin calling, asking for *khau pheb* and other kinds from when they were young, kinds Ia still grows.

Now, in October, if the person who calls is one of those poseurs who shines to her only this time of year, Ia may say she's already sold out. If the person is a true friend, Ia will tell her to try again next week. Inevitably, though, even friends will end up empty-handed. The only certain way to buy this rice is to be in front of Ia when she has a bucket ready to sell. Once, as Alice slipped out of the house in the dark early morning to catch the school bus, there were already two older women waiting on the street, clutching their handbags. As their heads nodded sheepish greetings, their eyes were pleading: *Now can we knock?* It worked. They drove away with rice.

For weeks, customers and photo caravans fill up the driveway. By the last week of October, though, the visitors trickle off as the farm is sheared back to dull reality. As workers have swept across the fields, the rice plants have been cut from lush and magical to middling and stubby, once again revealing the gray blur of traffic on the adjacent road. In the shed, the nonstop bustle of harvest has manifested as trash that flows out of the overstuffed garbage bags and into the rice fields, a river of empty Jimmy Dean bacon packets and Chicken McNuggets boxes, cucumber rinds and a thousand plastic water bottles. The sheaf of early rice that Ia cut so fondly back in August remains tucked into a rafter, though the stems' romantic arc has dried and cracked so that the bouquet now hangs, artlessly, straight down. The white grains, once pearls of promise, are blackened with creeping spots of mold.

Along the driveway, the makeshift tent where the widow Mai Der threshed her rice has disintegrated into a pile of debris. She left for the Green Mountain, where there's gold rush work to be had on the pot farms. Her rice harvest wasn't finished, but she was dependent on a ride that wouldn't wait for her and the choice was too clear: slog it out doing a second cutting of her own measly crop of rice, or rake in thousands of dollars trimming someone else's crop of marijuana. Unwatered and abandoned, the grain in her field has dried out and bleached from rich yellow to plain brown. Just a touch, and the seeds shatter to the ground. The birds help themselves.

Even before Mai Der left, Youa, too, headed to the Green Mountain with her husband. At around the same time, the OG grandma finally coerced Ia into doing a shaman ritual for her, after which she flew home to Minnesota. Pao Houa, rejuvenated by her time at the farm, also left, having finally been recalled by her children, who needed her to resume babysitting their kids.

With their cumulative departure, the life of the harvest dried up. No more storytelling in the field, no more lunches filled with warm laughter. Ia's kids and daughters-in-law and their children come to help on some weekends, but with their feet dragging. Ia did hire some strangers when things got busy, and they will keep showing up as long as the money flows. And loyal Jimmy comes seven days a week, roasting bucket after bucket of rice with a wordless grimace. Chou Lor is here most days, too, but beyond Ia's criticism of him, what conversation there is between them stays purely logistical. Most of the time he drifts through the background like a low-level employee: Disposing of the rubbish Mai Der left behind. Loading the hearth fire's ashes into a sieve and sifting out nails and other saleable scrap metal. Fashioning irrigation piping and stray clothes into impotent scarecrows, which hang limply as every bird in Fresno arrives to feast upon the rice.

In this company, harvest ceases to be a time to savor and becomes a time to endure. Ia would like to be out there cutting rice with the hired women—even if they are strangers, their company is better than no company at all. But the planting of *nplej niam tais,* "grandmother rice," has only just matured and is spitting out a bumper crop; someone must absorb the torrent of rice coming out of the field.

Daily Ia limps out to the field and shuttles hundreds of bundles of harvested rice to the back shed. Really the shed is just four sheets of plywood held up by a half-dozen posts. To make an actual room that could contain the harvested rice, Ia rigged up tarps to serve as walls and a floor. She did not prepare for the abundance of the grandmother rice, though, and on the last Monday of October, the shed holds a pile of these bundles as high as her belly and twice as long as she is tall. When she empties her basket on top, the heap spills right to the edge of the plastic.

Her job is to thresh the rice, which means beating each bundle against a milk crate so that the grain falls off the stalks. She thwacks each one four, five, six times. When all that's left in her hand is a tuft of stems with ragged, empty ends, she chucks it over her shoulder into a separate mound of discards and grabs a new bundle, begins again. Over the course of each day the mound of golden grain in the threshing shed grows outward and upward, with Ia sitting atop like an emperor on her pile of treasure. The head-spinning abundance should only make her smile.

And yet: Her burning stomach. Her inflamed ankle. Her miserable hip. The darkness creeps in.

When her rainbow of illnesses returned in late September, Ia realized it was not the hungry soul of Chou Lor's late uncle who was causing her harm. She determined it was in fact her own parents. Back in June, when she asked for their help with the failing long bean crop, she had promised to make an offering to them in exchange for their assistance. This kind of exchange is an acceptable way to call upon the ancestors, and it stays safe as long as the living person makes good on her end of the deal. Ia's parents seemed to hear their daughter's cries, and the plants flowered profusely. But then the beans themselves came, and the heat, and as the season got the better of her, Ia never followed through. Angry at her for neglecting their agreement, her parents must be causing this pain—that's what Ia figured. But then she made a hearty offering to them in early October, and still there was no relief.

With eyes bloodshot and her skull crushed by headaches, Ia turned to the doctors at Fresno PACE, only to receive the same ill-fitting results as always. They took X-rays and drew blood, sent her home with instructions to do a stool test. One doctor diagnosed that one of her feet was suffering from extra bone growth while the other had a hollow space now filled with swelling. After another doctor argued for surgery, Ia replied with the worry that an operation would leave her immobilized. He responded by offering to provide an electric wheelchair—an electric wheelchair that would not make it three feet down a row of rice plants before it pitched sideways into the mud. Ia told the man she would be better off "at Belmont"—the cemetery on Belmont Avenue where most of Fresno's Hmong are buried. The doctor then offered a bulky, four-footed cane and a fitting for orthopedic shoes. Neither took root. The only treatments that achieve sustained usage are those powders and balms given to Ia by loving relatives. Those she swears by.

Still, even as she grows dependent on the indistinct Chinese medicine that her oldest daughter sends from Oklahoma, Ia knows that there is no lasting treatment for the real source of her suffering. With each new lonely day on the farm, she allows the truth to surface—or perhaps cannot stop it from doing so. When honest with herself, she acknowledges that this illness recurs every year, slipping its arms around her just as the rice stalks shoot up from the leaves, then slowly strangling her until the field is empty. It assumes different forms, afflicting her stomach one year and her feet the next. Really, though, the problem is her heart. Not the organ itself, but the vessel that aches, the one that is broken.

When the rice crop opens a door into the past, Ia does not just peer in. Instead, something inhales her through the passageway. She is safe when with friends, the other women a firm tether to this world of the living. Alone, though, Ia slips too easily across the threshold, and from there she slides into a separate dimension. The rice brings her back to when she was a child in Sa Na Oua, safe with her parents, before marriage and beatings and dislocation. Before danger.

When Ia relives this childhood feeling of safety and belonging, her soul is not satisfied to simply touch the memory and hold it for a spell. Her soul wants to quit the sadness of this life and return to her parents' embrace. And so it wanders, away from Ia, beginning the voyage to the land of the ancestors. Traveling backward on the path of this body's life, her soul searches for Sa Na Oua. What it's looking for is Ia's placenta, in the dirt that was once the floor of her family's house, right where Ia's father buried it the night his youngest daughter was born. Just as this "birth shirt" swaddled Ia in the womb, so will it clothe her soul for its voyage to the afterlife, where at last she will reunite with her parents.

The danger is that if Ia's soul succeeds in leaving her body and returning to the ancestors, her life on this earth as this woman will end. Ia will die. The farther away her soul travels, the sicker Ia gets with these headaches and stomachaches, these throbbing joints—it is the very kind of illness that she, as a shaman, heals in others. The farm is a cauldron of memories, and every year her struggle repeats, as predictable as the flowering of the rice. Possessed by longing, she will brazenly cry out to them, right there in the field. *Mom and Dad,* she says through tears, *the rice is ready! Come and eat!*

It is one thing for a person to negotiate with the ancestors for help, as Ia did when she asked her parents to save her failing bean crop. It is another to summon them like this, as if they were here in the world of the living. The only place a person can do that safely is at the deceased person's grave; to do it here at the farm is perilous. If her parents hear her pain, they may try to heal it by seizing her soul and bringing it to the spirit world—which would also mean her earthly death. She invites them anyway, even as her own children implore her to stop. *Mom and Dad, the rice is ready!* If only her parents came, they would see her sitting atop this heap of gold. They would finally know all that their youngest daughter has become, how she matters now. *Come and eat!* she calls out again and again.

But that is all she says. Even in her anguish, Ia knows some limits. There is more to say—much more—but it must wait. Instead, she returns to the threshing shed, returns to the seemingly endless work. As her hands beat bundle after bundle of rice, her mind imagines flying away from all this sadness and trouble, like in her dreams. She thinks about it often this time of year. In those shamanic dreams there is no flapping of arms or really effort at all, just gliding on the benevolent currents, far away in the sky. She flies so high that the world looks different, the mountains mere lumps under a tousled green quilt, the great rivers meandering ribbons of blue and brown. The land below is Laos, always Laos. Sitting on top of her mountain of rice, Ia imagines how if the dreams were real she would simply soar into the air and fly somewhere new, somewhere she could start all over.

———

At last, with a final weary whack and a toss, Ia's hours of work are finished. Sun pours into the back shed from the edge of the earth, flooding the room with rich light. The mound of finished rice is as tall as a toddler and threatening to spill beyond the edges of the twelve-foot-long tarp. Ia, sunk into the top, is covered in dust that has turned her black hair gray and faded the brilliant flowers on her shirt. The heart-shaped gold pendant that normally rides her neckline has tucked itself within her bosom, out of sight.

After a few breaths of rest, Ia staggers to her feet, sloshes down the side of the slippery mound, and turns to face the rice. Last year, thieves drove up in the dark one night and filled their Toyota sedan with as many buckets of rice as they could before the farmer next door chased them out to the highway. Knowing this, Ia pulls a wrinkled tarp over the whole thing. She covers the tarp with spent bundles of straw, then throws milk crates on top to make this look like a heap of nothing. For good measure, at the edge she parks a sorry wheelbarrow, its wheel shaft bandaged with orange twine.

Turning back toward the fields, Ia smooths her hair and gathers it into a fresh ponytail. From a hook on the wall she selects a harvest apron made from dun fabric that looks like a polyester deer hide. Tying it on over her money bag, she walks into the rice plants. This hour of day is always a reward for the many that have come before. With the sun now dropped from the sky, the harsh shadows are gone. Instead, the soft light of evening seems to allow everything to glow. The skin of Ia's cheeks and the grains of rice equalize into the same tanned shade of gold.

In the pouch at Ia's waist is a small knife that Chou Lor made. It's a flat half circle of wood, darkened with dirt and sweat. The round edge has been whittled smooth, the straight edge inlaid with a razor blade. Fastened to her hand with a loop of homespun cord, the crescent holds hard and tight against her palm. She raises her hand to a stalk of rice, curls her middle finger around the stem, and severs the plant simply by twitching back over the razor. Cupped in her fist, the knife is invisible. As she glides through the field selecting one stalk and then the next, it appears that the rice simply falls into her hands.

Just two bundles are cut. This is not rice to be threshed. It is seed, which she will store over the winter and replant as next year's crop. Since the beginning, this is how farmers have helped their plants adapt—and, in turn, how farmers themselves have adapted. Each year the crop faces a range of challenges, from drought and pests to scorching days and early frosts. What seed makes it through the gauntlet of the season is saved back, carrying with it the knowledge of the previous year's troubles.

The seed she is cutting right now already carries the memory, from years ago, of a freak hailstorm that stripped the rice from the plants just before harvest. Ia carries that memory, too, of finding an entire year's work dashed on the muddy ground, unrecoverable. The day it happened she wept into the tape recorder, telling her mother how she had worked so hard all year.

We're going to be hungry, Ia cried to the cassette. *We're not going to make any money.*

Her mother sent back a tape with words of comfort. *It's out of your control.* Those words so familiar from Ia's youth. *Don't worry,* she told Ia, *next year you can start all over again.*

Of course, before her mother's reply arrived, Ia had already done what any farmer would: collected every seed that had managed to hold on to the stalks despite the hail, so that she could plant them the following spring, each one with the storm now written into its story. That's how it works. Annually, the cycle repeats, the rice that endures accumulating data, adding layers of memory—of knowing—that help it to survive the next season. Gradually, Ia's rice becomes less of a stranger to this industrial semidesert, more of a resident. The skin toughens.

She carries her two bundles of seed to the rear of the main shed and pauses, looking for space. Bundles like it are laid out to dry across the rotting plywood benches and the piles of fence posts and old sofa cushions abandoned on the ground. Others are stashed in buckets, in barrels, in a cardboard box that once held plastic straws, and in another that held baby carrots. The bundles that have already dried are stuffed into feed sacks leaning against the flat surfaces; from behind the blue sky printed on an old Hmong Lady rice bag, more gray stalks of seed stick out.

Ia picks up a dishwashing tub that was abandoned when they ran out of soap. She carefully nestles the two bundles of seed inside. In the driveway, Chou Lor waits behind the wheel of the farm truck, its engine running. Ia hangs her apron on a nail. Walks stiffly to the truck. Hauls herself into the passenger seat.

As he drives they are quiet. Between them, pinned to the ceiling where others might have a picture of Jesus or the Virgin of Guadalupe, is a laminated photo of General Vang Pao superimposed over an American flag. The image splits away from its backing, the edges worn over so many years—they hardly even know it's there anymore. Ia's head is turned toward the window anyway, her gaze falling blankly upon one dark almond grove after another.

In time, Chou Lor steers onto a two-lane highway, which becomes a six-lane freeway, which eventually spits them out onto a six-lane thoroughfare. There are dozens like it in Fresno, each one mile upon mile of traffic lights, the asphalt clogged with drivers driving the biggest cars they can afford. They pass Burger King, then Starbucks, then Denny's. A no-name gas station with hand-placed letters on a marquee reading CRITICISM IS THE PRICE YOU WILL PAY FOR LEAPING PAST MEDIOCRITY. Stopping and starting at one intersection and then another, they follow the concrete as it traverses the flat, gray city, all the way back to Creekside Ranch. Home.

Tomorrow at dawn they will return to the farm. In the days to come, Ia will beat every last bundle the grandmother rice produces. Once the workers have cut their way down the last row, she will make one more pass through the fields, stripping the stalks with her fingers to wring out any remaining handfuls of grain. Jimmy will roast bucket after bucket until there is none left. While Chou Lor hits the salvage yard to cash in the plastic water bottles from a summer's worth of thirsty afternoons, Ia will sell the precious last rice to the most persistent aunts and grandmothers. Finally, once her money bag is packed hard with dollar bills, she will tick off the shortest days of a long year, waiting, anxiously, for her soul to return.

PART 3

SISTER

In the middle of harvest, Hmong news channels across the United States lit up with a big story: On October 11, 2017, a Minnesotan named Seng Xiong was sentenced to seven years and three months in prison for a scam called *Hmoob Tebchaws,* "Hmong Country." In YouTube videos and on Hmong radio, Xiong had outlined his plan for the creation of a Hmong homeland in northern Laos. To join, there was a simple online application and, of course, a fee. In exchange for $3,000 to $5,000 deposited into Xiong's bank account, in the new land these "founders" would receive ten acres of land, free health care and education, plus something like Social Security for seniors. For lower-income subscribers, there was a payment plan costing $20 per month.

Seng Xiong was one of many who had sprung up to fill the vacuum created when Vang Pao died in 2011, the same year as Ia's mother. The general was eighty-one and over the years had been weakened by a stroke and a coronary bypass, as well as diabetes and high blood pressure; after countless armed battles, what finally killed him was pneumonia. Members of the Hmong community petitioned to have his body buried at Arlington National Cemetery, but the Department of Defense denied the request on the grounds that the site was strictly for U.S. service members.

Instead, Vang Pao was given perhaps the most elaborate Hmong funeral the world has ever seen, in Fresno. While two T-28 jets flew overhead, a horse-drawn carriage paraded his body through downtown to the convention center. Ten thousand people from four continents crowded in to mourn—and that was just the first day. Over six days and nights, thirty men helped guide Vang Pao's soul to the land of the ancestors, and sixty cows were offered as food for his journey. Women and men alike wailed with the grief of orphans. "It is like we have lost our sun," one relative eulogized. "The sun will never rise again."

Still, the hope that Vang Pao embodied lived on in the hands of lesser leaders, like Seng Xiong. This man claimed to have taken a diplomatic approach to securing a return to Laos, calling not for military action but for the creation of an independent Hmong state in the nation's northeast. He told supporters he was working with partners in the U.S. government and the United Nations, and that the realization of the plan was imminent.

After the FBI began an investigation, law enforcement scrambled to warn the Hmong community that Xiong was a fraud. Of course most already knew, this being simply the latest in a decades-old pattern of schemes that exploited so many Hmong people's deep longing for home. And yet when the FBI arrested Xiong at Los Angeles International Airport, en route to Thailand, more than four hundred Hmong across the United States had already signed up to the tune of $1.7 million.

Within months of the sentencing, Xiong's supporters were threatening another lawsuit, this one against the government: they wanted the money seized from Xiong to be returned to those who had originally given it to him. The would-be lead plaintiff, named Dao Moua, claimed that the plan to establish a homeland was already being revived; many wanted their money back so they could reinvest.

The Hmong calendar has just one holiday, New Year, traditionally celebrated after the rice harvest is in and people can finally take a break. In the United States, there are celebrations in various American cities, some of them elaborate multiday affairs with traditional courtship rituals alongside dance competitions and fast-food stands. That has been happening on various scales since Hmong first arrived in the United States.

But in 1992, when the United States and Laos reestablished diplomatic relations, those with the means began traveling back to the old country to celebrate the New Year. Now, each November and December, the most common airline routes from Fresno to Vientiane have a noticeable swell of Hmong travelers. Mostly they are older couples, born in Laos and still with relatives there. They stay a few weeks and tour the country, filling themselves on all the sweet, delicious, and long-familiar things they have missed. The women who plant rice in the United States find new seeds to smuggle back in their carry-on bags. More than a few men fly home engaged to a second or third wife, young and fresh—or at least return with their intimate desires slaked.

Ia makes the trip in years when she has earned enough money to afford it. When she boards the plane in November 2017, she is still hobbled by her myriad illnesses. And yet despite multiple flights and a fourteen-hour time change, she does not suffer jet lag—just pops up at dawn on the first morning. In the years when Ia flies directly into Vientiane, soon after waking she will hit the street and make her way down the block, chatting with every food stall woman as she buys little nuggets of pork and rice wrapped in ti leaves. At the morning market, she will stroll each lane and chat and buy until the plastic bags looped onto her wrists are so heavy with fruit that the handles cut into her skin. In theory, her bags are filled with stuff that can be bought at Asia Supermarket in Fresno—rambutan, lychee, mangosteen—but in practice, those fruits are a world away from how they taste here.

Chou Lor usually joins Ia on the trips, even as he complains that they are too expensive. This year's harvest, fortified by the grandmother rice, has allowed them to bring their two middle daughters for the first time. Song, the elder at almost thirty, is a princess of hair bows and lotions, at once warm, twinkling, and brashly outspoken. One year younger is Mee, who tends more toward flannel pajama pants and careful, alert silence.

At the last minute, they were joined by Thao, the fourth oldest of Ia's children and the oldest son who lives in the house at Creekside Ranch. Like Jimmy, he nearly always wears baggy shorts and a comic book–themed T-shirt, the hero's torso stretching out over Thao's considerable belly and the legs hanging down the loose fabric below. His face looks just like his father's except younger, without the etchings of old troubles. Indeed, at least publicly, Thao is relaxed and jovial, quick to unselfconsciously laugh his laugh that is several decibels louder than that of anyone around him. When he says something funny and others laugh, he says the funny thing again—just as his mother does. Other siblings say he is Ia's favorite child.

Thao first visited Laos two years earlier, in 2015, when he came in search of a wife. He found one, but because their wedding was performed by Hmong relatives rather than state officials, getting her a visa to the United States has proven to be a slow process. He calls her day and night, and when they are not talking she is the home picture on his phone, a porcelain beauty gazing up from beneath the rim of a pink sun hat.

This year's trip began in Thailand, and the kids' phones are filled with photos from two weeks of sightseeing. There was the night cruise on the *Chao Phraya Princess* and the Las Vegas–style production in Pattaya, complete with dancing elephants. The family hired a guide to take them to the site where Ban Vinai once was, all three of the kids having been born there, but that was anticlimactic. The refugee camp has long since been razed and the land is now a rubber plantation.

The day after Ban Vinai, they headed to Laos. As they crossed the long, concrete Friendship Bridge over the Mekong River, the water below seemed flat and listless. Its only objectionable quality was its color, like the effluent of an industrial dishwasher. Mee remarked that it didn't look the way Ia had described it in her story of swimming across to Thailand: vast and merciless, swollen with invisible dangers. As Ia gazed down at the water, she could only reply that, somehow, the river used to be bigger.

In a Hmong village outside Vientiane, Ia hires a driver and his van. It is worn but, in comparison to the open-air bus most people take out of the city, opulent. The first stop is to pick up Thao's wife, who is living in a lowland town until her visa is granted and she can come to the United States. Having collected her, they now drive east and north and east and north, each road narrower and more potholed than the next. Outside, the forest climbs over itself in a dense, dark tangle. Inside, the family sleeps: Ia and Chou Lor upright but slack, heads bobbing. Daughters draped across new bed pillows still in their plastic covers. In the front seat, Thao with his arm around his wife, her body curled into the negative space of his bulging frame.

The final ascent is marked by a sharp incline that feels as if it is made solely of rocks and the holes between them. Everyone is knocked awake. Then, without warning or announcement, the road flattens, the forest clears, and the landscape is occupied: first one small home, then another—perhaps one hundred households in total, each with six, nine, twelve people. Some houses have woven bamboo sides and shaggy thatch roofs. Others have been upgraded, with corrugated metal roofing or walls of stacked concrete bricks. In the spaces between roam nervous chickens and piglets with swollen bellies and packs of nearly identical dogs in the generic light brown that seems to be the mean average of all the colors a dog can be. At the edges of the village, tall forest trees curl their limbs wildly into the air. Beyond, the mountains are a wall of green.

Aside from the main road there are no streets—virtually no one in town owns a car, anyway. Instead, between the houses are cobwebs of bald paths where the scrubby grass has worn away under motorbike tires and the white ground has been pounded smooth by footsteps. When Ia says so, the van lurches off the main road and threads its way downhill to arrive in a sort of driveway that ends at an unimproved thatch house. There is no crowd gathered, waiting, but from every direction, people stream to the van. Ia steps roundly out the door and directly into the thin arms of a nephew, from which she is passed into the embrace of one relative after another, every face wet with tears and tilted in awe of the moment. When Song and Mee climb out of the van, there are introductions to these dozens of relatives they have never met. A cousin places her hands on Mee's bare upper arm and runs them up and down the plump flesh, squeezing, smiling, in a sort of appraisal.

After a few beats, a man emerges from the house. He is Ia's same height, though a fraction of her weight, his dingy T-shirt hanging slack from his shoulders and his tan shorts loose around his hips. His rumpled black hair has the same faint curl in it that Ia's does, and his teeth, like Ia's, are those of their mother: small and white like a row of Tic Tacs, strong enough to last a lifetime. Due to his sun-aged skin and the wrinkles at his eyes, he looks older than his sister, but for the careless stubble on his chin and the cloud of slow, joyful ease encasing him, he is forever the younger brother. He is the only member of Ia's nuclear family still alive in Laos, and every trip to the country includes a visit to him.

The swarm of people around Ia parts to allow her brother in. His eyes turn red—in this family, tears come on like a flash flood. The siblings embrace, weep, then separate. The tears disappear as suddenly as they came, and Ia reels into the arms of the next relative.

The day in 1979 that fifteen-year-old Ia left the cave for good and began her long trek to Thailand, her younger brother, Tong, set out through the jungle, too, in the opposite direction. His parents—their parents—had received word that the larger group, including Ia, was leaving. They would join, but not without their other two living sons. These men were soldiers in the threadbare resistance, living deeper in seclusion, and it was Tong who went to retrieve them. He was just thirteen but by then he had lived in the forest for a year. He knew the faint paths through the dense vegetation, knew how to slide between the leaves. Soon the three brothers were back with their parents, and the next morning they set out walking to Thailand, alongside half a dozen other Moua clan families. Just as Ia's father had always promised: if they left, they would leave together.

Soon, though, they realized they had left too late to make it to the rendezvous point in time. This was when a son-in-law convinced Ia's father to take an alternate route through an area called Thong Nhai, which he promised would easily reunite them with the larger group. The path now unfamiliar, Tong stuck close to his parents and older brothers. Nearing the place where their paths were supposed to cross with the larger group, they hid in the forest and peered through the trees for signs of them. Night came, then again day. After two days, Ia's father made official what Tong had already guessed but hoped dearly was not true: the larger group that included Ia was long gone, and with them the chance to go to Thailand had vanished.

The elders led the group back into the deep forest. They moved into a cave not far from the one Ia had just left, with no plan other than to survive. It was the same wilderness her father had hunted in for decades. Now, though, they occupied the shadows as if they were animals themselves. They found the land barren, already picked over by so many scouring hands like their own. Every day the family foraged for coarse, wild roots to eat. When it rained, they collected the water to drink. Otherwise, they sat in their camp and stared back out into the world from which they hid.

Their hiding place was high up on a mountain, and from a certain spot Tong could look down onto the distant rice fields farmed by those loyal to the communists. It was too far for him to make out the people, but he easily registered the signs of the seasons: just after they arrived, plumes of smoke rising from the earth signaled the burning of trees to clear a field for planting. Once the rains began in earnest, the black clearing flushed with green rice plants. Months later, when the rains eased, the green gave birth to rich yellow.

One day, just as the far-off rice had turned to gold, his mother sat beside him, crying. She asked him, *When are we ever going to get to eat* mov nplej tshiab *again?*

Setting aside his own grief, he tried to offer her some hope. *It's okay, Mom,* he said. *As long as we don't die, we'll have a chance to do it again. We'll start over.*

"As long as we don't die." Tong, just thirteen years old, struggled with a constant state of worry: If his parents fell ill, how would they survive? With only roots to eat, how would any of them survive? Or would they live, only to be killed by the Vietnamese? They clung to the promise that General Vang Pao would return. They only had to stay alive until he did.

For a year they scraped by on roots and water. At last, Ia's father and the other elder men decided they could wait no longer: Vang Pao was not coming to save them, and if they remained in the cave, they would surely die of hunger. They began the long walk to the state-run settlement of Thatom Thongvia. Just before arriving, they cut a long pole of wood and tied a white cloth to the tip. Carrying this as a flag, they entered the village in surrender.

Ia's father had been there before, back when France still ruled Laos. Facing a mounting threat from communist resistance in the northern mountains, the colonial government prepared for war in part by designing roads that would allow their military access to remote areas. Of course it was not the French who cleared and dug and flattened the earth. Road building was *ua qhev,* slave labor, the danger of the arduous work compounded by the diseases that came with life in the tropical lowlands: malaria, typhoid, dysentery. Word had it that as soon as a man left for the road crews, his family needed to have a cow ready for his funeral. Still, when a government agent arrived in a village, each household was required to supply one male. When the road building approached Thatom Thongvia back in the 1940s, those agents came to Sa Na Oua.

Tong and Ia would be born two decades later; at this time, their parents had just one child, an infant girl, which meant the only male they could send to Thatom Thongvia was Tong and Ia's father. This left their mother alone to do the work of two adults, shepherding the rice crop and growing any food she and the baby were to eat for the months they were alone. But that was not the concern of French administrators. Their father was marched off to the lowlands. The labor was hellish, propelled by a sickening incentive: the harder one exerted himself, the sooner the job would be complete and the men and boys could return to their families. As long as they didn't die first.

More than thirty years later, when Tong and Ia's father led his clan down from the mountains and entered Thatom Thongvia under the rule of the Lao People's Democratic Republic, many of the old dangers remained. Malarial mosquitoes. Fetid water. The un-fed spirits of all those men who had died building the road. In Thatom Thongvia, children went hungry, entire households died from disease. Tong and his parents and brothers put their heads down and tried to adapt. They spent what money they had on what food they could buy. They burned the trees from a hillside and in the rich, ash-covered soil they planted rice, at last. They tended the crop through the rainy season, slowly building back to normal, until the pestilence found them. Tong's father developed a fever in his stomach. By the time the rice was turning into the golden harvest they had dreamed of from the cave, Tong and Ia's father was dead. Was it disease? Despair? Defeat? The illness was never named.

It was not long before the scaffold of family fell away from around Tong. One brother, a die-hard soldier frustrated by civilian life, had already fled to Thailand to join the resistance, promising that he would return to bring the rest of the family once he knew the way. The other brother led his wife and children back into the mountains to live as fugitives. That left just Tong and his mother in Thatom Thongvia. When a message came from the brother in Thailand, the two expected their deliverance. Instead, heartbreak: Returning to retrieve them was too dangerous, the brother said. They were on their own.

Tong was fifteen years old, the same age Ia had been when she left Laos on foot. Now he, too, was an orphan. In the unsparing view of the clan, Tong and his mother had lost all value. Without any adult man in the family, this woman and boy could not reciprocate in the clan's offering of rituals or labor; they would now be only a drain on resources. No longer invited to the funeral feasts and shaman offerings that reinforced belonging in the community, Tong and his mother were instead sloughed off. Tong did his best to take care of his mother, but if he was no longer a child, he was not yet a man. Because his small body was unable to cut down enough trees to clear new land, he and his mother reused the plot the family had stripped when his father and brothers had been there. They planted the same thin dirt repeatedly, watched the soil degrade and the harvests decrease.

Still, with each new season, Tong grew, now sixteen, seventeen, eventually a man in a body that could cut down the forest on his own. Tong married a woman who gave birth to one son and then another—mouths to feed today, but like him they would grow into men. With the arrival of these sons, the clan saw new value in Tong. In recognition of his manhood, they honored him by replacing his child's name of Tong with an adult name: Pha Kao.

In time, Pha Kao's oldest brother returned from the mountains, and together the two families multiplied their individual strengths. Bit by bit, Pha Kao was able to imagine better days. Within a decade, he had saved up enough money to buy two plots of paddy land, right by the main road. Even unplanted, the plots were beautiful—he could just picture how green they would be at the height of the season. With them, his family could cease farming on the mountain slopes; these verdant lowland fields would produce twice as much rice as their dry plantings ever had.

It was 1991, the year the U.S. State Department would broker a deal between Laos, Thailand, and the UNHCR to shut down the refugee camps and begin turning battlefields into marketplaces; this was the same year that Ia would begin leading her family from the refugee camp in Thailand to the United States. General Vang Pao and his forces of resistance had been blacklisted by the Thai government, but they continued to fight for control of Laos. Hmong guerrillas still operated from their bases in Ban Vinai and other refugee camps. Within Laos, one of their strongholds was in the mountains to the south of Xieng Khouang, not far from Thatom Thongvia.

Before Pha Kao could buy the rice paddies he had been eyeing, the resistance began attacking villages of upland people who had left the mountains and submitted to communist rule—villages like his. After nearly being killed in a midnight ambush, Pha Kao and his brother decided it was too dangerous to stay there. They filed papers with the government for permission to leave the region. Within the year, they had moved their families to a village one hundred kilometers to the southwest and started over from scratch. The rice paddies were sold to someone else.

The region they moved to was closer to Vientiane, and over the course of the war and its aftermath, tens of thousands of displaced people had relocated there. By the time Pha Kao arrived in 1992, it was already crowded. When his family settled near a triangle-shaped mountain called Phou Houad, they found themselves to be an unwanted layer deposited on top of the others, all needing that same land in order to survive. And it was only getting more crowded, with new roads bringing in more and more people each year.

As Pha Kao recalls, when he arrived, a person could still make a fire by the river, put a pot of water on, and by the time it had reached boiling, the person would have caught enough fish to fill it. There were so many squirrels a man could shoot ten in one outing. Wild boar. Birds of all sizes. No more. Today, he says, with all those new people having flocked here, most of the trees have been cut down. The birds, with nowhere to live, have flown away.

———

There are still Hmong resistance forces tucked into the trees of Phou Bia, but they are a mere shadow of the guerrillas who tried to win the region in the late 1970s. Back then, the resistance was such a force that the Lao government had to call in Vietnamese military as backup; the carnage so great that Ia and her family were driven from Sa Na Oua forever. In 2017, those who remain number perhaps in the hundreds, and that includes the women and children among them. Still hidden in the remote jungle, the rebels live hand to mouth, dressed in rags. When they are lucky, they eat rice that has been smuggled in; otherwise, they subsist on roots and any other wild food they can scavenge. When Western journalists make the trek to visit these "jungle Hmong," the men interviewed talk less about winning back the country and more about their desire to simply reintegrate into civilian life without having the government put them in jail or kill them outright.

While the government has not reprised the full-scale offensive of the 1970s, it has continued to attack and antagonize the dwindling population on Phou Bia. Since 2016, especially, it has sought to empty out the rebels by force so that the area can be easily opened to mining and other economic activities rather than cordoned off for security reasons. Really, though, the government's offensive against the Hmong and other people in the uplands is no longer military. It is economic.

The year Pha Kao moved to Phou Houad—1993, the same year Ia moved to Fresno—the GDP per capita per day in the United States was $69.64; in Laos, it was 65 cents. This was, in large part, because Laos remained a nation of small farmers: 90 percent of the labor force worked in agriculture, mostly growing rice at a subsistence level. In the 1990s, the nation shifted to a market-based system in earnest, in hopes of inviting investment, producing foreign exchange, and increasing state revenues—all of which would raise the standard of living. On paper it was a well-worn path of development economics for Asian countries: more rice would be grown on less land by fewer people, excess farmers would become industrial workers, factories would be built, incomes would swell, and global capital would flow as never before.

In practice, though, Laos had little prospect for industrial development. The country was landlocked, the government was corrupt, and on the most basic levels it lacked infrastructure and a professional workforce. The one thing the nation had in abundance was raw land: an area roughly the size of Utah, largely covered in rich tropical forest, underlaid with farmable soils and untold mineral deposits, crisscrossed with hundreds of rivers just waiting to be dammed for hydroelectric power. In short, it had the uplands. Recognizing that these natural resources were the nation's only ticket to the global economy, the struggling government fashioned a blunt strategy to wring them of profit.

The first step was to digest those people who occupied the land it desired. People like Pha Kao. People like him all over the world, really: anywhere the drive of globalized capital plowed into the margins and ran up against what was differentiated as "the rural poor," the story was eerily similar. These people were seen as both the ostensible cause for needing economic development and an impediment to it. In order to improve the nation by extracting its natural wealth—to "turn land into capital," as the Lao government's slogan would later put it—the countless communities of people who farmed that land needed to be removed.

The government proceeded to relocate villages in remote locations to new sites at lower elevations, often alongside roads. The government's stated intention was to give these "unsettled" people a permanent location, where they could participate in the new economy and have access to services the new economy would bring, such as medical care, education, sanitation. Another outcome, unspoken but widely understood, was political. Since the beginning of centralized power in Indochina, the mountains had been the domain of those who resisted being absorbed by the state; since the beginning of the Lao People's Democratic Republic, in 1975, the uplands had been home to the Hmong resistance and other anti-communist insurgents. Living in view of the government, these upland people would be easier to surveil and control.

Working under the dual guises of tropical forest planning and economic development, in 1990 the Lao government pledged to permanently settle nine hundred thousand people from the uplands—a quarter of the country's population. Villages were consolidated into larger communities and often moved en masse to new development sites, either in the lowlands or at least along a main road. For long-term survival, each family was assigned land on which to grow food. In many cases, though, the fields were too poor or too small or lacking sufficient water for irrigation to fully feed those expected to rely on them. Yet outside farming, the majority of resettled people had little training with which to join the new economy. When resettled people found themselves with neither the land to grow rice nor the income to buy it, the one-party state gave little answer except rigid repression of the people's anger.

Meanwhile, the government declared open season on the nation's natural resources. Mining and logging stripped the forests. Foreign corporations erected plantations of rubber and bananas. In the hills, rice was increasingly replaced with maize and cassava—feed for the livestock that were now in high demand among all of Laos's major neighbors, whose growing middle classes had a newfound budget for meat. The most valuable commodity of all has proven to be electricity from hydropower. In the last decade, more than fifty new dams have been built. Another eighty-seven are in planning and construction stages, all in a nation the size of Utah. Each time the water fills in behind a dam's concrete walls, the lives upstream must be relocated. In 2010, the World Bank predicted that from just the hydropower projects planned at that time, the number of people who would need to be resettled was roughly 280,000—one out of every twenty-five people in the country.

In 2007, the government announced that Pha Kao's village would be relocated. The dozens of households would leave their idyllic setting near the river, where it was easy to grow little plots of vegetables and even fruit trees, and move to a bald hillside where a road had recently been constructed. Two years later, they got electricity for the first time ever. Most households now have enough to run a cell phone charger, some fluorescent lights, and a single appliance, usually a rice cooker.

At the bottom of the village there is a primary school, where lessons are taught in Lao. Some kids continue on to a secondary school ten kilometers away. If they graduate, they must go elsewhere to find employment. A few people in the village do operate small convenience stores from the fronts of their homes, selling soda and cookies. There is a man who fixes motorcycles and sells gasoline. Girls and women sew piecework embroidery of the sort that Ia once made in Ban Vinai, which they sell to buyers from Thailand. However, the only formal jobs in the village are those of the schoolteacher and various people who administer state bureaucracy. Perhaps the greatest source of income is remittances sent home by those who have left. The biggest sums come from relatives in the United States.

There is still farming, though not like in the past. As a complement to its resettlement programs, the government passed policies that would make upland rice farming more difficult and thereby force farmers like Pha Kao to grow cash crops. The government did not, however, solve the issue that across the northern part of the country, there were few markets for these crops and little infrastructure for shipping them to distant buyers. When former subsistence farmers entered the commodity stream, they found themselves at the mercy of global markets and their local middlemen, with neither the capital nor the influence to compete. A few years after moving to the new village, Pha Kao managed to plant two hundred rubber trees. Before he ever tapped them, the market crashed, in part because of overproduction.

Upland communities found that regardless of government overtures about the bright future, in reality, there was little place for people like them in the new economy. Some farmers who could find the money moved to the lowlands voluntarily. Others went to work on the banana farms and rubber plantations, or found work in Thailand's factories. Plenty in the younger generation took the increasingly universal path to the city. Some, primarily young women, married people in wealthier countries—this seen by many as the most reliable path to securing income. The majority, however, simply continued growing upland rice at a subsistence level, as they had for as far back as anyone could remember. Despite the promises of the new economy, despite all the obstacles the government had erected, despite all those people and corporations crowding in and pushing them off the best land, their age-old economy was still the surest bet.

To reach the land that Pha Kao farms today, he and his sons and nephews and their families must ascend the sharp slope of Phou Houad. At the lower elevations, the road is blocked by cattle gates fashioned from bamboo; later, it passes massive transmission towers connected by long, slack power lines as thick as a man's arm, which transport electricity from the nearby hydroelectric plant to Thailand. It takes four hot hours of walking straight up to reach their plot of land, and even it is available to them only through the privilege of clan connections. Not everyone would be so lucky.

To prepare the land earlier this year, they did as they have always done. In late winter, Pha Kao and his family felled the land's trees. They saved what trunks and bamboo they would use to construct the temporary houses they would live in during the farming season. Then they set fire to the rest of it, all those leaves and vines and branches incinerated to ash. What remained were only knee-high stumps and a forest of blackened tree trunks strewn across the raw ground. Their thin, straight lines suggested the density of the forest that had been, where life was an elbow-knocking rush upward to reach through the canopy for sun. Bare like this, the land was revealed to be steeper than it would appear under the equalizing cover of treetops. And Pha Kao and his family had cut the mountainside to the very brink of possibility, to where the slope was nearly vertical. Below, their clearing stopped only where the land dropped off into the sharp crease of a streambed.

Their farm adjoins a dozen others, together comprising a deforested spot perhaps a mile across. It is one of about ten on the flanks of Phou Houad, one of maybe fifty in the wide swath of land between the mountain and Pha Kao's village. Seen from the air, the whole deep-green nation is mottled with these naked patches. International observers regularly point to this "slash-and-burn" farming as a central culprit in the staggering loss of Southeast Asia's tropical forests. To most outside eyes, the barren landscape is shocking, seemingly the result of grievous miscalculation or utter desperation.

In truth, this is more or less what upland farming has looked like since Pha Kao's and Ia's ancestors grew dry rice on the margins of the growing Han empire—really, all across the highlands of Southeast Asia. Farmers would clear the forest, cultivate the open space for a few years, then move on, allowing the forest to regrow. The practice evolved out of a landscape with such regenerative powers that every family who wanted to could shear a plot back to nothing and barely leave a mark; the vast, fecund land would absorb their impact. The difference between then and now is not the system itself but all those people that Pha Kao laments having descended on this place. Before the war, no one would have had to farm way the hell up on the side of Phou Houad. Even into the 1980s, this was all jungle. But while the land has stayed finite, the number of people who want it for one purpose or another has multiplied. People like Pha Kao, who have always occupied the margins, have been pushed right to the edge.

The act of growing rice here looks much as it did when Pha Kao and Ia farmed with their parents. Pha Kao now has a small chain saw with which to cut down the trees, whereas his father and grandfather used handsaws to chew through each trunk. He also has a tractor, whose invaluable gift is to truck all the sacks of grain back to the village at the end of the season so that the family need not haul it on their shoulders. Otherwise, the essential tools are those familiar for generations: the homemade dibble sticks, the quick hands, the aching backs.

Something else, though, is fundamentally different from when Pha Kao and Ia were young. It's not just the cruel grade of this farmland, nor the Thai power company's transmission towers marching across the landscape. The change is a state of mind that accompanies them. It is most apparent in the members of the family who are in their first few years of counting as adults. How, while planting, one will stop in the middle of the hill, dig out a cell phone, and hold it up in the air, praying for a signal; how those without phones will stop, too, to see if this other one of them will get lucky. These teenagers give the clearest, most unconflicted message that this life of farming rice on the side of a mountain is something to escape.

But it is not limited to them. Pha Kao's adult nephew and his wife are scheming to procure six-month visas to France so they can do seasonal farmwork and return home with enough money to plant a rubber farm. Less ambitious parents resign themselves to rice farming, but with the understanding that if they could do something else, they would. It is now widely accepted that this life is a path taken only when there is no other option. The old men in Fresno who cling to their glory dreams of winning back Laos, the old women who yearn for *yus teb yus chaw*—even they do not want to do this, here, as it is now. The Hmong tourists who return so gleefully each New Year's always eventually get on a plane and fly home.

Pha Kao, because he thinks of himself as an old man, accepts that he will live out his days farming this steep mountain. Still, he wishes his children had the chance to do something else. Wait to marry, continue their education, find work with a paycheck—anything to avoid the poverty that has defined his life. Or return to where he was born, where Ia was born, where the land was flat and open and free for the taking. Where they could change their fortunes by moving farther into the mountains. For the reality that they cannot, he blames the government, with all its regulations that bar people like them from the country's wealth of land.

For his own bad fortune, though, Pha Kao holds responsible just one person: his father. Like Ia, he traces his sad predicament now back to that fateful day in 1979 when the family was meant to flee to Thailand, but didn't. However, as Pha Kao tells the story, there was no tragic mistake. His father—their father—had never wanted to go to Thailand; he wanted to somehow return to the life they had lived before.

In Sa Na Oua, his father had accumulated wealth and status. He knew that in Thailand, he would have nothing. Beyond that, though, Pha Kao points to something deeper. Even during the war, his father would melt into the forest for a week at a time, maybe more. The man knew every hill, stream, cave, gully for miles, and within that landscape he could track, trap, shoot, or hook any creature worth eating. Every time his father returned to the village, laden with fish or game for his family to eat, he was more alive than when he had left. Thriving in these wild mountains was his gift, and likewise his deepest joy. His purpose. Removed from this place, what would remain of him?

Thailand promised safety from violent persecution, plus bellies reliably filled with rations of rice. At the same time, it promised dependence, confinement, idleness, and political impotence. Of course escaping communist-ruled Laos was the only sensible thing to do; their family had been hiding in the forest and fighting off starvation for months. As a clan leader, Pha Kao's father had been charged with deciding whether to make the trek to Thailand. When Ia's group offered the chance to escape, he had felt compelled by the others' desire to leave. But in his heart, he never accepted the idea.

According to Pha Kao, on the day Ia left, their father delayed his family's departure. And when they were too late to make the rendezvous, his father saw an opportunity: Following the alternate path to Thong Nhai was a surefire way to ensure that they would never catch up to the larger group. He knowingly sabotaged the family's chance to flee to Thailand.

As Pha Kao sees it, his father did this because of his refusal to let go of the life that had long since died—or, rather, his refusal to let go of the belief that that life might still exist, somewhere deeper in the mountains. In a sense, he was no different from Vang Pao's followers in Ban Vinai and, later, in Fresno. But by choosing to remain in Laos, Pha Kao's father was unwittingly choosing all the decades of enclosure, poverty, and shrinking margins that would come with it. This was the only inheritance he left for his youngest son.

When Pha Kao tells the story of that fateful day, he does not talk about the tragedy that Ia does: how she was separated from the only group that ever offered her safety, how she was consigned to the care of a husband who had brutally beat her, how she would forever after be an orphan. Pha Kao thinks Ia is the lucky one—she made it to Thailand and then the United States, where she had the chance to escape the inherent scarcity of their existence in the mountains. He is the one left in Laos, the last of the living. He is the true orphan, the poorest of the poor.

B eside Ia's hired van, the teary greetings go on until every combination of villager and visitor has been made, sometimes twice. When there is no one left approaching for a hug, Ia crawls inside the van and fishes out two Halloween-size bags of Dum-Dums lollipops. As she backs out through the doors, her gaze does not meet the eyes of the children who have clustered behind her. Instead, she walks purposefully through a growing cloud of anticipation to a spot of shade where her brother's wife is quickly setting out three red plastic stools.

Ia sits in the center, Chou Lor to her left and Song to her right. Before them the children crowd into a tight half circle, three deep. Ia wrestles the bag open, takes two Dum-Dums in one hand, and extends her arm toward the throng. Two dozen young eyes stare at the lollipops, as if they might be a trick. In front stands a girl in pigtails who, at about four years old, seems driven more by sheer desire than nerves. She reaches out and wraps her fingers around the two Dum-Dums. When nothing bad happens, a surge of hands reach out to be next.

Even after every child is accounted for, the first bag is not half-empty. So there are seconds, then rounds for the teenagers and the adults and the babies who are old enough to have a lollipop held in their mouths. There are also the rolls of Life Savers that Song has in hand and the pink shopping bags full of fruit in Chou Lor's lap, all needing to be disbursed, and soon the children are simply trying to figure out how to hold everything and eat it at the same time—rolling the loot up in their shirts, taking a half-sucked sucker out to devour a banana, handing off the extra to their parents. One girl stuffs five Dum-Dums in her mouth at once. For a moment, everyone—brothers and aunts, cousins and sisters-in-law—stands together in the bare yard of Pha Kao's house, bound in the collective sugar high. Seated at the axis of their arc, Ia pulls out the final lollipop and drops the bag on the ground. As she cracks the candy between her teeth, she is alight from inside.

Ten minutes later, the crowd is mostly gone. The adults have dispersed back to whatever they were doing before the van's arrival. The boys have gone off to play. Ia and her daughters are seated on the red stools, their only audience now a half-dozen little girls. Anytime there is a sliver of action in the village, there will be a cloud of these girls standing around the edges. They are silent yet watchful, absorbing the information into the sponges of their brains. When Song pulls out her phone, they crowd against her arms to see the pictures of Thailand, pictures of Fresno. Mee, shyly huddled with her own phone, is soon surrounded as well. Ia does not have a smartphone and is not interested in entertaining, but for each grandniece who approaches, she will peel a 1,000-*kip* note off her roll of bills and press it into the girl's palm like a shiny dime.

Ia's own audience is assured; they just take a little longer. Over the next few hours she will see a steady stream of relatives seeking her help, receiving them with patient sympathy and, for certain people, magnanimous counsel. A niece has recently divorced and weeps that she is left destitute and ostracized. A daughter-in-law explains that her strange illness has been diagnosed as the calling of shaman spirits, and she is nervous about receiving the summons. Pha Kao and his wife emerge from the house and present Ia with a baby boy in a shirt so white it can only be brand-new. When he was born a few months earlier, the boy was sickly, vomiting anything he was fed and refusing to grow. The family sent a photo of him to Ia in Fresno and explained his story: his parents—Pha Kao's second-youngest son and a girl from a nearby village—are teenagers; their tryst led to her pregnancy. Without delay, Pha Kao paid her parents a bride-price, the couple was married, and the girl moved in with her new family.

From Fresno, Ia diagnosed the child's spiritual illness and prescribed corrective measures. The family dutifully obeyed, and now the baby is happy and fat, so juicy with breast milk that skin bulges up around the brass bracelet on his wrist. As Pha Kao's wife proudly delivers the boy into Ia's arms, she says that he has been named Sao, meaning "thunder." Ia admires him for a polite amount of time, then hands him to Song. Behind them stands the new daughter-in-law, wiry thin from breastfeeding, her face as round and naked as a full moon. In silence, she watches the exchange intently and then ducks weightlessly back into the dark doorway of the thatch house where she now lives.

The house is made entirely from materials cut from the land: the posts and beams are tree trunks and limbs, the walls are bamboo slats that have been split and plaited by hand. It is naturally dark, the only light what comes in through the two doorways and what seeps through the spaces in the woven walls. The dirt floor is pocked from wear but swept to a smooth, hard finish. It is the same basic house everyone in the village began with—virtually the same structure Pha Kao and Ia were born in, and their parents before them, on back through the ages. Just a single open room, the year's harvest of rice in bags stacked up along one wall.

In one corner, there is a cooking fire atop a broad hillock of ashes, behind which the bamboo wall is a deep black from countless baths of smoke. This is the place to which the new daughter-in-law returns most often, including now, amid the commotion of visitors.

If she has found a nest, this is it, the natural hub from which to perform her role of cook, server, and dishwasher. There is a corner like it in every home in this village, and most often a young woman like this daughter-in-law within. Back when Ia was newly married, she would have inhabited a similar space in Chou Lor's family's house.

Before the girl moved in, the person who occupied this corner was Ia's son Thao's wife, who is also Thao's cousin: Pha Kao's daughter, Ia's niece. As a baby, she was named *Ib,* meaning "one." Because the village had another, older woman by this name, they were differentiated by age: the older woman was *Ib phauj,* or "one aunt"; the younger was *Ib ntxhais,* "one daughter." Over time, people dropped her given name and called her just Ntxhais, "daughter." For anyone who doesn't speak Hmong it's a tricky word to pronounce, and so as she grew up and passed into the world outside her home, the larger world changed her name again, to Chai. These days, though, at least in the village, everyone calls her *Nyab Thao*—Thao's wife.

Chai is a few years older than the moon-faced daughter-in-law, born the same spring that Ia started farming in Fresno, almost two decades ago. She was born in the old village, before the road was built and the power lines erected. Of the children who survived she was fourth, after two brothers and one sister. Following her came one brother, the father of Sao, and then the final brother.

For that last birth, Chai's mother was brought to the nearest hospital. All Chai remembers is that when her father returned home, he insisted that she and her siblings go away and play—he didn't want them to see their mother's lifeless body, didn't want them to cry. Chai was not yet four years old, too young for concrete memories. There was a photograph of the woman, and in the years that followed Pha Kao used it to show Chai who her mother was. To this day, though, she cannot independently picture the woman's face or conjure the sound of her voice. It's almost as if she never had a mother.

For most of her life, Chai was raised by two other women. First was a stepmother, Pha Kao's second wife—the little wife, as such women are called. Pha Kao married her while his first wife was still alive. As he explains it, the arrangement was not about passion so much as practicality: he took her in hoping that she could help raise the children, so that he and his original wife could devote more time to farming and thus improve their lives—more of a nanny than a mistress. He says Chai's mother even agreed to the arrangement. But then everything changed.

When Chai's mother died in childbirth, the baby boy survived. The little wife had no children, and she convinced Pha Kao to let her raise the boy as her own. While she poured herself into mothering the child, at the same time she treated Pha Kao's five older children as orphans. Indeed, the little wife became notorious for her cruelty and violence toward the kids.

The extended family believed that the root cause of the little wife's wickedness was her own barren womb, but it could not be denied that she herself had suffered: After her own parents died and left her an orphan, her brother agreed to make her the second wife to a man she had never met. After that marriage ended in divorce, her family married her to an older man, who promptly died and left her a widow—all this before she was twenty years old. When Pha Kao's first wife died, the little wife came into power for perhaps the first time in her life. Chai and her siblings bore the brunt.

When the little wife was exceedingly harsh toward the kids, Pha Kao would intervene. Most days he did not, however, and the children had to be defended by the only person left: their grandmother—Ia's mother. This was the woman who really raised Chai.

Ia's mother shielded her grandchildren with her superior rank and, at times, her aging body. Most days, though, her tactic was to bring her grandchildren to farm with her, for even as she grew more frail and lost her eyesight, she continued to tend a garden, just as she had when Ia was young. As they worked, Grandmother told the children stories—folktales, ghost stories, true tales of wartime and the ragged years that followed. Ia aimed to support her mother by regularly sending money from Fresno; the old woman used the money to buy necessities for the kids. This particular act glows bright in Chai's memory because without her grandmother's generosity there would have been no new clothing, perhaps no shoes at all. Living in the old village, so far from any road, there was little opportunity for adults to earn money without leaving home. As Chai understood it, the only way one got cash to spend was by having a relative in the United States send it. Her grandmother, funded by Ia, was a lifeline.

After Chai's grandmother died, things changed. Ia's money was sent to—and stopped with—Pha Kao and the little wife. When the little wife erupted, the children had no protector. Chai escaped north and west to Xayaboury province, where her eldest brother worked as a teacher. But within a year, she moved home. Stepmother notwithstanding, home was where Chai felt happiest because it was where she was surrounded by the rest of her family. When she and her two younger brothers were teenagers, the three of them moved to the village where the closest high school was located; still, many weeks they would skip classes on Fridays and walk home a day early. Chai didn't mind that they had little money, because in her experience, life was all but free.

Chai didn't dream far beyond the borders of the village. She knew that in theory, getting an education might afford her the chance to transcend her parents' poverty. And yet from what she had seen, regardless of her schooling there was a single path ahead that consisted of getting married and farming rice. If the future was indeed preordained, she figured the best way to influence it would be to at least marry someone she liked.

There was a boyfriend—svelte, handsome, educated in the lowlands. Chai was not his only girlfriend, though, and she suspected that marrying him would lead to a life of heartache. Then there was Thao, whom she had met while she lived in Xayaboury. Ia had brought him to Laos with the intention of engaging him to Pha

Kao's oldest daughter, Chai's older sister; marrying between cousins was still seen as a protective arrangement, just as it had been when Ia's parents determined she would marry her mother's brother's son. By the time Thao arrived in Laos, though, the older daughter had married another man.

It didn't matter, because Thao immediately fell for Chai. He was moonstruck by the glossy black waterfall of her hair, which cascaded to the middle of her thighs. She had small, straight, almost baby teeth, set against soft pink gums. Chai was sweet and chatty and funny, with a hint of a temper that made the whole sauce of her *piquant.* She laughed easily, never covering her mouth but always curling her chin into her shoulder, as if to contain the intimacy of her smile. Nearly a woman, yet still shy like a girl.

Of course, when Chai met Thao she *was* just a girl, seventeen years old and twelve years his junior. Thao was not dashing, but he was genuinely nice to her. And she liked how unreserved and gregarious he was, social even among strangers. In a way, he was still a boy. When he arrived in the United States at six years old, he had immediately fallen in love with Godzilla. He drew the monster over and over—won a prize at the county fair for one rendering—then moved on to making up his own fantastical creatures. His dream job was to work in movies. He did study animation at community college, but when he tired of sitting in a chair all day long he dropped out and started a gig as a security guard. When Chai met him in Xayaboury, he courted her with drawings torn out of his sketchbook. And jokes, lots of jokes. After he returned to the United States, he messaged her devoutly. For that first year, there was nothing but kindness.

When Ia proposed that Thao and Chai be married, Pha Kao shocked her by demanding a bride-price paid in cash, and a steep one at that. Ia was infuriated by his greed and ingratitude—she had, after all, helped support his family financially for decades. Not to mention that, once married to Thao, Chai would be able to move to

Fresno and send even more money back to her father. Still, Pha Kao argued that because he had had to pay bride-prices when his sons married, it was only fair that he should receive one for his daughter. A bitter fight ensued and was ended only by Thao. Bawling, he pleaded with his mother to pay whatever Pha Kao asked. Ia yielded. A year after Thao and Chai met, they were married in the village in a traditional Hmong ceremony.

In the eyes of the American government, their vows were not official or legally binding. To bring Chai to Fresno, Thao would have to apply for her to be granted a K-1, or "fiancé," visa, so they could get married in the United States. Knowing that the application process would take time, Thao quit his job as a security guard and took a job at Hot Wok Express so he would have more flexible vacation time with which to travel to Laos. He made some changes for Chai, too, moving her to a village in the lowlands, where she would live with members of his family. It was the proper thing to do, now that she had joined his clan. Plus, she would be closer to the embassy, where she would need to go for interviews and paperwork. She would also be four hours away from the evil little wife.

That was two years ago. Today, returning to the yard of her father's house, Chai looks different. In the village, the standard women's wear is a wraparound skirt in Lao fabric and any shirt, scrubbed as clean as is possible without laundry soap. Emerging from the touring van with Thao and his family, Chai wears a dark jean jacket over a bright white T-shirt that says I ♥ PARIS, the I a drawing of the Eiffel Tower. She wears lipstick. Apple-red fingernail polish. Flip-flops, like the other women, but hers are bejeweled.

Still, as meal preparations begin, she pulls her long, long hair methodically into a ponytail and folds up the cuffs of her jean jacket. Without anyone asking her to, she drags a collection of spindly logs from behind the house to the far end of the yard, away from where Ia receives her supplicants. She arranges the logs on the ground like spokes of a wheel and, with a lighter from her purse, sets the center aflame. From the blackened hearth corner of the house she retrieves a five-gallon pot and a sooty tripod for it to sit on, sets the rig atop the fire, and begins boiling water for the night's feast.

All afternoon into evening, Chai will stay here tending this fire, pushing the long pieces of wood deeper into the flames as their tips burn away. Even as the makeup on her forehead thins with sweat, a group of the little girls, her nieces, will cluster at her sides to study and idolize her. Chai, in turn, will show them how it's done.

———

Across the yard from Chai's fire, the younger men are gathered in a space next to the house, the boundaries of which are marked by twelve soaring columns of concrete reinforced with rebar. With more money from Ia, this will become Pha Kao's new house, complete with concrete walls and concrete floor, shuttered windows and locking door. Similar buildings are going up throughout the village, both to accommodate the growing population and simply to upgrade out of the old thatch dwellings.

For now, though, the unfinished concrete frame serves as a makeshift garage for Pha Kao's red tractor, a luxury that Ia paid for a few years back. On the front loader, the younger men have laid a table, and on top of that, a freshly slaughtered hog. Ia bought that, too, hauled it up from the lowlands in the back of the van, packed under the family's luggage. It is twice the size of the rough-haired pigs that range around the village, its skin pale pink. The men crowd around it.

Presiding over the group is Thao, who loudly tells stories as he butchers the hog. He has been cooking since he was young, when he learned by helping Chou Lor make meals for the rest of the kids while Ia worked at the farm. By his own measure, Thao can watch a dish prepared once, then re-create it flawlessly; as a cook at Hot Wok Express, he tries to bring his own flair to the standardized recipes. This evening, on the front of the tractor, he is executing an elaborate personal recipe for what he calls a pudding: a soft, pale concoction fashioned from minced brains, tongue, ear, and cheek meat. For just the right consistency, he improvises a sous vide by putting the brains in a plastic bag and slipping that into Chai's boiling soup pot for a careful minute.

For hours, the visitors play their roles: Thao as master chef, Chai as tender of the cook fire, Ia as wise benefactor, Song and Mee as exotic aunties. In the driver's seat of the tractor, Chou Lor takes a snoring nap. The moon is bright white in the night sky by the time the women arrange three low dining tables in a line down the empty center of the house. After a man arrives with a rack of beer in tall bottles, Pha Kao and the rest of the married men file in to take their seats. Normally, the two meals each day here are rice with whatever vegetables are growing in the garden down by the river. What piglets and chickens each family has are reserved for ritual purposes and special occasions. Tonight, though, these men sit down to a showcase of pork, no piece of the pig unused. There is grilled leg and ribs with the skin on, spicy minced *laab* and soup with intestines, stomach and liver that has been cooked with bile to make it bitter. And of course the pudding, which Thao instructs the guests to scoop up with a piece of meat. There are heaping, steaming bowls of rice on the table but nothing else, vegetables in attendance only to flavor the meat.

Chou Lor sits at the head of the table, and each man takes a turn thanking him for bringing this food, blessing his family. Thao sits down the row from him. In the dark background, the thin mother nurses baby Sao and with blank eyes watches the men pour beer into small glasses. The women stand outside with the rest of the food in the makeshift garage, in a wide circle of light from a fluorescent bulb overhead. Chai shuttles full bowls inside, making sure the men's feast never dwindles.

When the men start to slow their eating, mothers set out two low tables just within the circle of light in the garage. They set each table with a bowl of rice and two bowls of pork and call the kids to eat. The pudding is long gone, but the children don't notice. Kneeling on the ground, they jostle and reach, so hungry this late in the day that they don't wait for spoons, just dip their fingers into the food. In the darkness surrounding them, dogs edge in toward the younger ones, hoping to thieve their way to more than discarded bones. Also outside the circle of light, Ia stands by herself. Restless, she picks up a pole and whacks a creeping dog on the haunches, sending it shooting off into the night.

Before the women can eat, they must clear the children's food, clean the tables, and consolidate the uneaten food into the new bowls from which they will dine. As the mothers work, Ia finds the only stool not in use by the men inside and settles her round bottom back onto it. She whacks two more dogs who are merely slinking around the periphery, and with a lunge in her hips dares the other mongrels to try. In a small gesture of dignity, of distinction from the children, a woman disappears behind the house and emerges with four small blocks and two boards to set atop them as a couple of benches. At last the women sit, if just inches above the dirt, and eat. Ia shuffles her stool into the light, bends over in her seat, and reaches down to dip her own spoon into the bowls.

The next day begins in the dark, when the most junior woman in each house rises to build a new kitchen fire on top of the old mound of ashes. First light lifts the highest mountain peaks from darkness, then wakes the green ridges below one by one. On the cement floor of her nephew's newly built house, Ia comes to life slowly. She sits up, legs still under her blanket, hair rumpled from sleep. Before long she is surrounded by a circle of the female relatives and neighbors who congregate before she goes to bed and as soon as she wakes. The house's only door is open and white morning light pours into the dark room, over the backs of the visitors and onto Ia's face like stage lights.

These women and girls come to visit, but rarely just that. They seek Ia's advice. They ask questions about life in Fresno. They watch as if this American family were a traveling show, the youngest girls staring from the doorway as Ia's daughters undress and style their hair and apply scented creams and climb into yet another set of clothes. Ia stays under her blanket, twisting her bed head into a skinny braid and, trying not to seem sleepy, politely keeps the conversation going.

This village is not Ia's village, these relatives not her family so much as her brothers' families. What draws her back here each time she travels to Laos is her mother, who is buried in the nearby forest-lands. Visiting her grave will be the day's main activity.

Chou Lor, whose chronic stomach illness has flared up, does not join. Thao and Chai stay behind as well. After breakfast, Pha Kao fires up the red tractor for those who will go. Flat boards have been attached to the front and back as makeshift benches, onto which half a dozen relatives sit and brace themselves. Ia and her daughters are given the only official seat, a plank behind the driver with a railing to hold on to; they try not to flinch at the diesel smoke belching out of the pipe at their backs. While no one says it out loud, it is known that if not for the visitors, the group would easily walk.

The route to the grave site is a series of ever less formal roads over which the tractor bumps and clangs, each person gripping whatever is closest in order to stay aboard. Past the old village, now overgrown, Pha Kao cuts the engine at the edge of a stand of trees and they proceed on foot, through the dark forest and then out and up a steep rise. A nephew trained in geomancy chose the top of this hill as an auspicious grave site where Ia's mother would rest undisturbed. Since the burial, though, the living have also found it desirable: first outsiders who began clearing the land for a rubber plantation, and then villagers who burned the ground to plant rice. Ia paid for Pha Kao to take the issue to court, and, after numerous fees, the family won rights to the burial mound and a two-foot ring around it. Pha Kao fenced the spot in barbed wire and on a post nailed a metal tag stating their permanent claim to this spot of earth.

As farmers have continued to plant every other square meter of this hill, the grave site has acted like an ecologist's exclusion plot, demonstrating what the land does when untouched. Only six years since the burial, it is a miniature forest of bamboo the height of a two-story house, and the barbed wire has long since been swallowed by vines. Leading the group, Pha Kao draws his machete and slices away the leaves covering the entrance. He pulls apart the middle fence wires, making an opening for people to climb through.

Within the chamber of bamboo the air is still and the light muted, the only view straight up to the sky. Below, a long bulge of dirt stretches from one end of the ten-foot-wide space to the other. Ia picks her way around the very perimeter, carefully crossing the head of the grave mound to stand alone on the far side. Pha Kao positions himself opposite her while the rest of the relatives clumsily pile up around the entrance. As if on cue, all the adults but Ia begin crying.

As the son, Pha Kao will voice the formal invitation for their mother to come eat. He lays out a plastic bag of cooked rice. Ia adorns the rice with a handful of pork from last night's feast. The other adults lay out plastic cups of orange drink, a packet of cookies. When the offering is set, Pha Kao wipes his tears and concludes weeping. It is then that Ia begins to cry.

Ia saw her mother just once before she died. It was twenty-three years after that fateful night when Ia left the cave without her parents and fled to Thailand. By the time she saw her mother again, Ia was thirty-eight years old, with eleven children and a rice farm in Fresno. Earlier in the year, on a cassette recording, her mother had recounted a dream. In it, Ia's father came to bring her to the afterworld. The meaning was clear: if Ia wanted to see her mother again, there was not much time left. Chou Lor protested that the trip would be too expensive—no one in the family had yet returned to Laos since they fled in 1979. Ia bought the ticket anyway. Her daughter Alice, just nine months old, was left in the care of the girl's siblings.

In the weeks before her trip, Ia anxiously, eagerly imagined re-uniting with her mother. She planned to recount every detail of every hardship she had withstood since being separated from her parents, pictured finally being able to lay the whole of her sadness in her mother's lap. When Ia arrived, though, her mother led with her own despair. It had been one year since Pha Kao's first wife had died, and misery gripped the household. While Ia's mother did what she could to save the children from the little wife's wrath, she herself was unprotected from the anger and neglect. She was ancient, blind. This woman who had once fought off a tiger with a machete now had to rely on a nephew's wife to bathe her. Her own son had shrunk away into the shadow of his new spouse's tyranny. All along, Ia had been sending money from the farm to take care of her mother, but it seemed Pha Kao and his wife had begun spending it on themselves while the old woman went hungry. Ia was shocked and furious that her brother would abandon their mother like this. The old woman now had just two sets of clothing; when one was worn, the other was washed. Both were rags.

Ia's mother begged Ia to bring her to the United States. There was nothing Ia wanted more. And yet immigration was an elaborate bureaucratic endeavor. *It's not like I can just sew you onto the collar of my shirt to take you with me,* Ia told her. *It's not that simple.* To bring her mother to the United States, they would need money, and someone to do the paperwork, and someone to act as a sponsor. Ia, with no legible income, no English skills, and no literacy in any language, could do none of it herself.

Instead, Ia did what she could. She bought an ox and hired a shaman to perform a soul calling for her mother; at the end, the shaman tied Ia's hands and her mother's with the same healing white string. Ia bought her mother three new outfits, then bathed the woman and dressed her in the best one, royal blue with a matching headscarf. *When I was a little girl, you were my mom,* Ia said gently. *But times have changed. Now that I'm grown, I'm the mom taking care of you.*

Inside, though, there were other feelings, harsher truths. A few years earlier, Ia *had* devised a plan to bring her mother to the United States: rallied some relatives to pitch in for a plane ticket, found a cousin with the necessary credentials—professional employment, fluency in English—to sponsor a visa. When given the chance, though, Ia's mother had chosen to stay with Pha Kao. His first wife had become like a daughter; her granddaughters, Chai and her sister, were her most beloved of all. As Ia understood it, her mother weighed the options and decided that her happiest life lay with her son. Chose him over Ia just as her father had chosen staying in Laos over following Ia to Thailand.

Ia knew her mother had always loved Pha Kao more. Perhaps it was because he was her baby, or because he had been sickly as a child. Or simply because he was a boy and Ia was a girl. A boy would care for his mother in old age and then carry her to her grave and feed her in the afterlife, whereas a girl would be gone from the household before she was fully grown. The bias toward boys was not uncommon—really, it was most every girl's inheritance—but still the acid memories ate away at Ia's heart. All those times when she had been left at home while her mother took Tong to farm with the rest of the family. All those other times her mother had sent Ia to the farm alone while she kept Tong beside her at home.

But now times had changed. Ia was older. She had eaten more rice, as the saying went, had seen more things and done a lot of thinking. She felt she had earned the right to speak up. *When I was a little girl, you didn't love me the way I loved you.* Ia said this to her mother. It was while she watched her mother combing through young Chai's shiny black hair, using what was left of her eyesight to pick out the nits so the girl would be free of lice. Ia remembered when she herself was young, how her mother had turned away from her own buggy hair in disgust. *When I was a little girl,* she said, *you only loved me enough so that I didn't die.*

At this her mother protested. Ia maintained that what she said was true, but she did not push back hard. The woman was still her mother, after all, and the rules of respect and deference still applied. Furthermore, this woman's anguish overrode everything. In days, Ia would return to her well-fed life in Fresno, while her mother could only stay here in her son's derelict custody, trying to subsist on meals of rice and gingerroot. There was no room for any more of Ia's sorrow. So she posed her mother in the best of the new outfits and pulled out the digital camera she had borrowed from her teenage daughter. Pushed enough buttons on the unfamiliar machine to freeze the woman in space. This way, at least, Ia could hold her forever. Once the photo had been made, instead of crumpling into her mother's arms and finding the comfort she had craved for so long, Ia resumed the work of soothing the weeping woman before her.

Today her mother is six years dead and Ia is standing beside her grave inside this tower of bamboo. In all the world, this is the only place where it is okay for Ia to address her directly. There is so much to say. Ia breaks off a section of toilet paper from the roll in her hands and wipes up her tears. Then she calls out to her mother in a joyless song. The tune is the traditional language of mourning, but the words rise out of Ia's unique heart. "I wish that this weren't real," she sings. "But this is not a dream. You are gone."

Beside her, Pha Kao commences offering the food. Having lost his father when he was young, he was never taught how to do such invocations, so he improvises. "Come and eat the food we brought for you, Mom, and when you eat, remember to protect us." His voice is calm almost to the point of vacancy, as if reading phrases someone else wrote.

The rest of the family stands across the grave, like an audience, listening as Ia moans wandering notes that wind over and under her brother's flat row of words. She draws out the end of each line in a long cord, as if grasping the words with her fingers and pulling them out as far as her arm can reach, until the words quiver. A dozen of Pha Kao's words fit into the space of one of hers.

From the smoldering fire, ashes float heavenward. Pha Kao steps away from the head of the grave, toward the rest of the group. Normally, this is when they would leave. Instead, they stand in place, shifting their weight from foot to foot. Smoke, trapped by the bamboo walls, clogs the air. A strand of saliva hangs from Ia's wailing mouth.

One after another, family members try to coax her away. Ia only retracts into her grief and begins singing a new story, the story of how, long before her mother died, she was orphaned for the first time: not by death but by choice, orphaned by her mother and father's choice not to go to Thailand with her, by their desire to stay in Laos. Normally, she tells the other version of this story, in which it is all a tragic mistake, but here she sings this dark truth out loud. Then she finally tells her mother how for fifteen years she waited for them in Thailand, searching for them, calling out to heaven and earth, telling herself if she could just stay alive they would be reunited.

No more pauses now. Ia rushes through the sobs to get to the next line of this mournful ballad, as if she must purge the words on her tongue to make room for the next ones rising up from inside. She sings of when she and her mother were reunited, finally, how she dreamed of being able to describe her suffering then, how at last she would sing her orphan song—and how she choked it all back, swallowing her tears so that her mother would not have to shed more of her own.

Ia's eyes are gone, sunken into her swollen face. Her song breaks apart as if dropped into water, the drowning words climbing out only two at a time. She sings about her life now, about this orphan girl farming rice, all alone, no one to help her as the sun beats down on her back, the heat so relentless she no longer feels it. About how the rice only makes her miss her parents more. How she fears she will forget their faces, that when at last they are reunited, they may not recognize her.

"Oh my mother, how much longer must I be an orphan?" Ia calls. "I must be an orphan until the day I'm able to join you."

At this, the family rustles. They have been waiting, variously patient and bored. Now even those who were chitchatting to pass the time click to attention at this mention of joining the parents in death. This is the opening that malevolent spirits look for, when anguish lays a soul out naked, ready for the taking. Even the well-meaning spirit of her mother might relieve Ia's distress by pulling her orphan daughter across into the afterworld. Just moments ago, the family was immune to Ia's grief, but even they see she must now be restrained from the brink, retained by the world of the living.

"Let's go, Mom," Mee says across the grave. Then, to Ia's nephew: "She's crying too much. Take her."

"You can stop crying," Pha Kao says flatly. "No matter how much you cry, they're not coming back."

The nephew grips Ia's shoulders and begins guiding her out. His grasp snaps Ia back to this place, this moment, and her role as caretaker of the group. Her voice shifts into speaking quick, tactical words to keep the spirit world at bay. "Mother, go back home now," she says. "I'm going to leave, but you stay. You and Father watch over us, be the barricade to protect us on earth."

The group masses at the exit, waiting for each one's turn to step back through the parted barbed wire fence. Ia is being directed forward but she calls back over her shoulder urgently, as if just realizing she forgot the most important part. "Make sure you watch over the son, so he is safe and he will have food to eat, so the son will be prosperous." She is being pushed through the fence. "There's only one of your sons left," Ia calls as she squeezes through to the other side. "Remember that you have only one son left."

————

The visit lasts another day and a half, centered largely on one meal after another. Gradually, the conversations slow down, the pauses idle longer, the meals end sooner. Without daily lives in common, this extended family reunion holds the awkwardness of any other. Ia's group decides that for vague and polite reasons they will leave a day earlier than planned, which injects the final morning with a last pulse of closeness. After breakfast, Ia is led to a nephew's house. There sits his teenage daughter, who has shamed her family with promiscuity and subsequently lost all her hair to an undiagnosed ill-ness. As the girl's parents look on, Ia performs a simple shaman ritual they hope will fix her.

When Ia is ushered to a different household for another last-minute ritual request, her family heads to Pha Kao's house to wait. Thao leans against the tractor and little girls circle him as if he is playing Santa Claus. He challenges them to thumb wars. They take turns punching his round belly, trying to make him flinch. He hands out a bag of Orange Crush drink mix packets he has saved for this moment, telling the girls that if they eat them they'll get fat like him, patting his gut, to which they respond by tearing open the packets, tipping back their heads, and pouring the day-glo powder straight onto their tongues.

Above them, in the tractor seat, sits Chai, playing gently with a different cluster of admiring nieces. She will not return until they are all much older, though neither she nor they know that now. In this moment, she is simply their beloved aunt, the only one aside from their own mothers whom they allow to comb their hair, to pick out their nits, to fashion their locks into intricate braids. After she gifts them the stubby end of her lipstick, they take turns painting their mouths a precocious red.

Pha Kao is in the house, also waiting. The final ritual Ia will per-form will be to protect him. He is a man plagued by bad luck: the one sued by greedy neighbors, the one who falls out of a tree while hunting squirrels. When a group of angry elephants charged at his family, it was Pha Kao—and he alone—who was almost killed. Years ago, a soothsayer foresaw that he would die in a tragic accident. Since then, to protect himself, he has ceased going to the wildlands outside the village, no longer hunting or fishing with his sons. These days, he will go to the farm, but otherwise he stays close to home.

He had a good spell, beginning back in Thatom Thongvia, when he married his wife, and together they made a house full of chil-dren. As a family they amassed money, eventually enough for him to marry a second wife. But the luck of those years belonged to his first wife, at least as Ia sees it, and when she died, her luck went with her. No more children were born to Pha Kao. What money he had stashed away was used to pay for his oldest son's wife. He became poor once again. His mother died, then his oldest brother. Today the protective web of family around him consists of a brother in Wisconsin who has no money to spare; Pha Kao's own sons and their families, who occupy their own thatch dwellings; and Ia. Her explanation is that Pha Kao's persistent poverty is written in the divine papers handed down to him at birth, just as it is written in her own life's papers that she will be lucky and rich. An immutable fate for each of them.

Pha Kao's latest piece of bad fortune was a dream in which he saw himself draped in red, the color of death. Today's ritual is meant to protect him from this, at least, by dispelling the bad omen the dream brought. While he and the others wait for Ia to arrive, Chou Lor stands at the front of the tractor, making preparations. He has folded an enormous piece of paper many times, precisely, and is cutting it into an intricate design.

Meanwhile, Pha Kao does what he can to fix himself up for the occasion. Even at New Year's he will wear grubby old clothes, but now he changes into a clean shirt, combs his hair. He enlists Thao to dig the electric razor out of his suitcase and shave the prickly hairs from around his crooked smile. When Ia arrives at last, Pha Kao moves into the dark room of his house and lowers himself onto a stool not far off the ground.

With Ia standing behind him, Pha Kao seems small, crouched. Or perhaps Ia just seems big: her belly round, her shoulders relaxed, leaning back on her heels as she lets a loud, sharp trill vibrate off her tongue long enough to get the spirits' attention. This is the same spot where the men ate dinner two nights before, where now a small crowd of adults and little girls has gathered to watch her perform.

Behind them all, taped to an armoire, is a copy of the photograph of their mother that Ia made during that lone visit years ago, which she gave to Pha Kao as a gift. The original was too dark, but this copy—enlarged and retouched—is saturated with white light, as if the subject were a divine apparition captured on film. As the old woman seems to look on, Ia begins to sing.

The song of a shaman is distinct. The notes ping-pong around the scale almost at random, producing a tune that is dissonant yet hypnotic. The phrases sung are composed of Hmong words but arranged in an arcane dialect that is unintelligible to the layperson. As Ia sings them, her voice is strong and sure as a tree growing straight toward the sun, without competition. Her words continue unbroken as Chou Lor approaches with the paper he has cut and the two of them gingerly pull the folds apart into a large, continuous ring. Unfurled, it reveals a design of standing figures linked by their hands. Soldiers. Ia lowers the paper over Pha Kao's head so that it hangs from his stooped shoulders and around his bent knees like a shawl, his torso enclosed by this fragile army.

Ia steps back and chants her commands: That these soldiers take away the funeral garments Pha Kao wears and replace them with armor. That they become a barrier to defend her brother from any misfortune that may come. That they serve as an umbrella to shield him from the heat. When Pha Kao must walk on fire, they must protect his feet. Without warning, Ia trills again, sharper this time, then slides the blade of the scissors up her brother's back and cuts the paper with a single snip. The soldiers collapse onto the dirt floor, and the omen is lifted.

Pha Kao, unsure of what comes next, looks over his shoulder at Ia. She picks up the paper by one end, walks it outside into the sunlight, and with a match sets the dangling snarl of paper on fire. When the flames lick up toward her fingers, she drops it on the hard ground. On either side of her is a little girl, and together the three of them silently watch the blaze eat through the paper until only an ashen skeleton remains.

And that is it. Without fanfare or delay, Ia and her family walk to their hired van. The same mass of people who swarmed the vehicle upon arrival swarm again now, again crying intently. From one household after another Ia receives the same gift: a freshly killed chicken and a bag of cooked rice. Even as the food piles up on top of the luggage, on the seat beside her, then at her feet, she receives each new bundle gracefully, with a loving smile of appreciation.

Pha Kao hands Ia the only thing of value that he has to offer: a sack of rice seed from his stores. It's another grandmother rice, given by his son's wife's mother. They call it "naked rice" or "red butt," for the dark spot at the tip of the hull. He and the rest of the family grow a little bit of purple sticky rice to eat at New Year's, but otherwise their entire crop is composed of the naked rice alone. The grain inside is unremarkable, just plain white. But according to Pha Kao, when cooked it makes twice the volume of other rices—leaves you feeling fuller, too. Plus, naked rice yields more than other varieties.

In Fresno this seed will bear nothing but a bouquet of bushy leaves, never flowering for mysterious reasons written in its genes. But Ia doesn't know this yet. She holds the bag with both hands, admiring its weight. Of all the gifts she has been given, this is the one she will hold close to her all the way down the long, broken road to the lowlands, across the Pacific Ocean, and back home to her farm.

April is never easy. When Ia arrives to begin planting, all the life that the farm held the previous fall has been scraped away. The bare soil that's left has been reshaped into a pattern of lifeless straight lines, whose perfectly flat tops dry out into a crust the color of sand. Here in Fresno, spring is less a time of promise and rejuvenation than of emptiness that must be filled—an annual reminder that if a person wants anything in this life, she must build it from the bare ground up.

Last year, with the widow Mai Der growing rice in the field next door, planting had at least brought a small crowd of friends and workers to the farm. On some days they had shared the work—you help plant mine, I'll help plant yours. This year, though, Mai Der has gone to the Green Mountain for the whole season. And Youa, the neighbor, is taking another year off. She did come out to lend a hand on the first day of planting, but she was so out of shape from not farming for a year that the work crippled her. The next day she couldn't get out of bed, much less return to the field.

There was a younger woman, who helped plant for a day in exchange for seed to sow her own crop on a farm nearby. Otherwise, the workforce is the same as for the final dreary days of last year's harvest: Ia and Jimmy get dropped off early, and Chou Lor joins at around nine, after he finishes the overnight shift at Foster Farms. But on Friday, the fourth day of planting, Ia pulls Alice from high school in order to just finish the job. For Alice, it's a net-zero equation, since she gets to skip a day of boring freshman-year classes, but only to labor here instead. This is, in a way, her life: doted on by her mother because she is the baby of the family, and at the same time expected to spend her free time serving her parents and brothers—cooking, cleaning, whatever else needs doing. In rare moments she gets fed up with being ordered around and shouts out a complaint in high-volume English. Mostly, though, Alice labors silently, earbuds in, appearing to refill Ia's water glass the minute it goes empty.

Jimmy's job is to punch the holes in the ground, using a special dibble stick that Chou Lor has fashioned out of steel pipe so it will withstand his son's power. The women follow behind, each carrying a foot-long tube of bamboo with half a pair of barbecue tongs inserted in the end—another Chou Lor original design. They drop seed in the holes and then smack the ground with the tong so that dirt collapses over the hole to cover it. Two hundred holes up one side of a row, two hundred holes back to the beginning. One hundred seventy-five rows. Seventy thousand holes in all.

Working their way down the field, Ia stays hinged at the hips, her back flat as a table, standing up only at the end of the row. Alice, who is at least six inches taller than her mother, stretches a leg out behind her to get lower to the earth. All day there is an iron pain in their backs, their hips, their calves. For days after the last seed is planted, the work will wear on as a memory in aching muscles and raw joints.

At ten thirty, Chou Lor arrives at the farm and walks to the field with a dibble stick in his hand. On top of his clothes he wears an oversize blue dress shirt. Across the fabric, lines of sweat from previous days make a picture like a mountain range. Ia interrupts her planting to stand up and yell at him.

She is still angry from this winter, when her body collapsed and her mind went dark and, in her telling, her family was deaf to her cries for help. The trouble began shortly after she returned from Laos, when a doctor at Fresno PACE diagnosed her with gout. As she understood it, the disease was incurable—when eventually the pain kept her from walking more often than not, she would be given an electric wheelchair, which she viewed as a certain kind of death.

At the same time came dreams that were powerful, crystalline, and, to Ia, obvious in their interpretation. In the most ominous one, Ia had returned to Sa Na Oua, where she had constructed a house, a building so fine that an old man, familiar to her in the dream, applauded her work. Even to someone who did not know Ia, the meaning was easily deciphered: to build one's house in Laos is a common metaphor for the soul's return to the place of birth, where it collects the placenta as the clothing it will wear for the journey to the land of the ancestors. The dream was communicating that in actuality, her soul had already gone home to Laos, meaning it was well on its way down the path to the land of the ancestors. As if to underscore the point, in the dream Ia wore the garments in which the dead are clothed for a funeral. She was certain the dream foretold her imminent death.

When she told the people in her real house in Fresno, they seemed not to care. In desperation, Ia kneeled at her altar and explained to her spirit guides that it wasn't time for her to go yet, that she had children to take care of still, that she had a husband who was still alive. She pleaded for the spirit guides to bring her soul back so she could continue this life. In return, she promised to repay them with an offering.

When she asked Chou Lor to perform that offering for her—a simple thing, just two chickens—he didn't say yes or no, just ignored her. Even after she went out and bought the chickens herself, he did nothing. Ia cried and cried, telling him how much it hurt. And when still Chou Lor made no move to help her, she raged. Grievances from decades before were hurled across the room. He had never loved her the way a husband should love a wife, never loved her the way she needed him to. *If I have to take these damn chickens and do my own offering,* she yelled, *I'm going to divorce you.*

When none of that moved him, Ia's hurt simply calcified, growing around her like armor. Alone like this, it seemed the world was out to get her. In March, the clouds gushed out twice as much rain as normal—two-thirds of the year's entire precipitation—casting a pall over Fresno and leaving Ia's fields a soupy mess. At the same time, she found out that her normal source for herbicides would not deliver this year, and she scrambled to find a replacement. Next, Pha Kao called saying he needed $2,000 to finish building the concrete structure to replace his thatch house. To top it all off, thieves looted the shed at the farm, stealing the rice roasting pans, several cooking pots, even the metal dishwashing basin, presumably to sell as scrap metal. When Ia bemoaned her cumulative misfortune, somehow it always came back to Chou Lor and his cold heart.

So when he arrives this morning at ten thirty instead of nine, Ia reacts from the raw wound of the winter. "Where the hell have you been?" she yells.

"You're lucky I came at all," he grumbles. "My stomach is hurting."

"Your stomach is always hurting," she snarls back.

"Let's just do this and get it done," he says.

He takes his place a row over from Jimmy and commences punching holes in the soil. Ia shouts that his dibble stick is too small, the holes it makes aren't big enough. Chou Lor keeps punching. Ia yells at him to stop making holes and instead come fix the rows whose sickly dirt has collapsed into the furrows. He drops the dibble stick and walks to the crumbled rows, which he addresses with the spatula tool she hands to him. When Alice escapes to the shed to cook lunch, Chou Lor silently takes her place filling holes with seed. Moments later, Ia says her back hurts and instructs Chou Lor to finish the last two rows on his own. She lumbers to the shed.

Crouched over one of the blackened pots that the thieves did not take, Alice deep-fries more chicken wings than they could possibly eat. Ia unpacks sticky rice and a Tupperware full of whole sugar peas that she has boiled and chilled. They don't talk much. Instead, Alice is thinking about a boyfriend she had for a short while, until her parents found out and told her to break it off. She is thinking about how she has been hanging out with the boy again, how she might sign up for summer volleyball because he plays, too. She is thinking about prom, which she won't go to this year—she is only a freshman, and besides, between tickets and a dress, it would cost hundreds of dollars she doesn't have. But she is still thinking about it.

When at last Alice has finished cooking, Ia sits in her customary spot at the center of the lunch table. Eventually, Chou Lor comes in from the field and takes his seat beside her. The kids fill their plates with a brick of sticky rice each and a few chicken wings. The parents fill their bowls with the soggy peas and their sweetish green liquid, eat it like soup. No one has much to say.

Yesterday the wind made the day so bitterly cold that they couldn't eat lunch at the table, had to move onto stools in the sun to stay warm. Today is nicer, hinting at summer. Ia, seeming eager for a good mood, turns on a monologue of stories and jokes to fill the space between them. When a story finally lands and everyone laughs at the punch line, she continues laughing even after they stop, letting it ripple through her. Then with each new story she tells she is more animated, food flying from her hands, her mouth. Soon she has unknowingly sprinkled herself with rice, which has landed on the shelf of her breasts, in her lap, on her round cheek.

Chou Lor keeps his head facing straight, turns only his eyes to look at Ia beside him. His lips stay pursed but the corners of his mouth turn up, smiling, the humor brimming inside. In a quiet voice that is somehow both mischievous and shy, he tries out his own joke: points at the food on her cheek and softly teases that she's saving it for later. Ia's eyes light up, first with surprise, then embarrassment, then delight.

"Right!" she says. A smile pulls back her lips, showing her little white teeth all in a row. "When I get hungry, I'll just take it off like this." She brushes a hand across her face. It only presses the rice to her skin.

Chou Lor turns toward her now, reaches his hand up to her face. His eyes are on her cheek but her eyes are on his eyes, for one second and then for another, as if she is caught in a feeling that she cannot name. As he delicately pinches the grain of rice from her face, it seems there is an invisible thread connecting his hand to her heart. He flicks the rice on the ground. The conversation carries on. But those two seconds hang in the air.

When lunch is over, all four return to the field without delay—the sooner these rows are planted, the sooner they can leave. Jimmy is ahead by himself, jabbing holes in the soil. Chou Lor is in the woman's role, sliding seeds off his fingertips in a single, fluid movement, broken only when he stops to roll his fists into the muscles of his lower back. Alice follows him, repeatedly falling behind to shoot out a round of texts on her phone and then slapping the holes quickly to catch up. Ia does her own row, planting with one hand and wielding the spatula in the other.

Everyone is exhausted, everyone's back hurts, and yet rather than become friction, the shared pain becomes another thread, this one holding the four of them together as they move up and down the rows. There is no bossing, no crabbing, no complaining except about the shared misery. The sun is sharp now, but for the remainder of the day they are cushioned by an invisible softness.

———

Pha Kao calls Ia and he is angry. More than two years have passed since Thao married Chai, and still the girl is languishing in Laos without the visa necessary to immigrate to the United States. Pha

Kao threatens that if his daughter has not been brought to Fresno by August, he will take her back. Moreover, for having broken the terms of the marriage, Ia will owe him $3,000.

Ia grumbles that Pha Kao assumes American officials can be bribed to deliver a visa just like those in Laos can, when in fact the process of applying for immigration to the United States is controlled by an impenetrable bureaucracy. The labyrinth of paperwork at times feels like a riddle at whose solution one can only guess. When Thao began the process, it was suggested that he hire a lawyer to facilitate things. Because that would have cost several thousand dollars, he resolved to do it himself, despite having little experience with government systems and procedures. Little did he know the process was about to get even more difficult. One year after the wedding, Donald Trump was inaugurated as president of the United States. Within days, the new administration's policies had begun constraining immigration across the board.

In the meantime, Chai has lived in limbo. It was understood that she would move into her husband's home—this is true for every bride. But she assumed she would leave her father's house only once her visa was granted. Instead, the day after the wedding, Thao instructed her to pack her things. She would live with Chou Lor's sister, who lived with her son and his family in a different village. It seemed nonsensical, given that they were not even part of the Khang clan, but because they were the closest relatives on Thao's father's side, they would have to do. To Thao, the move seemed logical.

Chai, however, was shocked and scared. When she appealed to Pha Kao, he threw up his hands. Thao's family had paid her brideprice. Spiritually, she had been transferred to their clan, which meant that as her biological father, he no longer had any say. His only advice was that Chai be obedient and do as she was told.

The village where Chou Lor's sister lived was four hours away, in the lowlands. It was just an hour from Vientiane, but in reality, it was far off the highway, down a rutted dirt road lined with trees embalmed in dried red clay. The village was announced by a row of stalls crowding the roadside, where brusque vendors sold SIM cards and dentures and fashions from China. Behind these shops, narrow lanes led into a thicket of houses separated from one another only by hot, still air. The view from each abode was simply the backside of another: walls of concrete blocks, fences made of corrugated metal, everything covered in clay. The house in which Chai would live lay where her particular lane hit a dead end.

Thao stayed with Chai in the new village for a week, then flew back to Fresno. *Why did I marry him?* she thought as she watched him disappear into the airport terminal. *He left me alone, to live with these strangers.* She reasoned that it was all part of the process, that Thao would do the paperwork and soon she, too, would fly to the United States. She told herself to be patient. She called Ia, who assured her it would be okay. That night, when she lay down within her partition of the strange family's thatch hut and cried herself to sleep, she made sure to do so silently; it would only make things more difficult if they heard her weep.

Because the family's children were all young, Chai understood that she was to become the de facto daughter-in-law. The next morning, she rose before daybreak and took her place preparing breakfast. After that, though, there was little to do. The family didn't farm or keep animals. The other married girls her age were sequestered in their own homes, out of sight. For company there was only the fifty-year-old woman next door. In the months to come, she and Chai would spend entire days doing the same piecework embroidery that Ia had done in Thailand. They sold the finished items for a price that worked out to a measly 50 cents an hour. And yet: what else was there to do?

Chai kept telling herself that this life in suspension was a necessary trade-off for the ultimate reward of moving to the United States. Already there were material benefits. Every month Thao sent her an allowance, part of which underwrote her share of the household's groceries; with this funding, they ate meat at every meal. When the family built a concrete house, Ia paid to include a private bedroom for Chai. And for the first time in her life, Chai did not have to farm. That was worth something.

Recently, though, at around the same time Ia was wrestling with the dark winter of Fresno, the walls began to close in for Chai. Her menstrual cycle had become increasingly irregular; when she did get her period, the pain was now intense. It began to nag at her that while she and Thao had tried for a baby several times, it had not yet worked. She began to worry that her body was faulty.

Ia paid for a spiritual investigation. The shaman determined that earlier, back in the home village, Chai had passed over a river while menstruating. A male spirit in the water had smelled her blood and entered her; to this day it remained inside. The shaman bribed the spirit to leave, but admonished Chai that he might return. To protect herself, Chai must not return to her home village until after giving birth to at least two children—otherwise, she might never be able to conceive.

Deeply afraid of imperiling her fertility, Chai accepted the diagnosis. But with it, she was forced to accept the further isolation it brought. The new village was a long trip from home, and she already knew from living there for more than two years that her family members would not come to visit with any regularity. Now that Chai was prohibited from going to them, her world shrank down to her eight-by-twelve-foot bedroom.

To have such a private space would have been a rare luxury in her home village. In practice, though, the room was a spirit-less place. The walls were bare except for a few photographs from when Thao and his family visited the previous year. Two pictured Chai with her sisters-in-law Song and Mee, all dressed in matching Hmong outfits, posing at a New Year's photo booth. The other two photos showed Thao in Thailand, where Chai had never been. In one, Thao stood with the beautiful hostess of the White Orchid

cruise boat, their portrait superimposed over a montage of Bangkok skylines at night. Even next to this woman who looked like a
princess, Thao was not smiling—never does for photos. Instead, he
made a face as if he were sighing for the camera, the corners of his
mouth turned down rather than up. His gray T-shirt was printed
with bold, capital letters that read, I'M NOT ARGUING, I'M JUST EX-
PLAINING WHY I'M RIGHT. Below the photographs was a single mattress on the ground, topped with a Winnie the Pooh pillow and a
red teddy bear whose fuzz had been loved flat. The rest of the floor
was a messy series of shopping bags and suitcases, filled with clothes
and other belongings, as if Chai were ready to leave at a moment's
notice.

Last summer, Thao said it would be just a few more months,
then in the fall that was revised to six more. Now those six months
have passed, and here Chai remains. She tests the waters of the shaman's diagnosis, asking if she can go home to her village for a short,
careful visit. Thao refers the question to Ia, who holds the shaman's
diagnosis with utmost seriousness. The answer is no.

Chai's frustration boils over. On the phone with Thao she is
angry: that she cannot see her family, that he has not brought her to
the United States, that she is growing old, wasting her life, stranded
in this lonely, hot village of strangers.

This is when Pha Kao calls Ia and threatens that if Chai is not
in Fresno by August, he will take his daughter back and make Ia
pay him for the damages. In all this, Ia sees a certain irony. People
marry their children to relatives because it is supposed to make it
easier to work through conflicts that arise from the union. In reality,
marrying Thao within the family has made it so Ia can't escape the
conflict.

Of course, on paper, Thao is the one who should take care of his
wife. But as the unofficial head of household and the bride's father's
sister, Ia is equally accountable for her daughter-in-law. She does not
mind the emotional responsibility. When things get heated between

Chai and Thao, the phone gets passed to Ia and she smooths things out. Indeed, the two women have grown close; when Ia was hurting so badly last winter, Chai was the first person to comfort her.

What wears on Ia is being financially responsible for another person, one who cannot earn more than the pittance she receives for embroidery piecework. Thao can afford to send Chai an allowance for food and minutes on her phone. However, his earnings from Hot Wok Express don't cover the big items, like the thousands of dollars to build Chai's bedroom, and the hundreds for each new set of documents related to the visa. Ia pays for those with money earned at the farm.

Ia does see an end point, in that once Chai arrives in the United States and completes enough basic schooling to get a job, she will be able to pay for herself. What's more, she will take over sending money to Pha Kao and the rest of the family in Laos. Until then, though, the new daughter is not profit but rather loss, just one more expense that can be paid for only by planting and growing and selling this rice.

———

It has been one week since the sunny afternoon when Ia and her family finished planting the rice. Already, Ia can tell something is not right. Sure, it is too soon to expect that every seed would have come up, but it is also too late for not a one to have sprouted and begun to grow. Morning after morning, as soon as Ia arrives at the farm, she goes straight to the field and finds it still barren, as if winter had never passed. While some of the rice does manage to send out a shoot, each one's little pulse of life is short-lived: the green quickly turns white, then gray. Their tragic bodies accumulate on the surface of the soil and mummify in the thickening sun.

The cause is not spiritual: it is human error—Ia doesn't need to visit her altar to determine that. When her regular source for herbicide fell through, an aunt in Florida filled the gap. But because the chemicals were sent in the mail, they were not the liquid to which Ia was accustomed; they were powdered. The aunt included instructions for how much to use, which Mee read to Ia and Chou Lor. There at the lunch table, the two of them portioned it out using the green plastic measuring cup left over from a bottle of another herbicide. For the first round they mixed it as told, filling the powder up to the second line. There in the cup, though, it seemed so little—too little. The next time they mixed the powder, Chou Lor instead filled the measuring cup to the fourth line, doubling the amount. Seeing this, Ia figured that as long as they were upping the dosage, they might as well go stronger. The next time, she filled it to the sixth line. For good measure, she returned to the areas that had received the proper amount and doused them again. They then waited the prescribed thirty days between spraying and planting, but of course that was not enough. Every seed they put in the ground would be poisoned.

Perhaps still lighthearted from springtime, Ia and Chou Lor make a joke of their shared stupidity. The punch line, of course, is Ia's redoubling their arrogance to put three times as much herbicide as was prescribed. When she tells the story, she shakes with laughter, her eyes filling with tears. Chou Lor, beside her, is tickled by it, too. Anyway, there is still more than a month to replant. As long as they get the crop in the ground before June, it will have enough time to mature before winter returns. They just have to go back and plant all four acres again.

This time, though, there is no one to help. Chou Lor must move on to laying out irrigation pipe and all the other necessary tasks of May. Everybody else who could be called on already gave what time they had the first go-around. It is left to Ia to make her way down each row alone, first with the dibble stick, then retracing her steps to fill in the holes, seed in her right hand and spatula in her left. After two grueling weeks, the farm has been replanted.

And again the seed fails. Here and there are sprouts that manage to stay green and grow, but overall the field remains gray-brown. This time Ia thinks the problem is the seed itself. Back in April, when that younger farmer helped plant in exchange for seed, Ia gave the woman a lavish amount—most of her extra, in fact, thinking she herself would not need it. When the farm's first planting failed to germinate, Ia scrambled to find more. An aunt who farms in Clovis gave her a sack of sticky rice seed that she promised was as good as the grandmother rice. Youa offered some of what she has been saving for when she returns from the Green Mountain. Both batches of seed smelled funky, but Ia didn't have the luxury of being choosy. Now she realizes it all must have been rotten.

With her field still mostly bare in the second week of May, whatever ease Ia accumulated since winter slips away. The gout flares up in her ankle. Her stomach illness rages back. Because of this she can't eat much, then has little energy. Laid over the stress of the seeds' failure is the larger specter of being too ill to farm the rest of the season.

Throughout it all, her phone rings. During the day, it is sick people requesting her services as a shaman. In the evening, it is relatives in Laos, among them Pha Kao asking for money to complete the walls of his new house. At night, in her dreams, even the dead come asking for help. One weekend when Ia leaves town to perform a shaman ceremony, in her absence thieves steal a pitiful booty from the farm: a rake, tarps, and the industrial-size garbage bag of recyclables. Grasping for compassion, she tries to reason that they probably need it more than she does.

For the third try at planting, Ia must sheepishly ask the younger farmer to whom she gave seed if there is any left over that Ia can have back. More uncomfortable begging also yields some drier seed from Youa. To fill out the supply, Ia digs deep into the stack of storage buckets in her garage and resurrects a type of rice that she didn't like but couldn't bear to throw away. They all go in the ground.

The seeds prove to be good, but in numerous spots they are eaten by birds or ground squirrels before they can come up. Elsewhere, perhaps where the herbicide was sprayed most heavily, the chemical's toxic effect seems to linger and the young plants die. With this new round of failure, Ia begins to grumble about how Chou Lor walks too slowly when he sprays herbicide, saturating the ground because he lingers too long. In her worst moments she spits out that this spring's disaster is his fault. So much is his fault.

By the last week of May, Ia stops checking to see if the last round of seeds will come up before planting more. The once-spacious deadline of having the entire crop planted by June 1 now feels imminent, and foreboding. Her mind churns with all the things that depend on this rice—and the people who would go hungry without it. She needs the crop to be able to pay for her own life, for starters. She needs it to be able to answer the needs of her relatives in Laos. And there are also her own children to care for. Save for Alice, those kids are now adults, and yet rather than releasing Ia from obligation, their adulthood seems only to have made their needs more expensive. Money for a little bit of meat every day in the refugee camp or for soda on the way home from school in Fresno has turned into thousands of dollars to pay the bride-price for Thao's wife or for the down payment on a car for Jimmy. Five sons, two daughters, and one daughter-in-law still live in the house. All but Alice are responsible for a share of the mortgage, and yet when they come up short, it is Mom who foots the bill. Or, rather, it is rice that foots the bill. Rice that foots every bill. For this reason, there is no room for it to fail.

The morning of May 29, Ia is running on a giant tumbler of milky coffee. She is redolent with the sharp, unfading smell of Tiger Balm. Six weeks now she has been planting, and her body is decrepit, her steps labored, her eyes vacant. The rows have gone from clean and mounded to now jagged and crumbling, pocked with four rounds of dibbling through the dried-out crust. As Ia makes her way down the row, she navigates a graveyard of old holes filled with skeletal seeds, even cobwebs. For the variety being planted today she has only a few cups left, and so resorts to a tactic she remembers her parents employing when she was young. Last night, acting as a sort of midwife, she wetted the seeds and wrapped them in a paper towel. This morning, they have swollen with moisture and shot out thin white tails, ensuring germination, at least. Into each fresh hole she pinches five or six of the sprouted seeds, no more, and packs the soil down on top of them.

This afternoon Ia will turn on the irrigation and let the water soak into the rows, all the way up to these embryonic plants. If all goes well, they will swell further, push up through the soil, turn into sprouts that become shoots that become plants and eventually a crop. And yet in a few hours, today will become the first triple-digit day of the year. As Ia plods her way back down the rows to plant, she carries an umbrella to shield her body from the sun. On this day, in this surging heat, it seems like a miracle that those tiny, fragile sprouts would survive.

There is no room to take chances. After Ia fills the holes, she goes to the lunch table and fits a black surgical mask loosely over her mouth. In a cut-off milk jug she puts several handfuls of brown seeds and a splash of insecticide powder. Pours in a half-drunk bottle of water and with a planting tong stirs it all into what looks like gravelly granola. There is nothing she can do about the heat, but she can do this: carry the jug to the field she just seeded and, every three feet or so, spoon a small mound of the toxic mixture on top of the soil. In places, there are similar mounds she laid in previous days. The idea is that the ground squirrels who lurk in the field and the birds who swarm above will eat these seeds instead of those she has planted. So far, it has worked. When Ia arrived yesterday morning, the sticky rice field was littered with dead pigeons. Seeing that some of them had leg bands—that they meant something to somebody—she discreetly tossed their limp bodies into a bucket. At day's end, she brought them home and buried them in her backyard without ceremony.

The summer that follows is objectively terrible. July is the hottest month ever recorded in Fresno. Not only is the record for consecutive days of triple-digit temperatures broken, but it is increased by eight days: twenty-nine in a row. When at last the streak breaks on August 5, it is probably only because smoke from another wildfire near Yosemite is so thick it blocks the sun's penetration. Alongside the county health department's customary heat advisory comes a cautionary health statement from the regional air district, both telling people to stay inside.

As in every preceding year, Ia and Chou Lor neither hear the warnings nor abide by them. The debacle of planting time turned out to have an ironic twist: overspraying the herbicides so delayed the rice's emergence that it allowed the weeds to get way ahead. As the triple-digit days were adding up, the fields were crowded with weeds; hidden within them, the rice was short and thin. Now, in early September, some stretches are the height they would normally be in midsummer, many of them still dwarfed by the weeds. In previous years, harvest would be starting any day, and yet this year much of the crop has not even begun flowering.

As Ia grimaces over the state of the rice, Pha Kao calls to say he has been bitten by a dog and needs her to wire cash to pay for three shots to prevent rabies. At the same time, Thao cannot afford his share of the mortgage for September, so Ia must pick it up. The good news is that Chai has been given an appointment for an interview at the embassy, after which she should receive her visa and finally come to the United States. The bad news is that Thao also cannot cover the cost of three immunization shots that Chai must get before the appointment, nor the fees for her blood work and a physical. Plus, the interview itself comes with a fee of $200. For all this, Ia digs deeper into the money bag sitting thin on her waist.

In any other year, Ia would be a wreck: saturated in stress, with every ailment resurfacing in concert. But this year is different. Surveying the anemic stand of rice, she is buoyant. As she scrambles for cash to pay the latest electricity bill, she is calm. Against all odds, her heart seems light. Just as the rice appears to have navigated successfully through this year of distress, so has Ia found a path to a kind of emotional survival. Peace, perhaps.

Oddly enough, it began with Fresno PACE, the painfully inept Medicare services provider that administers her medical care and has, over time, given her sleeping pills that sent her to the emergency room, recommended surgery for what later proved to be gout, and insisted they needed to x-ray her brain for reasons unknown. Because of this history, Ia is wary of their treatments, mostly refuses any concrete action beyond the medication for her high blood pressure. Still, she is willing when it comes to the consultative part of their care. Because she so desires liberation from her physical pain, she always shows up for the doctor's appointments that involve describing her symptoms and listening, through a mediocre interpreter, to the clinician's diagnosis. If one of the remedies recommended is to have a consultation with another doctor, she will go. Which is how she ended up seeing a physical therapist and, later, a "social work counselor"—a *therapist* therapist.

Hmong don't have a tradition of talking about emotions in a formal way, much less treating them as mental health disorders. There is no exact Hmong translation for the clinical terms "depression" and "anxiety." To say "therapist" requires a term cobbled together in recent decades: *Ib tug neeg kawm txog neeg txog kev nyuaj siab,* "a person who learns about people's difficult liver." The shorthand translation for *nyuaj siab,* this "difficult liver," is "stress," but really there is no exact equivalent word. For Hmong, the liver is the seat of life experience. It's akin to how Westerners' hearts hold love and sadness, but the Hmong liver is like heart, brain, and guts rolled together, the locus of everything from character and intellect to physical sensation and emotional experience. Broadly, *nyuaj siab* is the experience of feeling the weight of your troubles, but for each person that means something different. To heal it, a person could bring her *nyuaj siab* to a shaman for spiritual remedy, or present the associated grievances to a clan leader for resolution. Until recently, though, talking through *nyuaj siab* or any other set of emotions with a stranger simply for the sake of better understanding those emotions was an unfamiliar remedy for Hmong. For a woman to do that with a strange man was unheard of.

Ia wasn't aware she was going to a *therapist* therapist until she was in the room with him. PACE had arranged the meeting soon after she joined their program two years ago, told her generically that it was a doctor's visit. When she arrived, she was told that the doctor would ask about her history and try to determine what was causing her *nyuaj siab*—except not in those words, because they were speaking English.

The therapist was an Indian American man. PACE had hired an interpreter, another man, who was off-site and so on the therapist's speakerphone. The sound was terrible: too quiet, then too loud, crackly all the way through. Ia couldn't understand half of what the interpreter said to her. She could tell the therapist had the same trouble because she kept hearing him shout into the speaker, *What? What? What?,* after which he would ask what sounded to her like the same questions, over and over. She left the meeting more *nyuaj siab* than before.

Eventually, PACE improved the sessions, now with an interpreter in the room and a new therapist: an older white woman. Still, the questions were ill fitting, two-dimensional, as if Ia were an exotic species of human who could only be understood through the lens of war.

Were your family members rebels?

Did your parents die in the war?

Do you have nightmares about the fighting?

In the beginning, Ia didn't trust the doctors, nor did she trust the process of telling them her private history. She had heard that if you talked too much, the doctor would prescribe *tshuaj vwm*, "crazy medications," to quiet you. Further, if you appeared to be overly depressed, they might send you to the *tsev vwm*, "crazy house," where you would be kept in a room by yourself. The very thought of that as treatment both baffled and repelled her.

So every few months, Ia went to a therapy session with the old woman and played the dutiful patient, giving the answer to each question but never more. Or, when she didn't like the question, deflecting—*I don't know, I can't remember, I was too young.* Ia confirmed that yes, in her dreams she hears guns and bombs exploding, that the sound startles her awake, that in the dreams she just keeps running. But she did not offer the myriad other dreams: of flying over mountains and cliffs, of negotiating with the dead, of returning to Laos to build a home as a metaphor for her impending death. She figured the less she shared, the safer she would be.

Gradually, though, Ia opened up along the edges of the conversation. Perhaps it was the tantalizing comfort of having someone want to listen to her troubles. When asked about her family, Ia said that both of her parents had died, as had all her siblings save for her older brother who lives in Wisconsin. She did not mention Pha Kao; indeed, she kept private the existence of her entire extended family in Laos. Nor did she speak of how she misses her parents every day, so much it cripples her at times. But she did tell the woman that she feels as if her body is giving up on her—that even though she *feels* young and wants to work hard, her body will not execute what her mind envisions. She did not explain that she feared her soul might be departing her body, pulled to the spirit world by grief and longing. But she did go further to say that as her body fails, she is less able to earn money. And that the less she has to give others, the less they seem to value her. *No money,* Ia explained, *no love.*

Most nights she can't sleep, Ia told the therapist. She wakes at two or three in the morning, with so many things running through her mind that she struggles to shut it down. She is up again at four, unable to sleep for fear she won't hear the alarm when it is time to rise to go to the farm. Wide-awake, she heads to the kitchen, where she cooks rice for the day. If she is lucky she then dozes off briefly before the buzzer sounds and her day must begin.

Over numerous sessions, Ia slowly unspooled her *nyuaj siab,* sometimes through tears. What the doctors heard, translated into English, was that Ia felt "stress." The therapist and physician together counseled her that this was the cause of her high blood pressure, and that she must reduce the stress immediately; if she did not, her high blood pressure could give her a stroke—*mob hlab ntsha tawg ua tuag tes tuag taw,* "a sickness of the blood vessels erupting, causing dead hands and dead feet."

What Ia heard, translated into Hmong, was that if left unresolved, her *nyuaj siab* could lead to her being paralyzed, doomed to a wheelchair. If she were in a wheelchair, she would be unable to farm and make money. Without an income, she would become invisible to her children. As she now understood it, she could no longer afford to engage with things that made her cry or kept her awake at night because she felt sure that if she were paralyzed, her children would not show up to take care of her. Nobody would. The elders had a proverb: "If you take care of your new clothes, they will remain new. If you take care of your sanity, you will live longer." Feeling urgency after the dire warning from her doctors, Ia translated this into her own, more concise saying: "I have to be happy so I won't be sick."

The doctors told Ia that many other people experienced similar emotions. This was comforting, and in time she recognized that feeling alone was in itself a contributor to her *nyuaj siab*. At times it seemed as though everything was entangled in it.

The doctors reminded Ia of something her mother had taught her when she was young: there are things we can control, and things we cannot. Ia resolved to let go of the things she could not control. Chief among these was the loss of her parents. She missed them as much as ever, but at last she was able to say out loud the sad reality of her loss: that no matter how long she waited, no matter how much she cried, her mother and father would never come back. Missing them only made her sick. She resolved to *ua ib siab*—let it go.

Further, she decided to let her children go as well, at least monetarily. The therapist had insisted that in America, once offspring turned eighteen they were no longer the parents' financial obligation. Ia's continuing to agonize over making money so she could give it to them would lead only to continued stress. Ia slowly embraced the idea, reasoning that although she felt a maternal duty to take care of her kids, it was true that they could, indeed should, support themselves.

She extended her thinking to her brother Pha Kao, resolving to stop sending him money. Her older brother in Wisconsin, Cher, had been encouraging a shift like this for years. *It's important to let him suffer a little,* Cher would say. *He won't know what strength he's got if he never has to put any effort into trying to survive.*

Now Ia felt the truth in his words, and with it found a new grit inside herself. *I'm not at Pha Kao's mercy,* she thought, *he's at my mercy. Let him work hard like I do.*

By late September, just as the rice is beginning to mature, Ia has resolved to cut everyone off. No longer would she allow them to depend on her for money. Only one commitment remained: getting Chai to the United States. But those costs would be done soon. The interview at the embassy was scheduled for the end of October, and a week later Chai would receive a visa, board a plane, and arrive in Fresno. Chai could get a job, maybe at Foster Farms, and take over supporting Pha Kao. After that, everyone would be on their own.

———

In the beginning of October, the rice in the field is turning golden and Ia is radiant, a new purple money bag bright on her hip. The crop is a month late, yet Ia is unfazed. While other farmers she knows have already cut all their rice, she is just starting to cherry-pick out the patches that have ripened first. Chou Lor makes an offering, and Ia jokes that it's probably better that the ancestors can't speak directly back—after the mistakes of this year, they would only scold her and Chou Lor. When, a week later, thieves strike again and stoop to stealing her mortar and pestle, she laughs it off and buys a replacement at Asia Supermarket. Nothing can sink this new feeling Ia has, this commitment to blue skies.

Nothing, including that the weeds are the worst they have ever been. In their midst, the full-grown rice plants reach only up to Ia's chest. When she cuts a handful of rice stalks and ties the ends together with a rubber band, the bundle feels light. When she smashes it against the milk crate, just a sprinkling of rice comes off; the shells where the rest of the grains should have been are empty. From certain angles, she sees herself not even making back the money she put out this year.

But Ia does not cry to her parents, asking them to save her somehow. Instead, she buoys herself with the therapist's words: *It's out of my control.* They are the same words her mother used when counseling Ia about being stuck in a poisonous marriage. The same words her parents used when the rice failed and the family faced a long year of hunger. Instead of surrendering to despair, her mother and father gave the situation a new framing: *We'll only be hungry for one year. Then there will be a new year and we'll have another chance.* Ia repeats her own version of this like a mantra, certain that if she floats away from this belief and begins to stress, she will drown. *Out of my control. Next year, new start. Let it go.* The specter of the wheelchair is never far from her thoughts.

It works. If the mantra is a flotation device, Ia is less like a man overboard and more like a kid in a pool. No gout in her ankle, no stomach trouble. What weight she lost to anxiety earlier in the year she has gained back. She wraps her hair in a baby blanket patterned with pert little birdies and moves easily into the field, where she'll harvest whatever there is. The seeds she covered in insecticide and laid out to poison the pigeons back in April have made plants that have made grain, and she cuts and bundles that along with the rest. When her friends show up to help cut the crop, there is no crying. The friends are all widows, and still they laugh like teenagers. Chou Lor and Jimmy are there, always, but they stay clear of this party in the field.

The conversation streams from one topic to the next for hours, and Ia doesn't even seem to mind that the center of attention is a sassy friend named Pa. This other woman farmed here until her husband died but then had to give up her plot because she doesn't drive. She wears a clean outfit suited for a luncheon, then an entire set of farm clothes on top. Another shirt is wrapped around her head to protect her skin from the sun. Underneath are fake pearl earrings the size of blueberries. Ia teases her about having her head in the clouds now that she has a boyfriend. Pa is dreamy and coy, saying she doesn't want to marry the man but also doesn't want to lose him by not marrying him. The women counsel that in order to maintain her grip, Pa must mete out her affections slowly and keep him interested.

"You just have to keep roasting the yams," Ia says, "keep them soft."

"But if you keep leading them on, they keep asking for more!" another woman counters.

"How do you not know how to make excuses?" Ia asks, laughing. "Just keep stalling. And when you can't put him off any longer, just give the old man a taste."

"No!" Pa shrieks. "What if we do it and it ruins my... my *privates*?"

"Oh, please," Ia says. "You're already old."

Over lunch, talk turns to a story from Hmong radio about using green bananas to make a homemade Viagra, with everyone weighing in on whether Pa should use this potion on her boyfriend. Voices shout over one another until they reach consensus that such a move could backfire, making the boyfriend so horny that he would wander off to other women. From here the conversation drifts—to lucky numbers for playing the lottery, to the headache of babysitting grandchildren, to wrinkles and waistlines. One woman says she can't eat Ia's sticky rice at lunch today because she did yesterday and when she checked her blood sugar afterward it was at four hundred. "It's okay," Ia says. "Eat the sticky rice but just don't check your blood sugar—if you don't know the number, then you don't have to worry about it." Everyone laughs.

Today feels like the first day all year that the weather is perfect: sunny with a light breeze, not too hot and not too cold. There are birds overhead and dragonflies down low, buzzing the tops of the rice. The porta-potty is surrounded by a garden of fat and knobby pumpkins, ready to be picked from the vines. Because the rice is so short this year, there is no disappearing into it, no sense of escaping through time and space back to Sa Na Oua. Instead, the view is of trucks rumbling by on the road, across the asphalt to the almond trees now naked of leaves. The view is of one another, laughing, old and young in the same breath. Today that is all Ia needs. She moves ahead of the group, selecting rice for seed, as if within the grains she can capture this moment. She means to pick just two bundles but fills a whole basket instead.

The day of Chai's interview at the American embassy in Vientiane, Ia is in the field harvesting by the time the sun rises. Beside her is Thao. He has taken the day off from Hot Wok Express in case there are last-minute details in Laos that need his attention. Rarely does he come to the farm to help, and his presence here today can only be read as a show of gratitude. Without Ia's financial support, he would have struggled to bring Chai to the United States—indeed, after she gets her visa, it will still be Ia who purchases her plane ticket to Fresno.

The interview will take place in the morning in Laos, which is the evening in Fresno, which leaves Thao and Ia the entire day to crackle with nervous, giddy energy. They are certain that Chai will pass, which means as soon as next week she could have a visa and be on a plane. Thao is hoping she'll arrive before his birthday, like a gift to him. They will mark her arrival with a soul calling ceremony to introduce her to the Khang clan ancestors and formalize their protection of her. Informally, the purpose is to have a party that introduces Chai to all the living relatives. Ia's oldest daughter will come with her family from Oklahoma. Song has already planned the elaborate menu, and she and Mee are test-baking the complicated pastries they will serve as dessert.

Thao spends the day at the farm heartening himself by reciting all the reasons his family is so confident the interview will be a success. The purpose is for the American consular employee to assess the authenticity of the relationship between the applicant and the American fiancé. Chai and Thao's relationship is genuine, but it is reassuring that it also *looks* genuine. They are a believable match in age. They have been paired up for years now, and have the documents to prove it: stacks of receipts for money wired, reams of phone records verifying that Thao calls Chai throughout the day and then several times a night. Thao believes the government draws out the application process in order to test people like him and see if he will visit his fiancée over the months of stagnant bureaucracy. Thao can show that he has gone to Laos as many times as he could afford.

Ia razzes Thao for having any doubts. She feels certain Chai will pass because she has enlisted the support of the spirit world. Ia herself made a promise offering to the *tim tswv teb chaws,* the spirits of the land; she also directed Pha Kao to call to his late wife, Chai's mother, for help. With their combined protection, Chai will do fine. Ia is so sure, she says that when Chai passes the interview, Thao owes her a trip to the seafood buffet at the casino in Jackson. He laughs and agrees.

Last night, on the phone, Ia reassured Chai, too. *The questions will be stuff you already know,* she and Thao reminded her, *like what are your husband's hobbies, what is his favorite color—they're just testing whether you know him for real.* Ia tells her to answer the questions simply and not say anything extra, not try to sound smart. Don't let them know you're related to Thao. Don't dress up. Don't wear pants. Don't wear red lipstick or the usual whitening face makeup. This last part Chai already knew. When she went to the embassy for her physical exam, she saw women who had failed their interviews, each of them sobbing, the gleaming white foundation running down their faces in dirty smears. That day, the only one who passed was a woman who was dressed in raggedy clothes and holding a baby in her arms. Her fiancé was younger, not an old man, just like Thao. Chai felt confident, too.

At four o'clock, Thao's phone beeps an alarm. It is six in the morning in Laos. "Chai must be leaving for her interview now," he says to no one in particular, staring at his phone. A heavy scrim of gray clouds slides across the sun and the wind picks up. The air turns cold. If this were a place with rain, it would feel as though a storm was coming on. Thao looks at his phone again and it dies. He puts it back in his pocket, nonchalant. He would prefer for the news to be delayed, anyway. Too much screaming with big announcements like this. He would rather wait until everyone has calmed down.

Thao and Ia continue cutting the rice, quietly now, up to and then past the time when the embassy doors would be opening at seven o'clock in the morning, past when the first interview would begin at seven thirty, past when the sun in Fresno slips below the clouds for a sliver of horizontal light, then disappears for good below the horizon. It is amazing how quickly the light drains out of the sky after that—all day long it is beating down, roasting your shoulders, and then in a moment it is gone. Without discussion, Thao and Ia stop cutting and wade out of the field to go home.

———

Soon after they return to the house at Creekside Ranch, Thao's phone lights up. It's Chai. Excitement surges through the living room as he answers the call, everyone eager to hear the play-by-play and begin the mad celebration. But that's not what happens. Instead, Chai tells Thao that she failed the interview. No visa, no plane flight, no party.

That morning, Chai woke before daylight. She dressed in a customary Lao skirt and modest blouse. She did wear makeup, not thinking she would be the one crying today. She arrived at the embassy well before the first interview began. It is a modern fortress of steel beams and windows, surrounded by a fence of narrow metal bars that are artfully staggered, perhaps to distract from the message that it is a security barrier. At the gatehouse, Chai handed over her cell phone to a navy-uniformed guard. Her purse passed through the metal detector. She walked a cement path lined with impatiens to the main building. When she opened the door and stepped inside, the air was icy cold.

When Chai's turn came, she entered an office occupied by an American consular officer and a Hmong interpreter, both men. The American asked her how she and Thao met, when they got engaged, if they were related. She answered simply and politely, exactly as she thought they would want her to. It seemed as if the American was ready to approve her application, then had a change of heart. He spoke with his colleague in English, back and forth, then took a paper from a tray on his desk, signed it, and handed it to her as the Hmong man interpreted: *I know you really want to go to America but I can't give you a visa at this time.*

Chai cannot read the paper she was given, which is in English. When she texts a picture to Thao, he finds its information almost equally indecipherable: just an X in the box that says her visa "does not comply with the provisions of the Immigration and Nationality Act or regulations issued pursuant thereto," with reference to a section in a statute in the U.S. Code. Because no one on either end of the phone understands this, they are left to parse every detail Chai can recall, searching for clues. Did the interpreter mix up her words? Or twist them around in sabotage? Was she too pretty? The two men had repeatedly looked at the photos of Thao and Chai from when they met three years earlier—had she gained so much weight since then that they thought the woman in the photo was a different person? Then there was this: the man took the paper from a tray on his desk, and yet her name and case number and the code for refusal were all entered by a computer. Was the rejection already printed—the decision already made—before she walked in the room?

Ia had heard that the American president was making it impossible for people to emigrate from Laos. The landscape was certainly different than when Ia had come to the United States, when she and others like her were given visas almost as reparations for the damage wreaked by the American war. The government had worn through that sense of duty even before President Trump took office, but it was true that his administration's war on immigration had made obtaining a visa significantly harder.

In fact, the Department of Homeland Security had an eye trained specifically on Laos: There were more than four thousand people in the United States who were to be deported to the country, but Laos wouldn't take them back. Most of them had immigrated to the United States on those original humanitarian visas, fleeing the communist government's post-war persecution; in Laos, that same government was still in power, and didn't recognize these people as its citizens. To retaliate, the State Department enacted visa sanctions against Laos three months before Chai's interview. The sanctions didn't specifically prohibit the type of visa for which she had applied, but they doubtless made the eye of the needle more difficult to thread.

In truth, the eye of the needle was already pretty narrow. Visa applications from citizens of Laos and other least developed countries receive extra scrutiny for the sheer fact that the applicants are, for the most part, poor. Because they lack opportunities in their home countries, they are assumed to have more reason to lie their way into the United States. K-1, or fiancé, visas are viewed with special mistrust because they are often the type that people use to fraudulently marry in order to gain citizenship. This can mean someone paying an American citizen to marry him or her in order to gain citizenship, but in the case of developing countries, more often wealth flows in the other direction: someone, most often a young woman, marries an American in exchange for the money and opportunity she'll have access to in the United States. In Laos, K-1s make up an abnormally high percentage of all the visas issued, more than in any other country. All of which means that fiancé visas reviewed at the embassy in Vientiane invite exceptional suspicion.

There are clear legal standards for fraud, such as when the engagement is not consensual, or it exists solely for the purpose of getting someone into the United States. But beyond those black-and-white standards, there is a lot of gray area. What if the man is very old and the woman is young but of legal age to marry? What if a couple has all the right receipts and photographs but seems to have met only recently? In this gray area, it is up to the consular officer to judge whether a marriage is real.

The measure is not love—the government could not presume to adjudicate such a fluid, individual experience. Instead, they assess "authenticity." That is still a pretty subjective measure, given the range of reasons for which people around the world marry, but the U.S. Department of Homeland Security is not designed for expansive cultural thinking. It is designed instead for getting to yes or no on a visa application—some say, during the Trump presidency, designed for getting to no. When the man in the air-conditioned office told Chai there would be no visa, there was nothing for her to do but go home.

———

Ia knows nothing more than anyone else about the bureaucratic reasons for denying Chai a visa, but in the days that follow the failed interview, she pieces together what is likely the underlying spiritual cause. As Chai approached the gatehouse outside the embassy, her phone rang. It was her stepmother, Pha Kao's little wife. The voice asked Chai if she had arrived yet, then the line went dead. Chai proceeded to the gatehouse, turned off her phone, handed it to the guard, and thought nothing more of the call.

The little wife had woken with a bad dream and wanted to warn Chai about it. If it was an omen, Chai would need to protect herself against the threat. In the dream, Pha Kao's first wife came to the little wife and announced she would be accompanying Chai to the United States.

You can't go with her! the little wife yelled. *You died when she was a little girl and I raised her.*

She will never be yours, Chai's mother yelled back. *She's mine and I'm going with her to America.* She grabbed on to her daughter, and the little wife responded by trying to push her off. Fiercely they fought, a tug-of-war over Chai. In the end, the little wife lost. Holding Chai, her mother looked back at the little wife and said, *If I can't go with her to America, then I won't let her go either.*

The little wife woke in shock. She called Chai, but as soon as she got through, her battery died. By the time she got it charged enough to call back, Chai's phone was turned off and stored with the gatehouse guard. Over and over the little wife tried Chai's number, but she didn't get an answer until after their fate had already been sealed.

Ia, too, had been visited. The day before the interview, early in the morning, she had woken up, made rice, and retired to the sofa in hopes of a little more sleep. As soon as she closed her eyes, a vision of Chai's mother appeared before her. It was startling, given that Ia had never met the woman. Ia woke Thao and told him to call Chai—it was evening in Laos—and tell her to call her father. Pha Kao had already made an offering to Chai's mother asking her to help Chai pass the interview, but Ia was certain he should do it again. She even dictated the words Chai should tell her father to use: *Please come help her with this interview, because when she gets to America, she will be able to help Lee and the rest of the family so they won't be so poor.* Lee, the son Chai's mother had died giving birth to.

Ia had thought Chai's mother would be an asset to the immigration process; it had not occurred to her that she might actually stand in the way. But days after the interview, when Ia heard the stepmother's dream, what had happened at the embassy made more sense. That's because Ia interpreted the dream not with the jealousy of a stepmother, but with the protectiveness of a mother.

She thought of how when Chai had called Thao with the bad news of having failed the interview, Thao had lashed out at her. He had blamed Chai, calling her stupid and hissing that she deserved to be stuck in Laos, to die there. This was not the first time Ia had over-heard Thao speaking viciously to Chai over the phone. Sometimes his yelling was so loud it woke Ia up through the bedroom wall.

In the beginning, Ia thought the marriage was the best thing that could happen for an orphan like Chai. Her life in Laos had a weak broth: poor father, cruel stepmother, single-track future that would find her farming rice and scratching by, just like all those who came before her. Ia thought marrying Thao would offer Chai the chance of something better. Over time, though, Thao began re-minding Ia of Chou Lor when she married him—the poisonous tone, the heartless ridicule. Ia watched Chai, still so young and yet putting up with the abuse, believing it was a tolerable cost for the chance to not be poor, and perhaps believing it might stop when they were finally together.

But Ia knew better. When Chou Lor had abused her, she had followed her own mother's advice: let go of the things that were beyond her control, try to not let another person's actions hurt her. What it had wrought for her was a life full of tears, and now she predicted the same for Chai. The relationship with Thao was au-thentic, and yet it seemed to lack that more essential thing the gov-ernment couldn't quantify: love, and the kind, gentle care that it brings. Maybe, Ia thought, Chai would be better off staying in Laos.

Ia had never said it out loud, though. Thao's temper was too wild, and Ia feared crossing him. But then the stepmother had her dream, and Chai failed the interview, and to Ia the explanation seemed clear. Chai's mother had recognized the same danger that Ia had, but she had acted on it. The mother had seen that in coming to the United States, her daughter would be leaving the protective cir-cle of her nuclear family and entering a world of strangers, all alone. In the dream, the mother said she was going to go with Chai, but of course that was impossible, she being so many years dead. So instead, she blocked the path, protecting her daughter from a life of tears.

When Ia realized this, she admonished Thao. He had to apologize to Chai's mother by making an offering to her spirit and asking her forgiveness—maybe after that the visa path would clear. Ia told Thao he shouldn't speak such harsh words to Chai, but she stopped short of telling him to apologize to her. That might have provoked him, and Ia dared not invite his wrath—it was too familiar to her, from so many years ago.

—————

For weeks, no one in the family understood why Chai was rejected, what the government was doing with her application, or how the process could be moved forward. After seeking advice from cousins and uncles, Thao believed the most expedient approach was to hire a lawyer who could decipher the rejection, petition against it, and deliver Chai without further ado. The obstacle was the cost—$6,000 to $12,000 was the ballpark figure he had heard—which was the same obstacle that had kept him from hiring a lawyer when he first began the application process more than two years earlier. His instinct was to get the money from his mother, but, pursuant to her epiphany about cutting off her dependents, the bank of Ia was closed. Short of taking out a loan from an actual bank, he had no other source for that kind of cash.

Thao remained buoyant. An uncle who had helped Hmong immigrants for years advised him to appeal to his congressman's office for help—this was the way things got done, he explained. Thao went to the office in downtown Fresno and was told he must put his request in writing. He wrote a letter stating his case, mailed it, and waited. *These things take time,* his uncle said. Before long it was December, and his uncle consoled him that nothing happens during Christmas. He must just wait until January.

Even before nothing arrived in January, Thao was on to the next plan, this one fail-safe. He and Chai would get legally married in Laos, then he would apply for a visa for her not as his fiancée but as his fully documented, incontestably authentic wife. It felt like so obviously the right choice—Thao marveled that most couples don't do it this way from the start. He was told the process takes eight months to a year and a half. That was longer than he imagined it would take to appeal the failed K-1 visa application with a lawyer, but this approach felt more concrete—undeniable. "And if you have a baby, they'll speed up the process for you," he told people with deep confidence. "With a baby, you go straight to the embassy."

The only hitch was that he couldn't go to Laos just yet—he didn't have the money for airplane tickets and filing fees. He needed to log more hours at Hot Wok Express and save up. Also, his tax refund would help, and that was just a few months off. He told Chai he would be there in March, maybe. As soon as he could.

Chai was left to simply wait for Thao to make the next thing happen. Increasingly, though, this passive life became intolerable. During the weeks following the failed interview, Chai barely ate. When Thao called her, she had little to say. The house on the dead-end lane in the dusty lowlands now felt like a prison.

She was willing to accept that the opportunity for a better life must come at the expense of being separated from her family. But for three years now she had only sacrificed, without reward. As she watched other young women she knew marry and receive visas, inexplicably, and move off to the United States and China, Chai wanted to know why her own life was on hold. In her darkest times, she threatened to divorce Thao so she could start her life over.

To these threats, Thao responded coldly that she would be screwed without him. *If you want to go back to your father's village and be poor, fine,* he told her, *I won't stop you.* Before the damage was done, though, Ia intervened with a more rational framing. She advised Chai to think carefully about leaving Thao. It was a reversal of Ia's own private thoughts immediately after the failed interview, when she thought perhaps their relationship was better off severed. But since then, Ia had incorporated the lesson of her own reckoning in Thailand decades earlier, after she vowed to leave Chou Lor but then was made aware of the limitations an already married woman faced. Now, over the phone, Ia offered Chai a pragmatic reality rooted in empathy but delivered bluntly. If Chai were to divorce Thao, she would be damaged goods, likely to remarry only as an older man's second or third wife. She would be condemned to living in the village, farming for the rest of her days. *Is that the life you want?* Ia asked her.

Chai knew implicitly that the chance for a better life should be seized when it was available. In truth, though, she didn't know the shape of the thing for which she was making this colossal sacrifice, didn't know what, exactly, it would feel like to be "less poor." What she did know was what it meant to be poor in the village, to be poor as a rice farmer. It doesn't somehow get better. The future feels fixed. *Is that the life you want?*

Ia advised Chai to be patient—with Thao's bad temper, with all the waiting, with a visa application process that was beyond their control. And so January became February, February became March, and still Thao was in Fresno. *As soon as I can,* he assured Chai.

In the meantime, a cousin in Minnesota with some knowledge of immigration documents looked at Chai's original visa application and determined that it was rejected because paperwork was missing. He assured them that after Thao submitted the necessary documents, Chai would be given a new appointment and the visa would be theirs. Thao took the necessary steps, and through April he held out hope that the government would surprise them with good news. But then came May, still with no word. The only good news was that it had been long enough that Thao had saved up the money for a cheap plane ticket to Laos. Seven months almost to the day since Chai failed her interview, he headed to the Fresno airport.

Just before he got on the first flight, Mee called him. The letter from the visa center had just arrived in the mail, and it said Chai's application had officially been canceled. Thao was not surprised. He was convinced that the American government had intentionally designed the byzantine process to force innocent applicants like him to pay fees multiple times, in order to generate maximum profit. The letter did not give a reason for the rejection; instead, it gave another number that referred to a section in a statute, which anyone who was not an immigration lawyer would have to look up on the Internet in order to understand. Mee promised to do the research and report back soon.

Instead, though, the next day Chou Lor was cleaning off the kitchen counter and mistakenly threw the letter in the garbage, which went out to the trash collection, never to be seen again. Mee reported this to Thao, who seemed not to care that he might never know the reason that the man at the embassy had rejected Chai's application. "It was probably something really stupid," he said. Anyway, it didn't matter now: he had arrived in Laos, and at last he had it all figured out. Marriage did not have to be so complicated, after all. Everyone, not least of them Ia, hoped that this time he was right.

PART 4

WIFE

After the buoyant days of harvest and her liberating resolution to let everything and everyone go, Ia passed much of the winter of 2019 seated at her dining table. Looking through drugstore reading glasses, her eyes would fix upon a strip of hemp fabric in her hands. With one tiny, perfect stitch after another, she embroidered an elaborate design of green and orange diamond shapes onto the cloth. It was trim for the jacket she'd wear at her funeral; she needed it to be exactly right, and the only way to make sure of that was to sew it herself. The previous winter, in the throes of feeling so hurt by Chou Lor's neglect for her spiritual well-being, she might have approached this work with vindictiveness or self-pity. Now, though, her tone was simply matter-of-fact. "I'm aging, I know my time is coming," she said. "I could wake up tomorrow and be dead." Best to be prepared.

Then one night Ia had a dream: She and Chou Lor were in a village in Laos—always in Laos, her dreams. Chickens and pigs roamed peacefully outside the houses, but the place was empty of people. Suddenly, Vietnamese soldiers were shooting at her and Chou Lor. Together the two of them took off running, down a hill and toward a big green lake that, somehow, promised an escape. The lake was

257

enclosed by a barbed wire fence, and as they hurried toward it, Ia told Chou Lor her plan: *We'll go through the fence, then we'll fly off over the lake.*

Ia crawled under the wire easily. *Hurry!* she said to Chou Lor, who was motionless on the ground. *Why aren't you hurrying?*

The barbed wire got me, he said weakly. She saw that a spike had indeed caught Chou Lor's heel and was lodged inside. He was stuck. The soldiers were drawing close.

From out of nowhere, a being appeared by Ia's side. *You've got to leave him behind,* the being said urgently. *We've got to go now! We've got to fly.* Ia obeyed, and soared into the air away from the danger. But she was reluctant, looking back over her shoulder at Chou Lor. He was still prostrate, helpless, and shrinking in her view with each passing second. The being urged her on, with this consolation: *You can find each other in the next lifetime,* it said. *If it's meant to be, you can find each other then.*

Ia woke up sobbing.

———

By summer, the farm's aura of doom feels familiar. The rains came early last fall and lasted all winter, which meant Ia's fields were too wet to be plowed until April, which meant she never had time to spray herbicide before planting. Then in May, a time when precipitation would normally disappear until winter, the rains returned. The month's rainfall was 500 percent of normal—just two and a half inches, yet to the gritty plants that grow wild here, it was a miracle monsoon. By Memorial Day, Ia's fields were growing the most lush, deep-green crop of weeds in memory.

Now, in mid-July, the fields look like low-grade hay, with gray-green sprangletop—the worst of all rice weeds—growing from one end to the other, uninterrupted. Their feathery tops knit together into a canopy, and in places where the earliest plants have already matured, they rain down seed to start the cycle of invasion all over again. Without question, the weeds are the worst they have ever been. Of course, last season, after the herbicide debacle, was the worst the weeds had ever been up to then. It seems a pattern is developing: each year, the record is broken.

The furrows are thick with yellowed grasses that Ia and Chou Lor have already stomped down and sprayed with the impotent over-the-counter herbicide, in hopes that the rice will surge ahead before the weeds can rebound. Today Chou Lor uses a flimsy weed whacker to crew-cut the weeds along the edges of the rows. He knows they will just grow back, but it is the most expedient remedy for a problem that is beyond their control.

Ia lowers onto her knees and uses a short sickle to saw through the soil at the weeds' roots. The labor leaves her hot and gritty, but it works. Once she passes through, all that remains are the scrawny rice plants, ready to grow unimpeded. After forty-five minutes, Ia stands and from here sees that she has made it only ten feet down the row. Doused with a mixture of fatigue and discouragement, she stares at the remaining 160 feet. Even if she did somehow make it all the way to the end, there would still be two hundred more rows to go. Though the sun is hidden by a scrim of clouds, it is 96 degrees and still morning. She gives up and heads for the shed. Walking, she passes row after row with this same pattern: ten feet of green success, then a wall of gray defeat.

Alice is in the shed, flipping beef ribs over a fire she has made from old fence posts and a healthy dose of lighter fluid. To hold the tongs, she must gently splay her fingers outward so as not to bend the blue and gold acrylic nails that extend an inch past her fingertips. A year ago they might have looked like silly dress-up, but next month Alice will start her junior year at Sanger High School, and she is changing accordingly. Gone is the hoodie she used to wear, drawstring closed tight around her face in the field. Today she wears a light-blue sweatshirt whose neck is cut away so it falls almost off her shoulder. On the front is a picture of a Native American dream catcher over the words DREAM BIG. She and Jimmy have been conscripted to spend the day tending the long beans, and after a full morning in the fields, her nails are somehow unscathed.

While Alice cooks, Jimmy lies on the bean shelf, disappeared into his phone. One by one, the others arrive from the fields to wait until lunch is ready. Youa, whose diabetes and missing teeth make it hard to eat much, brings her own insulated travel mug filled with thin rice porridge. Her husband, Neng Her, sets on the table a plastic container of cooked rice and a plate of cherry tomatoes from their field. This spring, after giving up on the Green Mountain and its promise of riches, they reclaimed their two acres from Ia and planted rice.

Having two more people at the farm every day brings a spark of life that the farm lacked last year. At the same time, the four adults together carry an air of decay, aging as if in a race to the finish line. In April, Neng Her went to the hospital for appendicitis and Youa had emergency surgery on her gallbladder. Even now in July, most days Youa remains in the shed at the farm, where she sits at the lunch table, head in her hands, dozing off.

May was Chou Lor's month. First an ambulance rushed him to the hospital because of pain so severe that the non-Hmong-speaking doctors at first diagnosed him with heart failure. When it was communicated that the pain was in Chou Lor's stomach, they found and cauterized an ulcer as wide across as three fingers. After a week in the hospital, Chou Lor went home; there the pain and vomiting continued. One evening, sleeping on the couch, he had what may have been a heart attack: chest pains, blacking out, falling to the ground. The only bright side was that he was able to grab the side of the coffee table on the way down instead of crashing into it with his head. "I almost croaked," he says with disquieting resignation. "Twice in one month."

Chou Lor is the last to arrive at the table for lunch. He peels off his sweaty shirt and seats himself at the table bare-chested, too hot to put on another one. His head and shoulders slump over, his whole torso held up by his spine. His belly balloons forward like a smooth mound of clay. He opens a bottle of water, takes a careless sip, and lets the water spill down onto his skin.

As the food is served, the others stab at conversation here and there. About old people's aches and pains. About how kids these days are glued to screens. About how they were all farming here already when Ia was pregnant with Alice. As they talk, Jimmy stares into his phone, Alice taps out text after text with her thumbs. Between topics there are long pauses, filled with only the sounds of tired chewing.

Conversation turns to Seng Xiong, the man who ran the scam that involved taking Hmong people's money in exchange for promises of plots of land in an autonomous Hmong country that he would create. His partners have resuscitated the plan, updating the vision with plans for both gender equality and economic and agricultural development. Xiong himself remains at the Moshannon Valley Correctional Facility, a federal prison in Pennsylvania. He regularly records extended audio messages for his followers, in which he insists that if they believe with all their hearts, the dream of a Hmong homeland will eventually materialize.

It's all the same old scam—everyone around the table agrees. No different from Vang Pao's guys who come around asking for donations for military orphans and widows, with a wink, wink that signals the money is for the resistance. But if General Vang Pao couldn't win back the old country for the Hmong, Ia scoffs, why would any of these nobodies be able to get the job done?

"Every night those scammers are on YouTube," Youa says. "Every night they're there! I just think, *Idiots.*"

"There's no land for us," Ia says, raising her voice. "You want to get land where you can live forever? The only land you're gonna get is at Belmont." Everyone knows she means the cemetery where most of Fresno's Hmong are buried. Each year, more and more of their friends end up there.

Chou Lor is quiet through lunch. He eats a huge bowl of rice, spooned over with a slush of watermelon and melted ice. He cautiously nibbles at a grilled rib, but can barely enjoy it for fear of what it might do to him. His stomach has only worsened since spring. Regularly now, after eating, his abdomen will expand like a balloon and the food will come right back up. He bounces between pain and fear of what the pain means. Every day he is a little weaker for lack of nutrients.

Ia continues to believe the problem is spiritual in nature, though she has yet to pinpoint the source. She is unsure whether the ancestors are punishing Chou Lor or simply hungry themselves and striking him to demand attention. She will make an offering to some late uncle, Chou Lor will feel better the next day, then before long he'll be sick again. Frankly, the more the cycle repeats without lasting results, the more Ia questions its relevance. And yet the doctors at Fresno PACE have not offered a more compelling explanation. Chou Lor has been warned against eating a whole list of foods including anything acidic or spicy, and avoiding them does seem to help. Still, sometimes even water will make him throw up.

Chou Lor seems agnostic on the root cause, preoccupied as he is with his discomfort and, increasingly, worry. The vomiting and consequent weakness have made it difficult to work a full shift at Foster Farms, and he has run through all his sick days for the year. He was planning to retire next summer, after he turned sixty-seven, so his Social Security benefits would be greater. But because of his illness, as soon as he turned sixty-six this year, Mee filed paperwork with the government so his retirement benefits would begin. Once Chou Lor received the first check, two weeks ago, he gave notice at Foster Farms.

Tomorrow is his last night. He thinks they may give him a cake at the end of the shift, but that's it, no company-sponsored retirement benefits. Indeed, twenty-two years on the graveyard shift and the only pay raises he ever received were to meet government-mandated increases in the minimum wage. He finished at $11 per hour, which leaves him with Social Security payments of less than $1,000 a month; additionally, the government will send a small amount to Ia and another to Alice, at least until she turns eighteen in the spring. Altogether, the payments amount to less than the family received in welfare when they arrived from Laos twenty-five years ago. This cut of several hundred dollars per month from their monthly income has preemptively sucked any of the joy out of finally ending two decades of gutting, skinning, cutting, and packaging chickens from midnight to eight in the morning, five nights a week. Retirement will not mean Chou Lor putting up his feet and getting some rest. Instead, he'll shift to working full-time here at the farm, in hopes of making a little more money to cover the loss.

After lunch, Chou Lor is the first to return to the field. He finds a gray T-shirt from the clothesline at the back of the shed and pulls it over his head. He tugs his tube socks up to meet the cut-off slacks he wears as shorts. He unscrews the cap from a bottle of water and pours it on himself, first wetting the tops of the socks, then soaking the gray shirt—makeshift air-conditioning for the work ahead. Over the wet shirt he dons an oversize gray work shirt stained with great blooms of oil and sweat, then across his face a dust mask, and over his head an oversize sombrero like those the hired workers wear in the orchard across the road. When he is ready, the only bit of him left uncovered is his eyes, and they are cast down on the ground.

———

Ia sits at the table a little longer, her gaze going right past Chou Lor getting dressed to the blue-gray ocean of weeds. She is happy about having him come to work on the farm full-time, without the competing demands of the night work. But she, too, is worried about the bottom line. If the farm had to support only Chou Lor, Ia, and Alice, they could get by. As ever, though, the financial equation is much bigger than the three of them.

The wall of resolution that Ia erected last fall, when she vowed to cut off those who relied on her for money, has been breached. She held out for a while, even changed her phone number so her family in Laos wouldn't be able to reach her. After Thao, not thinking, shared her number with Pha Kao, Ia stopped answering her phone when she saw the calls were from Laos. Her relatives responded by blocking their numbers so she wouldn't see it was them calling, and so Ia stopped answering her phone altogether, unless she saw the number of someone she knew wasn't going to ask her for money. After that, Pha Kao's youngest son began messaging Mee through Facebook. He would ask for Ia, who would be sitting just across the living room from Mee, at which point it felt wrong to lie and say she wasn't there. So Ia would use Mee's phone to call the son, who would connect her with his father, and before long she was sending Pha Kao money and then fielding calls for more.

Last week Pha Kao phoned to say that his rice crop was overgrown with weeds and he needed $200 to hire workers to help him get it under control. Ia hardly knew what to say, having spent every day in recent memory in her own weed-infested fields, either on her hands and knees in the dirt or in the shed trying to summon the energy to go back out. She managed to hold a line, telling Pha Kao with exasperation, "I don't have that kind of money!"

The truth is that she had already given it all to Thao for his trip to Laos. He had saved money over the winter and pocketed his income tax refund, which was enough to cover an airline ticket but not weeks on the ground in Laos. Nor did he have enough for what they knew from experience would be an endless series of costs associated with government paperwork. Rather than force her son to take out a formal loan from a bank or a less savory funder that would charge interest and penalties, Ia gave Thao several thousand dollars with the understanding that he would pay it back. She swore it would be the last time.

She also ended up sending Pha Kao just a tiny bit of money

to put toward his weed trouble. And then, when Thao's trip went longer than expected and he ran out of cash, she wired her son a few hundred more. And just like that, the great revelation of last fall—about breaking away from all the people who depend on her for money in order to take care of her own health—that revelation evaporated into the heat of the Fresno summer. It was replaced by something else, this time not an explicit protocol but rather an internal acceptance that forsaking those who come to her in need is simply not who she is. For a moment it had felt liberating to try on the revelation's very American stance, that literal self-interest, but it never fit Ia right. Even as the people whom she serves so plainly take advantage of her, she forgives them over and over. Keeps giving. Because it is her divine occupation to help others. But more so, because that's what her heart tells her to do.

There is one exception to this rule: Chou Lor. Perhaps the only person who has never asked her for money is the lone person she cannot forgive. Of course, that is not how Ia sees it. In her view, she has forgiven her husband, if indirectly, by staying married to him after the cruel words and the beatings. This concession she made for the sake of the children. Had she left him, the kids would have lived the lives of orphans—either mistreated by the second wife that would have replaced Ia or, had the kids stayed with her, abandoned by the clan as children without a father. Ia could not have rested knowing her sons and daughters had been relegated to such a life. So for forty years she has stayed, sacrificing her own wishes, forgiving Chou Lor for the survival of the group.

Alice challenges this explanation. She is nearly a woman herself now, already the veteran of a few high school romances. Drawing on books of poetry, she counsels her friends on matters of the heart, telling them, for instance, that every relationship is like a rose that must be watered by both partners; not cared for, it will perish. Should this happen, the dead flower cannot be revived. Instead, both partners must plant a new one together.

This is where Alice sees her mother's fault. After Chou Lor beat Ia in Thailand and she tried to divorce him, he swore he would never abuse her again, and he never did. What's more, in the many years since then, he has changed into a person who wouldn't hurt someone else. But even if Ia has technically forgiven him, she has refused to give him a second chance. Alice, who knows Chou Lor only as a gentle father who will wire her flip-flops back together or smile softly at a joke, feels that he deserves one.

Ia's heart is not fresh and full of poetry like Alice's. To her daughter's bright metaphors, Ia would respond with a Hmong saying that means essentially, "You will remember the bad things that others have done to you but not necessarily the good." In a way, the saying proves Alice's point. But Ia means it in the way that proves her own: the abuse, physical and verbal alike, will always stay with her. Her heart will never *not* be broken—time has only hardened this position. Every other minute of the day, Ia will surrender herself to the service of the group, even as her generosity is abused and her kindness is gobbled up without gratitude. But with Chou Lor, she unfailingly sacrifices their group of two and instead honors her own individual, private pain. Indeed, she guards it ferociously.

The tinny whir of the weed whacker calls out Chou Lor's presence in the field. The rest of the group has also gone back to work; only Ia remains at the table. Her eyes are now fixed on the dirt ground before the hearth, loose in their gaze. The heat is rising even as she sits there. She dreads returning, knows exactly what it will feel like, having been there so many times before. But she cannot *not*. If the weed whacker weren't so loud, a person could almost hear the weeds growing, choking out the rice. She wraps the fingers of her right hand around the worn, stiff handle of her sickle, and with both fists pushes herself off the bench.

————

Getting a marriage license in Laos proved to be more complicated than Thao had predicted. Soon after Thao arrived, the man who was facilitating the process for him determined that crucial documents had been forgotten. The Lao government required a written marriage proposal and parental consent, both of which seemed rather old-fashioned to ask of a man in his thirties. But then the Lao government would prove to be a fusty, lethargic machine whose every form was filled out in longhand. Because the government alone had the power to legally certify a marriage, Thao followed orders.

His solution was to call his sister Mee in Fresno and convince her to serve as his secretary. She felt she had no choice, since the other siblings refused. Using the computer at the Walmart where she worked, Mee googled "sample marriage proposal." In the first hit she found one that seemed sincere, beginning, "This proposal is only a humble declaration of the love I feel for you. You mean the world to me. I cannot imagine life without..." She copied and pasted it into a Word document and changed the names to make it personal: "Dear Jenna" became "Dear Chai," and "Love, Robert" became "Love, Thao." Then she typed up a bare-bones statement of parental consent, and drove Ia and Chou Lor to sign it in front of a notary at the Clovis Pack & Ship. After waiting an hour in line, Mee overnighted the two sheets of paper to Vientiane for the cost of $140, which Ia paid. Thao promised to pay her back.

Once Thao's stack of papers was complete, he and Chai submitted themselves to the pedantic robots who operate the people's democratic bureaucracy of Laos. At every step, there was a new fee. And at every step, Thao brightly forecasted that the rest of the process would be simple.

Four weeks in, they caught a break: Chai was pregnant. After three years of trying whenever they were together, this time it must have happened as soon as Thao touched down. At times, Thao groused that he wished it had worked three years earlier, so he wouldn't have had to make this trip in the first place. Most of the time, though, he focused on the way the pregnancy would grease the wheels with the Americans at the embassy, the way that discreetly proffered cash sped things up with the Lao paper pushers.

Chai was happy, excited, nervous, relieved. Beyond the pregnancy, she was also just high on having her man with her in person for once. As she and Thao waited for the papers to make the rounds, she enjoyed being in the lowlands in a way she rarely had. They went to a theme park and rented a little boat. They ordered platters upon platters of restaurant food. They went to a photo studio with rental garments and had a wedding portrait made: she in a flowing white gown, he behind her in a white suit, both of them posing against a backdrop of a grand staircase in a mansion. On each new adventure, Chai took selfies showing her glowing, practiced smile alongside Thao's soft, sighing expression. Friends on Facebook wrote that they were the perfect match.

Inevitably, it came time for Thao to leave. He had been in Laos eight weeks when they were told it would likely be another two or three months before the marriage license was issued. Thao needed to return to Fresno so he could work and save money, so he could come back once the paperwork was complete. The day he left, all the closest relatives piled into a van and brought him to the airport. Before he went through passport control, Thao bent down and said goodbye to the bump of Chai's belly. *You and Mommy stay behind,* he said. *I'll be back.* This time, Chai didn't cry. She knew he would return soon.

But in the months they were apart, the glossy joy of pregnancy gave way to the friction of reality. Chai, once in her second trimester, felt increasingly anxious that she might not have a visa before the baby arrived—and she was still counting down to nine months. No one had yet explained that she wouldn't be allowed to fly after seven months, which meant that at best they would have six weeks after they were married for the embassy to approve her visa and for her to fly to Fresno. Thao insisted the process would soon be easy and fast—once the embassy knew Chai was pregnant, once the two of them were legally married—but his assurances no longer carried them through. When Chai told him about the vivid dreams she had now that she was pregnant, Thao criticized her for sleeping too much. Over the long, humid summer, Chai was nauseated and in pain, always lamenting that she had no one to take care of her. *Stupid woman,* Thao would yell. *Why are you always sick?*

As Thao's voice throbbed through the walls, Ia could not sleep. It pained her to hear Thao blaming Chai for her suffering. *Why are you yelling at her like that?* Ia asked him. *Do you even have a human heart?* Trying another tactic, Ia appealed to his self-interest, reminding him that the bad words spoken to the mother can hurt the baby. This seemed to quiet his scolding.

Because Ia knew the rage might return at any time, she also counseled Chai. Having heard that people in Chai's father's village were encouraging her to leave Thao, Ia told Chai they were probably just trying to sabotage her marriage because they were jealous she had a chance to escape Laos. Ia reminded her how hard life had been before she married Thao. She reminded Chai that she was an orphan. While Chai had been shielded from the worst of that fate—by her grandmother's protection, by Ia's remittances, and more recently by Thao's money—if she divorced Thao, the support would end and her livelihood would be farming rice.

And the poverty won't end with you, Ia admonished. *It will extend through your children's lives and all the generations that follow.*

Ia pleaded with Chai to see her immediate frustration in light of the bigger picture. Marrying Thao had freed her from this dark fate. She must now find the strength and patience to wait for as long as it took for Thao to bring her to the United States—though this time, Ia revised the message she had given in the past. *By the time you get here, you may be too old to go to school and make something of yourself,* Ia said. *But in sacrificing your own self, you will have given your children the chance to have a better life than you did.*

Ia did not mention her own self and the cost of making a similar sacrifice by staying with Chou Lor for the sake of their children. Nor did she enumerate the tears she had shed over the years, the harsh words she herself had spit out. This was not a conversation about love; it was a conversation about survival. Chai would have to figure out on her own, as Ia had, how to shelter and defend the parts of her that remained fragile.

In early October, what should be the heart of harvest's glory, Ia's fields are not golden. They are gray. Someone driving by might guess that the farmer died and the crop was then abandoned. But just because Ia's crop is poor does not mean that the demands on it have ceased. Pha Kao called, saying he needs money to defend himself in a lawsuit brought by a rubber farmer, who says Pha Kao's cattle ate his young trees. Thao will soon need money to return to Laos, once his paperwork goes through. If all goes as planned, Chai's visa and the attendant costs will need to be covered. And Ia herself needs money to go to Laos, on a month-long trip with her four daughters planned for just after Thanksgiving. Given the dismal state of the rice the sensible solution would be to cancel the trip, but the airline tickets have already been purchased, in what now feels like a long-ago moment of extravagance—a moment when Ia assumed that her crop would come through.

Right across the driveway, Youa's crop looks picture-perfect, with barely a weed in the field. If anything, the rice plants are too tall, too heavy with grain, so sections have begun to fall over with the weight of their success. There is no magic ingredient behind the crop. It had the same wet spring as Ia's, the same weak herbicides, the same aged bodies doing the work. The difference is that while Ia farms eight acres total, almost half of it in rice, Youa and Neng Her have just two acres, small enough to tend like a huge garden. Married now for fifty years, they are an inseparable team, and all summer they crawl down each row on hands and knees to hack out the weeds by the roots. To beat the heat, they arrive at the farm at 4 a.m. and start work by headlight.

Ia must endure the daily trauma of seeing this evidence of her comparative failure. When the vanloads of strangers in Hmong costume make their annual pilgrimages to shoot portraits and sing their wistful songs to the rice, this year they go to Youa's side of the driveway. After the Hmong news channel broadcasts a video from the farm to show that the harvest is in full swing, customers call Ia asking to buy some of her gorgeous crop. She must tell them it was Youa's field they saw. "If you want rice, call her."

After weeks of staring down her failing plants, Ia does the cold, hard math and determines it will be more profitable to harvest Youa's rice than to hunt and peck through her own fields. It is the ultimate humiliation. Publicly, she reasons that her crop is mostly just late, and harvesting theirs will tide her over. When she asks Youa for the privilege—because she has to ask for it—she frames it in mutual benefit: the field being so very full, Youa and Neng Her cannot possibly harvest all their rice before much will be destroyed by heat and birds; why not have Ia and Chou Lor take on some of the work? Youa agrees but says she will charge for each row. Ia haggles down the price, fueled by righteous bitterness that she is being charged at all. Still, even at $200 a row, her bottom line will be greater than if she were to let pride constrain her to her own puny crop.

———

Ia believes that once her crop matures fully, her children and their children will come out to help on the weekends. And when she starts harvesting a lot of rice, Jimmy will come to roast it; until then, though, he is at home, having been tapped to babysit his infant niece while her parents are at their jobs. For now, at the farm it is Ia and Chou Lor alone. Yesterday the two of them stayed harvesting their rows purchased from Youa until after all the golden light of sunset had drained from the sky. This morning they are processing it—thrashing, winnowing, roasting—so that tonight they can sell it and put some cash in the money bag.

In front of the shed, a gray tarp has been fashioned into some-thing like a kiddie pool, with Chou Lor in the middle. Ia has given him the sitting job of beating the grains off the stalks. He performs his task with passive, almost reverse execution—not slamming the bundle onto the milk crate, but rather using his limited energy to lift the bundle up, knowing that gravity will inevitably pull it back down, shattering the rice into the gray bowl at his feet. Each time he makes a fist around a new bundle of rice, the dry skin of his hands turns a bit more to dust.

Months now of retaining little or no food each day has left Chou Lor a dazed, empty version of himself. There has been medi-cation, but with little effect. There have been doctor's visits, though likely too few. His next appointment is not for another three weeks. He would like to quit the contract that binds him to the negligent care of Fresno PACE and seek help from more attentive doctors, but the paperwork to disenroll will take months. Until then, Chou Lor is left to roll the dice on meals of plain rice porridge and hope that he comes up lucky enough times to keep himself from starving before he can see the doctor again.

Ia has had progress with her shamanic investigation only inas-much as she has been able to rule out some causes, so far confirming that Chou Lor's sickness is definitely not the result of his offending the ancestors, nor of the ancestors needing something from him. Her latest thinking is that the torment is being inflicted by a girl-friend from long ago. This is not uncommon. After the lover dies in real life, his or her spirit will attempt to finally claim the object of long-ago affection by dragging that person into the afterworld. As of this morning, Ia suspects the woman Chou Lor took as his girlfriend shortly after they were married.

As Chou Lor beats rice off the stalks in the kiddie pool, Ia stands nearby, loudly recounting the details of this affair to Youa, who is seated across the yard. Ia describes how the woman was short, with squinty eyes that were too close together, too ugly to get a man of her own—an old maid. How Chou Lor gave this woman gifts, promised to marry her as his second wife. How the woman gave him her virginity, stealing away with him time after time to have sex in a secluded cave, stopping only after she was married off as someone else's second wife. How shortly after her marriage, the woman died when her husband cut down a tree and it landed on her head—blunt trauma.

When Chou Lor has beaten his way through the pile of rice bundles, he comes to stand beside Ia, who is winnowing her way through a wheelbarrow full of grain. He picks up his own flat, shallow basket, scoops in some rice, and mirrors her motions: hands flick the basket up, the contents jump skyward; basket falls down, the heavy grains drop back in while the papery chaff flies away on the breeze. Their hands work from memory, the movements so old that they have become automatic. Ia doesn't skip a beat as she continues her story of Chou Lor's adultery, says it must be because he lied about how he would marry the woman that she's come back to haunt him now.

"It's because I'm so good-looking that all my exes are coming," he says, his voice low but sly. "They want me."

Ia chuckles to herself, stops winnowing and lifts her head, smiles. Her voice cracks as she makes the joke: "You fucked her then, now she's fucking you!" Ia laughs so hard she must put her basket down. When Youa laughs, too, Ia repeats the line and throws her head back in hilarity. Her belly shakes, her eyes tear.

Chou Lor keeps flicking the basket, keeps staring down at the rice. But the corners of his eyes crinkle and his mouth softens into a laughing smile. There is nowhere for him to go but toward this twisted ridicule of his debilitating, monthslong illness.

Ia, still breathless from laughing, asks him if it was worth it—all that sex once upon a time for the misery of now. His grin widens, as if he is transported back to the afterglow of seventeen and his trysts in a cave, of holding this woman he loved then. Still staring down at his winnowing basket, he murmurs, "Uh-huh." *Yes, it was worth it.* In his words and in hers, it is hard to disentangle the strands of hurt, cruelty, comfort, and love. Perhaps that's because, over so many years, they have all fused together.

The laughter dies away. After the moment has dried up, they are still here, still winnowing, just quiet. With the motion of the work, a clean cotton pouch on a string necklace bounces its way from inside Chou Lor's shirt to the outside of his sweater, where it lies on his chest. It is a protective charm—this Ia will not joke about, not even discuss. The white of it brings out the jaundiced cast of his skin.

Chou Lor says he has no energy, needs to eat. It is only ten in the morning, but Ia tells him to cook the food she has brought for lunch and hands him a bag of chicken parts. While she begins roasting rice over the hearth, he heats a pot of oil and plops in the meat. He leans against the shed for support, stares blankly into the bubbling fryer. Beside him, Ia turns the rice with a hoe, scraping the mound away from her to the far edge of the cauldron and then sliding it back across the heat, over and over, the metallic rhythm of it both hypnotic and grating.

After Chou Lor pulls the fried chicken out onto a plate, he pours the oil onto the ground and sits at the table. Before he has even touched his food, Ia barks at him: Why did he dump out the oil? Why didn't he also prepare the pork ribs she brought, the soup she planned? Where is the water she told him to fetch?

Chou Lor rises from the table. He receives the hoe from her and takes over roasting so she can commence cooking. Twenty minutes later, when the batch on the hearth is done, he picks up the gray tarp and spreads it out so that the finished rice can be dried in the sun on top of it. As soon as it is flat on the ground, Ia yells at him for choosing the wrong tarp. She grabs the correct one and shakes it at him. He seems to barely register her discontent. "Fuck it," she mutters. "Use the gray one."

———

It is a year to the day that Ia and her girlfriends traded recipes for green banana Viagra in the field and gossiped over lunch. So far this year, no friends have shown up. People call, wanting to work in the field, but there is not enough rice, nor is there enough money to pay them. Ia must turn them away.

Still, she makes a feast with three kinds of rice and two kinds of pork and Chou Lor's cold fried chicken, lays it out across the grease-stained table in bowl after bowl after bowl. The only guests are Youa and Neng Her, who contribute a small offering of denture-soft eggplant, and who are not actually real guests. Ia sits and commences pushing the food anyway, insisting they must eat ever more.

Chou Lor takes his place beside Ia, in front of an empty bowl. For a long time he sits motionless, staring beyond the table into a private middle distance. His hunger has been displaced by something else. He tries mixing cold rice with bottled water into a tepid gruel. He tries tearing shreds of fried chicken off the bone and feeding them between his lips. Mostly he slumps forward, chin on his hand, silent as Ia eats noisily beside him. Eventually, he stands up without ceremony and returns to beating bundles of rice in the yard.

By the time he comes back to the shed, lunch is over and Ia has resumed roasting rice. Chou Lor drops onto the bench. When he opens his mouth, his voice lifts only enough to push the heavy words out. The pain in his stomach is not going away.

"Do you want to go home?" Ia asks in a voice that is softer than normal.

"I don't know," he says. "I don't have any energy left."

"Do you want to go home?" she asks again. "If you want to go home you can go." A pause. Chou Lor looks miserable. She can't stop raking the rice in the pan or it will burn.

"If you need to go home, go home," she says. "When it's time, I'll come home." Another pause. "I'm not going to go home, but you can."

"I don't know," Chou Lor says. "It's just my stomach…it's fine. It seems like I'm just—I have no energy."

He remains on the bench. She continues roasting. What else is there to say?

Ia keeps a distance between herself and Chou Lor's sickness, as if it is a child she is babysitting until the real mother comes back. She asks Chou Lor how he's feeling, and reserves a portion of her mind to worry about him at all times. But even as he punches new holes in his belt to adjust to his shrinking waist, it seems Ia cannot afford to fully acknowledge the severity of his condition. The system is too fragile as it is. With just the two of them picking—and with Chou Lor at half-mast—they'll harvest less rice, and inevitably miss some that could have been picked if only there were more people. As a result, they'll make less money, and the system will strain further. When Ia gets home each night, her family members tell her to just quit farming once and for all.

Her only path forward is to keep picking and roasting and selling, trying to block out the stress. The lightness and joy of last year's deliverance is out of reach, but the specter of a stroke and a wheelchair still looms. So she reaches for the bright side, saying that the rice in her fields actually looks pretty good given the amount of weeds, that the crop is mostly just late, that the full harvest still lies ahead. When she finishes roasting the rice they picked yesterday, she suits up and heads out to the next of their rows in Youa's field. Chou

Lor follows her. They reason that if he were to go home, he would just sit there with nothing to do but watch TV and simmer in illness. Here at the farm, work will distract him from his pain.

Wearing heavy rubber boots, Chou Lor stands in the flooded furrow and faces the rice like a wall. To stay out of the water, Ia steps up onto the row, above him, and wedges herself between plants so that she is picking them from within. These rows she chose are grandmother rice, planted from Youa's seed, and it is the same as Ia's in its best year. The plants all arch with the same perfect curve, so tall the grains hang down in front of Ia's face like a beaded curtain. Even fresh on the plant, they have a fragrance that is warm and browned as a campfire marshmallow. The red-winged blackbirds watch from the telephone wire. Dragonflies hover straight above.

For the afternoon, Ia and Chou Lor act out the scene in which their crop is as rich as it has ever been, laying the bundles to dry in the field, hauling heavy basketsful back to the shed. But the abundance is only on the surface. Ia can't have friends come to help, because then she would have to share this precious haul. She is not moved to call to her parents to join her, this being someone else's crop and not something of which she feels proud. Thao calls on the phone to ask where Ia's EBT card is, so he can buy some groceries. Otherwise, this whole afternoon it is just Chou Lor and Ia. They discuss logistics in short, lifeless spurts. Aside from that, they say little.

As they pick in silence, Ia keeps her eyes sharp on the plants before her. The rice is too precious to reserve the most perfect specimens as seed; everything that is mature will be roasted and sold. But when Ia comes upon a stalk that is past ripe and too dry to eat, she clips it and tucks it under her arm. When there are enough of these clutched against her side that her elbow sticks out and she risks losing her grip, she unloads them into her wicker basket. By the time the sunlight drains out of the sky, the bottom of the basket holds a thick layer of these seeds. Back in the shed, she will store them in a plastic bag in an old plastic container. Next year, she will take them out and plant them, and maybe things will be different.

———

For a whole month, Ia combs her fields for what rice it has produced and wrings out a paltry harvest. Finally, a week into November, she is ready to sell the last of it. She stores the buckets of rice in the garage, where she will mill it after dinner. Some women who call themselves her relatives are coming this evening to buy.

In the kitchen, daughters and daughters-in-law are slicing scallions and pork for pho, while the unmarried sons play video games in the bedroom they share. In the living room, one person holds the infant granddaughter for a while, then the next person does, and so on.

Chou Lor sits leaden on the sofa, more tired than usual. For days he has not been able to hold down any food, and while in some ways that is the new normal, tonight something seems more acute. Song is the first to notice. His skin is pale yellow. His breathing is heavy, now heavier. Before long, he can barely respond.

When Song tells him she is going to call 911, he summons a voice to protest. Seeing his pain, the family agrees she must make the call anyway. Fifteen minutes later, ambulance lights set the dark street ablaze. Paramedics march into the living room and quickly march out wheeling Chou Lor on a stretcher.

The children know their father has been sick; they have watched him disappear in an ambulance more than once this year. Somehow, they know this is different. A blue desperation falls over the house. One after another they cry out in shock and distress, *My dad's going to die!* Ia echoes them, softly, *He's probably going to die.*

Nobody knows what to do. The daughters finish making pho. Everybody eats. In an absurd act of hope, the women pack a serving to go and Jimmy leaves for the hospital to deliver the hot meal to his father.

Ia retreats to the garage and switches on the rice milling machine. Other women use food processors to get the hulls off their rice, burning through two or more of the little machines each season. Because Ia grows on such a grand scale, a few years ago, when she and Chou Lor went to Laos, they stuffed into their suitcases the various components of a mill. Here in the garage, Chou Lor patched it all together, rigging it to a lawn mower engine that now bellows like a machine gun as it strains to spin the belt that runs the rollers that split off the hulls so the rice can spit out clean and pretty from the chute.

The whole contraption shakes with effort, and behind it Ia's shoulders shake with weeping. The noise drowns out her sobs. She feels helpless, with no way to influence the situation: can't help treat Chou Lor's illness because she doesn't understand what's happening to his body; can't discuss it with the doctors because she doesn't speak English; can't even deliver him the hopeful bowl of pho because she doesn't have a driver's license, nor does she have a car. So she keeps ladling rice into the hopper of the mill until one bucket is full, then another and another. She packs the rice into old feed bags until there is a wall of them across the entrance to the garage.

When the women arrive to buy rice, Ia doesn't tell them a thing. Instead, she curls up her swollen face and makes pleasant conversation, until at last the women dip into their handbags for cash and stuff every last sack of rice into their cars. The season is now officially over. The long winter begins.

There are no seasons in a hospital, no indication of fall versus spring beyond the holiday decorations on the nurses' station or the clothes worn by those who visit. Temperature is constant, routines invariable. The sun itself—rising, setting—is apparent only to those who have a window and, more, choose to look through the glass.

Ia sits in a chair, facing away from the window. Above her is a painting of a country road lined with trees whose leaves have turned the reds and golds of autumn, half of them already fallen on the ground. Beside her is Chou Lor, his cotton gown lying in loose folds over his bandaged abdomen. Ia's days are spent waiting for good news from the doctors, then nights are spent trying to slip beyond the incessant beeping of machines in order to fall asleep on the plasticky couch. Morning nurses' rounds start the cycle over again. She and Jimmy switch off at this post; the one who is off duty tags out mostly for real sleep at home, to enable his or her return to the hospital. First it was weeks of this, now months. New Year's has come and gone, and still, they are no closer to bringing Chou Lor home.

The doctors have chased the illness across Chou Lor's midsection, starting at the original corrosion in his stomach and following the trail of malfunction to duodenum to bile duct to pancreas. After the first surgery, the doctor predicted Chou Lor would be discharged in days. With the second surgery, there were promises this would all be over soon—so much that in late November, the children shooed Ia off to Laos on the trip she had planned with her daughters. When she returned, exhausted and broke, Chou Lor was worse than when she had left. After the third surgery, though, the doctors repeated a mantra: *If all goes well, he can go home this week.* And yet it never goes well. Or it does, then the progress is erased—the Jell-O he could eat yesterday is verboten today. Gradually, his face thins into sharp relief. His eyes lose their shine.

Ia observes this all intently, but her actual information is limited. By law, the hospital is required to provide an interpreter twenty-four hours a day. Each time, though, this service must be requested and then waited for. At times, there is a Hmong nurse on duty who can fill in. Otherwise, the surgeons use diagrams to explain what part of the digestive system they will extract next, and the nurses just wait and communicate with Ia's children when they come, assuming they will relay everything to the parents. Instead, the kids skim off a portion and feed it to Ia and Chou Lor in small bites. Ia thinks it's because they want to protect her from the worst parts or from the magnitude of the trauma. But that is assuming they themselves understand the doctor's concerns about the hepatic duct or the need for a cholangiogram. Or, if they did understand, that they would know how to translate terms like "gastric bypass" and "contrast medium" into Hmong. Ia gives her children questions to ask of the doctors to clarify, but, similarly, the kids transform her many words into few, or none. She suspects that they are too shy to query the doctors, or that they think she is being pushy.

When her children are not there, Ia sits on the couch with her legs dangling over the side, not long enough to reach the floor, and silently watches the nurses attend to her husband. Her torso is still, her eyes hawklike, but her bare feet twitch wildly. Her mind is screaming. *Why haven't you given him pain medication yet? Why is he not allowed liquid today? When will the doctor be here? Can't you see he is in pain?*

Then the nurses leave and she and Chou Lor are alone, sometimes for hours. Ia massages his aching legs as best she can; always he begs for more. Sometimes she turns on the TV for him; sometimes she cries to him. Often they are simply just there, he staring straight out from the two o'clock angle of his bed, she sitting in the simple chair with her back against the same wall as he, her eyes fixed on the same empty space ahead. In these times, she returns to one topic over and over, kneading it with her thoughts. *Why are we alone? Where are the people who are supposed to be here?*

Not the children—she understands that they must work, and they come as often as their schedules allow. It is all the other relatives, the web of clan members who should be here bringing food and crying along and showing that Chou Lor's little family is part of something bigger and stronger than just themselves. Back in October, Ia's phone never stopped ringing, with all those people calling her "auntie" and "daughter-in-law" in order to get at what little rice she had to sell. Now it seems they have forgotten her.

The absence of visitors saddens Ia, as it would anyone in her situation. There is more to it than just her hurt, though, and this is the territory where her brain ranges wildly during the long hours at the hospital. The clan is the foundation of Hmong life and its elaborate fabric of ceremonies and gatherings. But the Khang clan is small, and Chou Lor's place within it is weak; that his brothers were all dead before he even left Laos means he has no automatic allies within the group here in California. If the clan is not showing up at the hospital while Chou Lor is still alive, one can guess they won't be there if he dies. And yet the complex ritual of the funeral can be performed only by clan members; without them, Chou Lor's soul could not be properly guided to the land of the ancestors. Ia could not bear for him to suffer like that, eternally wandering the gray world between life and afterlife.

The clan members should be bound by duty to perform the funeral—she hopes that will prove true. Even so, their absence at the hospital suggests a more tangible, more blighted fate. It could be that once Chou Lor dies, the clan will abandon Ia and her children, just as her mother and Pha Kao were abandoned by their clan after her father's death.

It is not supposed to be that way; clans are obligated to take care of all members. And yet it is all too common. Protocol is for men to call men with invitations to gatherings, and without a man to call, it is easy to forget the rest of the family. So it is said. Perhaps more true is that when this happens it is because other families have little use for widows and their children, unless the sons have come into their own power within the clan—and Ia's sons have not. The orphan family may not be invited to participate in rituals and gatherings because, without a spiritually competent man to perform the cere-monies, the family cannot reciprocate with rituals and gatherings of its own. When this happened to Ia's mother and Pha Kao, the result was poverty and hunger.

Ia has plenty of food. What torments her during the unending hours at her husband's bedside is imagining her devaluation: having worked so hard for so long to elevate her family—despite Chou Lor's addict father, despite Chou Lor's own slow wit—only to be demoted to worthless widow simply because the man beside her died. At times it feels as though Chou Lor has been her life's greatest obstacle. Yet without him, she fears she will no longer exist.

She agonizes about this to Chou Lor and her children—not the whole chain of consequences, but the lack of visitors. Thao urges her to let it go. If she has already summoned Chou Lor's relatives and they have failed to come, worrying about it is not going to make them materialize. Thao tells her, *We, your children, are here.* But that does nothing to beat back the fire raging inside Ia's head. She obsesses over her abandonment as if it has already happened. At times over the winter, Thao worries more about his mother than he does about Chou Lor.

Perhaps it is not a coincidence, then, that when the lease for Ia's farm comes up in early January, she pays down the coming year's rent without hesitation. Her kids try to dissuade her from farming as she has in the past, saying that with Chou Lor in the hospital the family system of covering for one another is already maxed out; that because they all have jobs (and Jimmy is split between the hospital and babysitting the youngest granddaughter), there will be no one to help her during the week, and they don't want to relegate their weekends to farmwork. Ia rents the whole eight acres anyway. It is possible Chou Lor will be healthy again by spring, she argues. Even if not, she will at least hold on to the land for the following year.

Then in February, because the weather is dry and she doesn't want to get rained out like last year, Ia pays out more to have the furrows laid, after which—factoring in what she had paid in November for disking—she has invested a total of $6,000. She reasons that the only way to make the money back will be to farm this year. She reasons further that if Chou Lor were to die she must farm to support herself—where else would she find an income? Also, she must farm to support Alice, who is still in high school, and to whom she has promised a down payment on a car. And like that, the idea of farming this year slips from the hypothetical to the inevitable.

From the outset, the logistics are taxing. The farm is twenty-five minutes from their house, without traffic. Ia rides along as Mee brings the second-youngest granddaughter to school, then Ia is dropped at the farm. Jimmy spends the afternoon babysitting the infant grand-daughter, and after the girl's mother comes home, he drives to the farm and picks up Ia. If Ia sleeps at the hospital, Jimmy has to drive all the way north to the hospital to get her in the morning, then all the way southwest to the farm, which means either rising at dawn or slogging through rush-hour traffic. More and more, Jimmy is the one to stay overnight with Chou Lor so Ia can sleep at home.

Chou Lor is hurt that Ia is leaving him alone at the hospital. But as she sees it, spending day after day at his bedside is pointless. She can't have a conversation with anyone beyond the Hmong custodial worker who comes to remove the soiled linens. And ultimately it is the doctors who are treating Chou Lor, not her. *There's nothing really that we can do,* she thinks. *It's not like if we're there he's going to get better, or if we're not there he won't.*

So, quietly, she shifts her time from the perpetual autumn of the hospital to the vital, dynamic winter of the farm. There the rains for which Californians wait all year are summoning life from within the gray dirt. Last year's rice plants and weeds endure only as dried-out bones, buried in place, but from their remains sprout green grass as bright as Astroturf.

———

For Thao, there is finally good news. The paperwork required for him to marry Chai is complete in early January. It's later than origi- nally expected, but that doesn't matter now—the rest will happen so fast. Thao laughs about the process for the fiancé visa, which seemed easy in the beginning and then later became impossible. Getting married is proving to be just the opposite: a maze of bureaucracy to start, and now, nearing the finish line, a breeze. "There are no sur- prises at the end," he says solidly. Soon he and Chai will be married and then the embassy cannot reject her.

Chai, annealed by the repeated disappointments that have pre- ceded this moment, is more pragmatic. She knows that once she and Thao are married and the paperwork is delivered to the Americans, there will be more physicals, blood tests, drug tests, scheduling, in- terviews, and likely more waiting between each step. "It will take time," she says stoically. In the months that have passed since Thao left, Chai has also become more pragmatic about their personal relationship. When they argue, she accepts it as an innate part of their marriage—almost structural. She unloads her frustrations on him, and when he can no longer handle the conversation, he passes the phone to Ia.

When the paperwork goes through, Chai has entered the aching-back stage of pregnancy, the no-position-feels-comfortable-for-sleeping and peeing-in-your-pants stage. Thao says she is being a wimp—teases her that when he comes to Laos, he will have to take care of two babies, the little one and the big, mama one. Still, their conversations are buoyed by their rapidly crystallizing image of the child that is due to be born on February 26. Chai can see the feet kicking, can feel the hardness of the head as it pushes her belly out. Thao shows people in Fresno the ultrasound photos on his phone, excitedly interpreting the images that are unreadable to anyone but him and Chai. Though the fetus is sitting high and therefore pre-senting as a boy, the doctor says it is a girl. Ia tells them that's a good thing. When they are tired from working, a daughter will make sure dinner is cooked by the time they get home. A son would claim he doesn't know how to cook or that he's too young, and they would have to forgive him. Boys, Ia says, are overrated.

Now Thao's main concern is that his father will get well enough to return home before he must leave for Laos. He pushes his departure to February, figuring that way he can do it all in one trip: get married, have a baby, get the visa. The three of them will fly home together right around when the rice is planted in Fresno. After Chou Lor's third operation takes place in mid-January, the doctors say, *If all goes well, he can go home this week*. But the Jell-O is again given and then taken away. At the end of the month he still has not eaten. By the time Thao must leave for the airport on the tenth of February, no more progress has been made. He says goodbye to his father in the hospital room.

Once Thao is on the plane, a different urgency sets in. Chai's due date is more than two weeks off, but she has been having contractions for a week already. The challenge is that once Chai gives birth, she must remain in bed for thirty days. By law they must be married in Muong Cha, now called Xaysomboun, which is the capital of Chai's father's province, where Chai legally resides—and which is four hours away. For this, Thao timed his flight so he would arrive two weeks before she gave birth, leaving ample time to make the trip, get married, and file the paperwork; in the plan, the thirty days of bed rest doubled as a month of waiting on the embassy. If they can't get married before Chai goes into labor, the plan will be delayed a whole month by the bed rest, and who knows what other obstacles might arise during that time? The day before Thao's flight, the doctor informs Chai that the baby has dropped and rotated into position. "Any day now," Thao says nervously, "this balloon is gonna pop."

At the last minute, Thao's cheap ticket through China is rerouted through Taiwan and Vietnam—a longer trip, but he arrives a day early, on a Wednesday evening. First thing Friday morning, Chai and Thao are driving the four bumpy hours to Xaysomboun. Before noon, they are assembled in a spare room within the provincial government building. It is February 14, Valentine's Day, and while that is a meaningless distinction in Laos, the local official who performs the perfunctory ceremony declares that, numerically, it is an auspicious day to be married. The union is witnessed by two additional government workers, plus the man and woman in whose house Chai has been living for the past few years. Pha Kao is not there. In his place, Chai's oldest brother has come to give her away.

The event does not look like the wedding portrait that Thao and Chai had made in the photo studio. She wears a long, blue, flowered dress with a lacy collar and a high waist to accommodate the baby bulging out from her middle. Thao wears black pants and a black golf shirt. The backdrop is a window covered in a grate, with a weed whacker below it on the ground. But in this portrait, they hold the paper with the exact Lao words and the necessary signatures and the stamped, passport-style photos that altogether prove, at last, that they are bound to each other for life. In this portrait, their smiles are not posed; they are irrepressible.

One week later, Chai gives birth. The baby is healthy and Chai comes through the delivery unharmed. When they are allowed to leave the hospital, they return to the house. The windowless bedroom where Chai has spent the past four years with her bags packed to leave becomes the first home for the new family.

Thao himself adjusts to life as a parent as best he knows how. He can't bear to eat only chicken and rice each day, but he is willing to cook the customary meals for Chai in order to set her and the baby off on the right track. When his enthusiasm for this caretaking job begins to lag, Chai gets on the phone to Ia and then Ia gets on the phone to Thao, telling him to work harder—and he does. Ia pays for a shaman to perform the ritual that calls the baby's soul into her body. Now complete, the child is given her name: Emma, which, being American, means nothing in Hmong. As February becomes March, it feels as though everything is falling into place, at last.

When Thao's flight to Laos was rerouted, it was because the United States had suspended all flights to China. A novel coronavirus had surfaced in the city of Wuhan, and the air travel ban was intended to prevent its migration to North America. The day Thao checked in at the San Francisco airport was a milestone: the virus had killed one thousand people worldwide.

One month later, Fresno has its first case of the coronavirus. While the illness is present in eighty-four countries, the shape of it is still unknown. The danger to nursing homes has been recognized, but not yet the danger to meatpacking plants. The Centers for Disease Control recommends that people avoid gatherings of 250 people or more but discourages the use of face masks. The *Fresno Bee* publishes a video interview with a barefaced infectious disease specialist who reiterates the now constant message that people need to wash their hands religiously and cover their mouths when they sneeze. Otherwise, he cautions, viewers should not overreact.

One week later, Fresno County declares a state of emergency. Schools close. California's governor asks seniors and those with chronic illnesses to isolate at home. Shoppers crowd stores to stockpile toilet paper, hand sanitizer, disinfecting wipes, canned food. And rice. Commodity futures are sinking globally but the price of rice is rising, as people from Hanoi to Hong Kong to Saint Paul buy as many sacks as they can get their hands on. To even enter Asia Supermarket in Fresno, customers must first wait in a line that stretches the length of the building. When the store imposes a limit of two fifty-pound bags per family, some families magically split into two so they can buy double that.

Fresno's shamans are suddenly booked solid with sick people wanting treatment and healthy people wanting protective rituals, both unknowing that the ceremonies themselves—for which dozens of relatives are gathered into stuffy kitchens and living rooms smoky with incense—are optimal conditions for infection. Hmong radio crackles with recipes for preventive herbal tonics and assurances that Hmong will not contract the coronavirus because they have strong immune systems from living in the mountains in Laos. Local government agencies scramble to translate public health information into Hmong, Spanish, and Punjabi, finagling their own spots on Fresno's non-English radio stations and Facebook pages to push out their countermessage that, in fact, the coronavirus can infect anyone.

Ia has never been one to listen to the news, and she is not worried. The family is so consumed by Chou Lor's illness that by the time Ia's daughter-in-law rushes out to Costco, the shelves are bare. The family laughs that when they run out of toilet paper they will just use water from the sink. And rice is taken care of: even though last year's harvest was meager, many bucketsful saved for the family's own consumption remain in the garage.

After a son warns Ia that the police might arrest her if she goes to the farm, she resumes spending most of her time at the hospital. Social distancing restrictions mandate that only one person is allowed in the room with Chou Lor at a time. Because Ia can't communicate with most of the medical staff, her main source of daily information is the Hmong custodial worker. The woman tells her that Fresno now has two coronavirus patients, and one of them is being treated in this hospital, on this same floor. She advises Ia to wash her hands often.

———

After his third surgery, Chou Lor was moved to a new room with a different painting of autumn leaves. Now around his wrist is a jumble of bracelets: hospital ID bands in numerous colors, as well as pieces of string tied on by well-wishing relatives, who finally came when his condition began looking grave. Ia tries to help him by conducting a thorough shaman investigation. She also buys a medicine supposedly made from rhinoceros bile and sneaks it onto his abdominal wounds. Nothing prevents his deterioration.

By mid-March, Chou Lor's veins collapse under months of IVs. His legs are more bone than meat and they ache without respite. For pain the hospital gives him Tylenol every four hours; ninety minutes after swallowing the pills, he pleads for more. *Take me home,* he begs Ia. *I can't stay here anymore.* When a doctor visits the room, Chou Lor becomes excited, telling Jimmy to pack his things because it's time to go at last. But over and over, to the point of cruelty, the doctors say Chou Lor will be able to leave soon and then rescind the order—because his temperature is too high, or his final lab work comes back wrong.

In the third week of March, Chou Lor finally breaks. *I'm not going to go home,* he cries to Ia. *I'm going to die here.* After he alarms the staff with erratic behavior, nurses tie his arms to the bed as a caution against self-harm.

Two days later, Chou Lor becomes fixated on a desire to eat pho. *Let's go,* he says to Ia and Song. *We'll sneak out of here.* They say no, of course, and he says please, and they say no again. Gradually, Ia soothes him, steering his mind away from pho and back to the hospital room, where his arms are still tied to the bed. After some time, he seems to surrender. Then Song tells him it is time for her and Ia to leave, and that they will return tomorrow.

Don't come back tomorrow, he says. *I'm not going to be here.*

Song tells him again that she will come back the next day.

I won't be here, he repeats. *I'm going to die tomorrow.*

Then he addresses Ia. *I'll be the first to go. You will be the second. Don't worry, I'll wait for you.*

The next day Chou Lor is still there, lying in the same hospital bed, tortured by the same din of beeping machines and clacking keyboards, by the anonymous moans floating down the hall and into his room. As Ia sits nearby, he rattles his arms under the restraints, trying to break free. Then, suddenly, he stops. Ia looks at his face: his eyes are white. She shakes him. He is limp. She yells for the doctors. She cries for an interpreter.

The doctor listens to Chou Lor's heart, then runs to the door and yells his own pleas for help. The room fills with people, but there is little they can do. After so many surgeries, Chou Lor's torso is too delicate for chest compressions. Ia watches them give him a shot but it seems to have no effect. A man arrives and begins praying beside the bed. There is an interpreter now, and he tells Ia that the doctors say for her to stop crying, that Chou Lor has been suffering for so long already, that his body is tired of fighting, and she will have to let him go. Ia grabs Chou Lor, holds him, and cries more.

In the chaos, Ia called Song and told her to rush to the hospital with the rest of the children if they wanted to see their father one last time. Now Song enters the room and weeps alongside her mother.

As they tell the story, Chou Lor's heart has been stopped for twenty minutes when he opens his eyes. He tells them he has been to heaven. At judgment, the justice told Chou Lor that he was innocent and loyal, and therefore it was not his time to die. Chou Lor was sent back to earth. *I'm not going to die anymore,* he says gleefully, crazily. *I'm going to live forever and everything will be okay.* The doctor is aghast. Song is overjoyed. Ia feels she might pass out.

There is no miraculous recovery. Chou Lor has ups of sleeping at night and downs of insisting that it is time for him to go. His legs continue to ache, and the Tylenol continues to be ineffective. Ia now has a hospital-issued tablet with which to contact an interpreter by video, but the voice only relays back the nurses' message that there is nothing more they can do to help Chou Lor. At the very end of March, in the middle of the night, he stops breathing again. Ia is awake, watching over him, and sees that he has turned stiff, cold. Nurses rush in, doctors try everything, and eventually Chou Lor is resuscitated. This time, though, he returns with no divine message, only silence.

Chou Lor can still understand when he is spoken to, but his own voice has become fragile. Ia puts her ear to his lips in order to hear. Even as he must drag each individual word out from the back of his throat, he continues to declare his desire to go home. Song is in charge of all medical decisions, and so it is she who petitions the doctor to allow the family to bring Chou Lor home. The answer is unequivocally no. Twice now Chou Lor has had to be resuscitated. Were a similar episode to happen at home, there would be no one to help him. He would not survive the wait for an ambulance and the transport to qualified care. The doctor cannot sign an order that he knows could likely lead to death.

The doctor believes that to live, Chou Lor needs another operation, to remove his spleen. But he has grown so weak that he looks as though he is made out of paper. Before he can undergo surgery, he will need to regain his strength. The doctor explains that the hospital is not a good place to convalesce, and as he speaks perhaps he pictures the storm cloud of coronavirus gathering on the horizon. The best place, the doctor says, is a rehab facility, where Chou Lor can get fresh air and physical therapy, with round-the-clock medical care. The hospital will begin looking for an open room at a local facility.

When the state of California issued its shelter in place order on March 19, it deemed agriculture "essential work." Farmworkers did not receive the window signs of gratitude or car parades that health care workers and teachers did, but they were free to continue their labor while the rest of the state stayed home. When Ia heard from others that everyone was back at the farm, she suddenly felt that she was behind schedule.

When she returns in April, the bare, open ground of the farm no longer represents possibility and life. Rather, it lays out very starkly that every single thing that needs doing between now and the end of the season—all the watering and weeding, planting and harvesting—has yet to be done. Further, it will more or less all have to be done by her—she is reminded of this every time a son or daughter drops her at the farm and then promptly leaves for an obligation elsewhere.

As Chou Lor has become thinner, Ia has gained weight from sitting on the plasticky couch and worrying all winter. Her cheeks have turned to jowls; her stomach hangs down enormously. There is no specific injury in her body, but she moves listlessly from the shed to the furrows, hauling armloads of plastic sheeting or pushing a wheelbarrow half filled with dirt. She laments that there is no man here to do the heavy work. In truth, though, she is stymied equally by muscle and by knowledge. The farm is her creation, and yet it entails so many necessary tasks that she has never done: engineering the network of irrigation pipes and tubing, leveling the furrows so they are neither too deep nor too shallow. They are the things that Chou Lor always did in the background of her mighty, bossy days. Now Ia must learn how to do these things, and do them all herself.

At the hospital, she puts her ear to Chou Lor's lips. He whispers that he wants her to stop farming. It's just her now, and it's too much. *Besides,* he says, *who cares? Let it go.* Ia sits up and replies in her normal voice that she has already spent a lot of money on the season, too much to forfeit. She offers that if he is not better by June, then she will skip planting a whole plot of long beans. If he is not well enough to help her next year, they will quit farming altogether. This year, though, she will plant rice and just a few vegetables, the melons that are already in the soil, some peppers and pumpkins. He pushes out one word: *Okay.* Then she leans close to him, and after a pause he tells her, a few wispy words at a time, how to fix a section of the long bean field that flooded last year.

With his voice in her head, Ia returns to the farm. First she must shovel out the end of the furrows, where the tractor driver allowed the dirt to mound up. After that she'll need to run the irrigation to make sure the water doesn't pool, then cover the rows in black plastic, then employ her children or hire workers to drive in fence posts every eight feet and crisscross twine across it all to make a trellis for the beans. Three acres of this, more than two football fields' worth. When she digs into the mounded end of the furrow, the dirt comes up as a single hulking clod. She places it back down, whacks it with her shovel, and it crumbles into dozens of little nuggets, which she must then scoop like slippery beans up and out onto the path. Every few rows, she flattens out the dirt she has placed on solid ground; as she rakes her shovel across the clods, dust flies off in the breeze like smoke from a fire. Her eyes fill with tears.

The memories of how Chou Lor beat her still occupy the same places they always have, sitting low and hard on their dark thrones. Between them, though, there are now openings where other memories can emerge. Ia recalls how last fall, when Chou Lor couldn't even eat, he still worked alongside her until the rice was all in. As this space in her mind opens, she recognizes that in fact he has been her partner for far more of her life than he has not—every night that he worked the graveyard shift at the chicken plant to pay their rent, but also back further, into their childhood: When he pulled her across the Mekong in the middle of the night. When she followed him through the forest of thorns. When he stood watch with his rusty rifle as she gleaned rice from an abandoned field.

This revelation is bittersweet, of course, for the new space in her mind comes only out of the empty space created by Chou Lor's absence. Ia is able to see how essential he has been to her because she knows he may soon be gone for good. When talking to him at the hospital, she stays upbeat, telling him that if he were going to die it would've happened already. *It's been months now and you're still here,* she tells him, *so I think you'll be okay.* But when she looks at his withered legs, she can't imagine how they could ever be strong again. In her heart, she feels certain that this monthslong story at the hospital has a bad ending. And when she imagines losing Chou Lor, she can't picture how she will then be able to carry her own life forward.

Ia spends more and more of her time at the farm. She throws down hundreds of dollars more for plastic sheeting and herbicides. She coaxes her youngest children to spend their weekends helping her. When she finally goes to the hospital to visit Chou Lor, he beckons her close and whispers, *How come you never come to visit and stay with me? How come you're always at the farm?*

She replies as honestly as she can. *Don't you know it's because of the farm that I'm still alive?* she says. *If it weren't for the farm I would have died first, before you.*

———

By the middle of April, the coronavirus SARS-CoV-2 has become a global pandemic. There are now two million cases in roughly 180 countries. Citizens of all nationalities watch in horror as the worldwide death toll creeps up daily, hitting the unconscionable number of a hundred thousand dead on April 9—and then just climbing more. The International Monetary Fund predicts the greatest global economic contraction since the Great Depression. At the same time, the price of rice hits its highest mark in seven years, as the world's top exporting countries pause selling their grain outside national borders for fear of domestic shortages. In Fresno, frantic women call Ia begging for seed so they can plant rice crops this year to ensure that they will not go without. *Name your price,* they say. *We'll pay whatever you want.*

For Thao and Chai, life continues relatively unchanged. Laos has only six confirmed cases of the coronavirus, and while there will be economic pain to come from the stalled global economy and its diminished need for the things the country has to sell—rubber, timber, electricity—that is still in the future. Thao and Chai spend their days eating papaya salad and luxuriating in the blissful bubble of new parenthood. They primp their infant daughter in one frilly dress after another. They cocoon her delicate hands in tiny mittens, her downy hair in a white turban decorated with hearts.

Thao's grand plan, or at least hope, was for them all to leave for Fresno on April 16—he envisioned walking into the embassy with the baby and being handed visas for her and Chai. But at the end of March, Laos went into lockdown as a precaution. The American embassy in Vientiane was shuttered indefinitely: no paperwork, no interviews, no visas. Thao could leave on a charter flight to Los Angeles arranged to evacuate American citizens, but Chai and the baby could not. Thao feels ripped in half. He aches to go home, knowing that his father appears to be dying in Fresno. But Ia counsels him to remain in Laos. Now that he has his own family, he must put them first. Because his bank account is nearly empty, she wires him some money to live on.

In California, life has been turned upside down. For a month, people have been ordered to shelter in place, leaving home only for essential services. Optimists are forecasting that the curve has been flattened and President Trump prepares to unveil his reopening plan for the nation's economy. And yet no one even knows for sure how the illness is contracted. Can the virus be transmitted by touching one's face? By flushing a toilet? How many asymptomatic carriers are out there right now? Is the coronavirus vastly more widespread than is known and thus totally overblown? Or is it actually more deadly than anyone realizes?

One thing that is known is that the San Joaquin Valley is especially vulnerable. The population has drastically high rates of the poverty-related, preexisting conditions that predispose coronavirus patients to severe illness and death, among them diabetes, obesity, hypertension, and asthma from the gray valley air. At the same time, the valley has a chronic shortage of hospital beds and medical professionals; should one doctor be lost to the coronavirus, it would have a resounding impact. Three weeks after the first case was reported in Fresno, local first responders were already running low on personal protective equipment. The county health department pleaded with residents to donate any unused gloves or masks they had at home.

It is against this backdrop that Ia's family finally gets their wish: the doctor says Chou Lor may go home. It is not because Chou Lor is well enough to leave the hospital—he is still barely more than a skeleton. But when the doctor insisted that the family send him to a rehab facility, they refused. They knew well enough that doing so might be sentencing their father to death, and not just because of the virus. Under lockdown, no one would be allowed to visit Chou Lor; he seemed just as likely to die from the isolation as from the disease. At the same time, Chou Lor's pancreas showed the first signs of repair. This opened the door for the doctor to change his position. He said he recognized that in addition to all the other ailments, the patient was suffering from acute homesickness. For that, there was only one cure. Maybe once home, the rest of the body would follow in healing.

Or maybe the doctor recognized that there was no safe option for a body this compromised in a system this broken in the face of a burgeoning pandemic. This hospital would surely soon swell with coronavirus patients, and likely have too little protective gear to contain their contagion. Nursing homes were known to be incubators for the disease. And yet Chou Lor's home would hardly be a sterile environment. There would be relatives coming and going from work, children with dirty hands, teenagers flouting commands to socially distance from their friends. Every path that lay before Chou Lor was perilous. Perhaps the doctor figured the man should at least feel happy.

The day that Chou Lor is to be released, his family speaks in code. This way, whatever evil spirits have been plaguing him will not know to follow his body home from the hospital. The family speaks of bringing him to pick vegetables, and never refers to him by name. Further, they do not tell their father in advance, for if the doctor changes his mind at the last minute again, that alone might finish Chou Lor. Alice goes to the hospital and slowly changes him out of his gown and into the clothes of a healthy person, mumbling something about how he needs to get dressed for an X-ray. At home, Song prepares the hospital bed that Fresno PACE has provided.

When there are no more possible barriers, a hospital social worker informs Chou Lor that he will go home today. He still can barely talk, but he smiles back at her as brightly as a tree in springtime. When his wheelchair passes through the hospital's sliding doors, it is the first time in five months that he has breathed fresh air. Here in Fresno, it is a perfect Wednesday, in the high 70s, with pure sunshine. In every direction the horizon is dingy with smog, but it is easy to look past that. Straight up, the sky is only blue.

———

Ia is not at the hospital, nor is she waiting for Chou Lor at his destination. Other wives would be, but this is the week that the Hmong farmers begin planting rice—it's the same every year. Ia started on Monday morning, returned on Tuesday, and today she's at the farm again.

In truth, she is compelled as much by custom as by urgency: Jimmy is effectively the only man she has now, and as soon as Chou Lor is home, Jimmy will switch to serving as his father's nurse.

Before Ia loses him from the farm full-time, she needs to squeeze as much work out of him as possible. There is also the larger urgency, the perpetual urgency, of money. Ia is broke from paying multiple shamans to help Chou Lor. Thao needs her to send money so he can feed his new family in Laos. Pha Kao also says he needs money, to repair their father's grave. And each morning Ia wakes up with all the thousands of dollars she has already put into the farm this year staring her in the face, reminding her she needs to earn them back.

So Ia enlists Jimmy to punch the holes in the ground where the rice will be planted. To fill the holes with seed, she hires a stranger, a grandmother who lives in Minnesota but is stranded in California by coronavirus restrictions. Ia informs the woman she will be paid by the row, not by the hour.

And of course Ia is there, too, bent over at the hips, shuttling rice into the ground as fast as she can. She holds the seed at her waist in the old pouch that suggests a polyester deer hide, in places now rubbed bare of its hair. On top of it, though, is a new black silk money bag, embroidered with a Chinese seal the color of dollar bills and fastened with a gold safety pin. On her shirt, another, fatter gold safety pin has replaced the cheap drugstore one that normally fastens the V-neck. The heart-shaped pendant her children gave her for Mother's Day years ago has been swapped out for a hefty gold medallion she bought herself. Her chest is as white as fluorescent hospital lights, and against the skin the new necklace glows.

The field has also had a good luck makeover. At no small cost, each of the 160 rows has been covered in skintight black plastic that blocks out sunlight, so that weeds cannot grow. It is a blunt weapon, more mercenary than artful. Altogether, though, these armored rows present the farm as something more formal than before, something to be taken seriously. From the road, they read not as more dull dirt in this dry desert but as rolling waves of dark water, a shining black ocean reflecting the blue back into the sky.

Ia hopes the plastic means the rice will not drown in weeds come July; it is her only hope for farming this almost four acres of rice without Chou Lor's help. The trade-off is that the punishing work of planting is inflamed by all the extra steps required. The combination of the stretched plastic and the soft soil underneath means that the hole that Jimmy's dibble stick makes is both too small and too deep. The women must use both hands to rip the opening in the plastic into a wide gash, then fill the hole with soil, and only then sift in seed and cover it over as normal. The process takes six seconds instead of the normal three, which seems manageable on its own but when multiplied by sixty-four thousand holes means roughly four extra days of work, four extra days of purple pain spreading exponentially across the lower back, the hips.

No one says out loud that the finished product looks like a treasure map for pigeons, each hole in the plastic marking exactly where they should peck for rice. Ia cannot think about that, especially since last year's poor crop left her short on seed. She keeps her back flat and her eyes straight down. Right hand budgets out six seeds per hole, left hand covers it with soil using the little tool made from one side of a pair of tongs. Two hundred holes up the east side of the row, two hundred holes down the west. Three rows, maybe, then a rest in the driveway. Ten rows, then a break in the shed.

Ia and the hired woman go in together, but mostly Ia acts as though she's alone—talking on the phone, quiet on the bench. Beside her on the lunch table is Chou Lor's hat, grimy with dust. Outside the door, the bundles of twine that only he would have wound into tidy coils. On the ground, a bucket full of crooked nails and other scrap metal that he sifted out of the hearth's ashes and never had a chance to redeem for cash.

Ia is in the middle of a row, deep in the afternoon, when her phone rings from inside the money bag. She stands up and answers, "What is it?"

She listens to her daughter's voice.

"Okay."

A pause.

"So he just got home now? It took all that time?"

A pause.

"Okay, as long as he's there."

That's it. She doesn't say goodbye, just slips the phone into her bag as she bends back down to face the earth. Her face is blank, as if hardened against expressing anything. She dips her hand into the pouch at her waist and reloads her fist with seeds.

Other wives would act differently in this moment. But Ia is not thinking about right now. She is thinking about what comes next—not *wife,* but *widow.* She knows too well that the word is nearly the same as the word for "orphan." And she has already been orphaned too many times for one life. Other wives might accept the abandonment that awaits them once their husband is gone. In a sense, Ia's life's work has been to make it so she doesn't have to. Of course she is here at the farm right now, and of course she will continue planting until the blue fades from the sky. With this rice, she will never be alone.

For a while, it seemed as though everything was going to be okay. Fresno PACE had assumed they would be arranging hospice care for Chou Lor, but the family insisted that he be set up to live. In addition to the hospital bed, Song made sure there was a wheelchair and a visiting physical therapist, to get him walking again. His torso was a mess of tubing, with a drainage in his front and another in his back, plus a G tube to his stomach and a J tube to his intestines. Within a day, Ia dispensed with the prescribed packets of nutritional formula and began feeding him real food by mouth. When he said he wanted pho, Song cooked it for him from scratch. Chou Lor devoured the meatballs and slurped down the rich broth, emptying his bowl. He told them all defiantly, *I'm never getting sick again.*

A few weeks in, the drainage tubes dislodged from his torso and Chou Lor was brought to the doctor. The family members in attendance murmured that yes, they were feeding him nutritional formula as directed. In their minds, though, the visit only vindicated their approach: a CT scan showed that his pancreas was healing, so much so that the drainage tubes were not replaced. When, a month later, the J tube fell out, it was also retired. The doctor was pleased by

Chou Lor's progress. Back at home, the physical therapist cheered as Chou Lor walked five feet and then ten, to the kitchen island, then to the front door, then around the kitchen island and to the door and all the way back to the sofa.

As spring turned to summer, Chou Lor was able to put himself in the wheelchair and go to the bathroom without assistance. He gained weight. He held his infant granddaughters. He walked a record seventy-five feet. One evening, when Ia came home from the farm late, Chou Lor asked if he might leave the hospital bed and sleep with her. Ia was taken aback. Even before he became ill, they had not shared a bed for years. Now, he said, he missed being in the same room as her. She could only answer yes.

In the new, private space of their bedroom, they began to dream out loud. *I'm going to help you with the rice again,* Chou Lor said at first. *We'll scale back and work smarter, so we can have more time to do other things, too.* Ia saw that his legs were still shriveled, that his skin was dried out, but she looked past that and focused instead on the feelings his words gave her. Hope. Happiness. Warmth. They both had worked so hard for so long.

In the weeks that followed, what grew from their bedroom conversations was the promise of something new. *Let's give it all up,* Chou Lor would now say. Ia was ready. They could get by on his Social Security payments and the donations she was given for performing shaman rituals. When he was better, she would quit farming altogether. They would travel to Laos again while they were still young enough to enjoy it. Hell, they would travel the world. Their lifetime of labor would be over. Instead, finally, they would just live.

———

All spring in Laos, Chai and Thao felt their life together was at the precipice of finally beginning. Thao had repeated the words to himself so many times they were gospel in his head: *Once you have a baby, you just go to the embassy and they hand you the visas.* Because of the coronavirus, though, the embassy was closed—they couldn't even make an appointment for a date in the future.

Because most commercial airline flights had been suspended, the embassy's website was publicizing charter flights out of Vientiane on which American citizens could get out of Laos and make their way back to the United States. On his phone Thao watched the announcements come up and the tickets sell out. Though he yearned to see his father again, he was the only one with the documentation that would allow entry into the United States, and he would not consider leaving alone. So instead, their family of three waited, as the two months Thao had planned to be in Laos turned into three and then four, as his bank account drained down to double digits and Ia was summoned to replenish its funds.

Finally, in the third week of June, the embassy receives them. Baby Emma is given a visa without complication; her father is American, which automatically qualifies her as a citizen. Chai is told she must fill out the I-130 form, which requests a green card for a spouse. Processing might take more than a year, perhaps closer to two.

They should have submitted this form the day after they were married, four months ago, before the coronavirus turned the world on its head. That way, Chai would already be four months into the process. As it turns out, though, it doesn't make a difference. As Thao and Chai will come to understand, on April 1, the Trump administration took advantage of the pandemic to further restrict immigration. In consideration of "the profound and unique public health risks posed by the novel (new) coronavirus known as SARS-CoV-2," the president issued an executive order doubling down on the visa sanctions he had imposed on Laos and other countries in 2018.

The earlier ban had been limited mostly to visas for dignitaries and other high-profile applicants—a shot across the bow of a weak nation. The new sanctions were a full-scale attack, covering essentially any visa application from a regular Lao citizen, including Chai. Before she can begin waiting for the embassy to process her application, she must wait for the sanctions to be lifted. With President Trump hoping to win reelection based in part on his hostility toward immigration, there is little chance of that happening in the foreseeable future.

Four days after their dispiriting visit to the embassy, a new charter flight from Vientiane to Seoul is announced. "We encourage US citizens who want to return to the United States immediately to book this flight," the embassy website advises. "We are not aware of any other commercial flight routes from Vientiane to an airport with connecting flights to the United States. The US Embassy is not organizing another special chartered flight." In Fresno, Ia and all the kids pitch in enough money to buy two tickets: one for Thao, one for four-month-old Emma.

Everyone insists it is the right decision. In Fresno there will be hospitals and medicine if the baby gets sick; there will be supermarket shelves stocked with infant formula and diapers. During the thirty days after the birth when Chai recuperated in their little bedroom, not a single relative from her home village came to help out. In Fresno, though, there will be a houseful of people from the baby's clan to share in caring for her. Of course Emma should go with Thao. In Fresno, she will have a better life.

Two weeks later, Chai accompanies Thao and the baby to the airport. Chai cries the entire ride there. She cries more when they arrive. Thao dons his face mask and checks in for the flight. He stands with Chai in the big empty lobby and bounces Emma on his round belly. When they can't wait any longer, he turns toward the doors that will lead him through passport control. This time, he doesn't kiss Chai's belly or tell her that he will be back soon. He can't even look her in the eye.

———

Chai cries all the way back to the house on the dead-end alley. When she walks in and sees the room where for months she has been living with Thao and Emma, the room where she will now be alone once more, she falls apart all over again. The rest of the house is no better: the wife in the family Chai lives with has just given birth and is now spending her thirty days at home with a new baby in her arms.

What was I thinking? Chai asks herself frantically. *Why on earth did I agree to this?* Almost as soon as Thao arrives in Fresno, Chai asks him to send Emma back. Thao yells at her that it is impossible—for so many reasons. She knows that, but she is desperate. She calls again and asks if she can at least leave the house in the lowlands for somewhere not saturated with painful memories. Staying there, she feels she will die.

Hearing her heartache, Thao tells her she should return to her village in the mountains. Maybe that will help.

So, in the middle of the rainy season, four and a half years after leaving as a new bride, Chai moves back into her father's home under a cloud of shame. Not only did her husband fail to bring her to the United States, but he left her right back where she started. The more venomous neighbors sneer that her husband didn't even build her a house of her own. Instead, Chai makes a space for herself in the dark, concrete house her father built during the time she was gone.

When Chai cries to her father, he reassures her that the baby is better off in the United States, for all the same reasons Thao's family listed. When Chai cries to the little wife, the message is repeated: in Fresno there is a whole clan of people to love her baby. Chai must just be patient, and soon enough she will be there, too. Chai tries to believe them, though as a mother her heart is never convinced. The only option is to find a way to survive until the embassy changes its policy.

———

Through July and into August, Chai continues to cry on the phone to Thao, and he continues to yell back at her to stop crying.

During one such conversation, the family in Fresno is gathered for dinner in the great room that makes up their kitchen, dining area, and den. Tired of the vitriol her brother is spewing into the phone, Song lashes out at Thao. *Why do you have to be so mean to her?* she asks. *In all the years I've been married, my husband has never yelled at me like that.*

Thao says nothing. Instead, Chou Lor speaks. His voice is soft—he is still frail, perhaps more than anyone realizes. He tells them that if he is sent back to the hospital he fears that he won't come back out. For that reason, there is something he needs to say to them all. *Let this end with me.*

The family is silent.

I was raised in a family that was abusive, Chou Lor says. *My father beat my mother. Then I beat your mother. Please, don't carry on this tradition. When I die, let the abuse end with me.*

Ia is stunned by his words. In their forty years together, he has never spoken of how he assaulted her. She brought it up just about every time they had a fight—in many ways, it is the inciting incident of her entire adult life. But Chou Lor always remained silent on the topic—until now. Not wanting the moment to vanish, Ia jumps in to affirm that yes, Chou Lor's mother suffered at the hands of her husband every day of their married life. *At the beginning, I suffered, too,* Ia says. *Not anymore, but I did.*

Chou Lor faces the group and agrees. *What your mother says is true,* he tells them. *I regret what I did. Now I beg for her forgiveness.*

It is a time of miracles, these few months after Chou Lor returns from the hospital. A time of possibility. Things that laid dormant for decades—and worse, rotted in the dark for all those years—suddenly crack through to the light and burst into bloom. As if Alice's book of syrupy love poems held some real truth all along. Forgiveness? Yes, Ia will forgive him at last.

———

By all accounts, Chou Lor's death comes as a surprise. *He was doing so well.* Then suddenly he is not, and days after that family dinner he is back in the hospital, back in surgery, back not recovering as well as the doctors hoped. Because of what is now known as Covid, the family is not allowed to see him in the ICU. It is the virus's deadliest week yet in Fresno County, with an average of five deaths each day. Only those in end-of-life care are allowed visitors.

By the time Song talks her way into the hospital, her father's fingers and toes are purple. Within days, the doctor is asking for consent to take Chou Lor off life support. The family is allowed into his room, two at a time. Ia and her daughters negotiate around the new tangle of tubing to dress him in a collared shirt and a three-piece suit of black wool that hangs loosely around his meager body. After he is clothed, they gently style his hair. When he is prepared to begin the journey into the next world, two by two, Ia and the sons and daughters say goodbye. Finally, in the stillness after midnight, their father leaves them for good.

———

In the weeks that follow, Ia's tears rarely stop. No matter where a conversation begins, she winds it back to the topic of Chou Lor's death and all that has been lost with him. A few words will make it out of her mouth, then the rest drown in her throat.

Gradually, the crying is compounded by other afflictions. Stomachache. Fever. Headache as if her brain is snared in a metal trap. The August heat switches the long beans into overdrive, but Ia doesn't go to the farm. Instead, she stays in her bedroom and sleeps all day. Barely speaks—barely able to.

The family enlists a shaman to investigate whether there is a spiritual cause for Ia's illness. The shaman finds that there is a soul to whom Ia made a promise. It seems that soul is coming to collect. Immediately, Ia understands.

During the pillowy months when she and Chou Lor shared a

bedroom again, Ia would rise before dawn to go to the farm. Before she left, she would always make a bowl of cereal for Chou Lor. One day, he woke her up first, asking for his breakfast. She went to the kitchen and returned with his bowl. When she offered it to him, he reached not for the food but for her hand. *Koj niam,* he called her—"sweetie." *If I die, will you remarry?* He was weeping. She could feel him wanting her to say no.

Of course not, she said.

Promise me that you are not going to remarry?

I promise, Ia said. *Wherever you are is where I will be. If you go, take me with you.*

But this was not what she had meant. Chou Lor had been healing, slowly moving back toward his full self. In those halcyon days, she saw their future in life, not in death—that was the meaning of her promise. Just as they had discussed, they would live out the years before them on earth with a new kind of togetherness. *Wherever you are is where I will be.* That she had told no one about the conversation makes her even more certain about the shaman's diagnosis. Clearly, she is sick as hell because Chou Lor is trying to bring her with him to the afterlife.

But Ia is not the only one to fall ill. In the beginning of September, Mee gets sick. Then her brother and his wife. Mee's employment at Walmart mandates that she be tested for the coronavirus, and the results come back positive. Thao will now have to be tested, because of his job; until he gets the results, he must try to keep baby Emma six feet away. One by one, nearly everyone in the house comes down with Covid.

Ia, now sick for more than two weeks, tests negative. And while her family gets better, she remains depleted—not dead, she says, but not feeling fully alive either. Even as the first of the rice is ready to harvest, she stays home. When her phone starts ringing with customers wanting *mov nplej tshiab,* the children intercept, at times confiscating the device to prevent any conversations that might set off more crying, and with it more illness. They need all their strength and energy in order to put on Chou Lor's funeral, so his soul can complete its journey to the spirit world.

Word has gotten out, though, that the family has Covid—*had* Covid, really, but it doesn't matter. The clan members who had agreed to perform the funeral use the opportunity to cancel, citing health concerns. It is not unreasonable: Hmong funerals include dozens if not hundreds of people, gathered indoors, for a process that can last three days. Earlier this summer, Youa from the farm also died, and her funeral proved to be a super-spreader event. One relative who flew in from Colorado became so ill he ended up on a ventilator.

Ia will hear none of it. When the relatives try to cancel, she is incensed. Already they had been dragging their feet. In the days following Chou Lor's death, none had shown up at the house to mourn or offer support. Before they agreed to perform the funeral, they required assurances of the money they would be paid. The abandonment that Ia had prophesied from the side of Chou Lor's hospital bed had materialized with searing accuracy. Now that her husband was dead, she and her children commanded no respect. They were orphans. When the relatives finally offer a compromise, it is that they will show up only to transport Chou Lor from the morgue to the cemetery for an outdoor burial—an observance suitable for a child, not a man.

A Hmong funeral is not a perfunctory event simply marking the end of a person's life. It is an essential ritual that maintains the soul's place in a continuum that extends from far before any of those of us on earth were born through to a time when we all will be long gone. The many complex steps must be executed by an array of specific people in the clan, many with specialized training. When complete, the funeral will convey the soul of the deceased to the land of the ancestors, from where it will later be reborn. Without the funeral, the soul will wander for eternity, poor and hungry.

Even when her children tell her the funeral won't be possible, Ia will not be mollified. Giving Chou Lor this spiritual deliverance is vital: Because he was her husband of forty years. Because he suffered for so long. Because she wants to set him free. But also for her sake. Burying him as if he were a child would be a great dishonor to the family. And if his soul wanders for eternity in the spirit world, she and the family will suffer here on earth. Even in death, Ia's fate is tied to her husband's—she knows this well.

When the negotiations with the relatives reach a standstill, Chou Lor comes to Ia in a dream. He says he is ready to leave, that he is cold—when will they release his spirit? Ia cries to him and explains that his relatives refuse to perform the funeral. She has begged them, but they won't listen to her. He must go to them, she says. He must change their minds. *We need to do this so you can find your way back home.*

Less than two days later, the relatives call Ia with the news that the funeral is back on. However, there are conditions. They will allow only the mandatory pieces of the ritual, for a shortened total duration. Further, they will not perform the ritual themselves: they will contract with people from another clan. It is an insulting modification, but at this point, Ia will take it. The date is set for the first weekend in October, right at the peak of what is normally harvesttime.

———

The weekend of the funeral, smoke from a massive forest fire blocks out the sun. In the east, there is no view of the far-off mountains. Instead, just a sky that is flat white, the color of a blank page. At the Sunnyside Banquet Hall, guests are greeted by three separate standing signs admonishing YOU MUST WEAR A MASK TO ENTER. In the entryway is a table offering multiple dispensers of hand sanitizer. One of Ia's daughters-in-law stands in the path to the door, apologizing as she points a digital thermometer at the guests' foreheads before she will allow them in.

The family has worked hard to make the function room look as dignified and normal as possible. The chairs are spaced six feet apart and covered in crisp white dressings, each tied with a gauzy gold ribbon that matches the drapes. The front of the room is crowded with massive arrangements of both real flowers and intricate paper creations on folding stands. Along the back of the room are three poster boards displaying photographs showing Chou Lor's happy life with his family: Sporting puffy 1980s sneakers in a carport with a minivan. Wearing a traditional outfit at Fresno's Hmong New Year festival. Standing among plaster penguins at a zoo.

Flanking this display of snapshots are two large framed portraits from the wall at home. One is Chou Lor and Ia as Lao royalty, draped in silks and gilded with gold jewelry. The photographer posed them in a formal embrace that suggests love, but the kind for public consumption: each of them with one hand placed on the other just so, while their bodies remain distant. The other framed photograph is the one composed like a military portrait, showing Chou Lor in a starched uniform with awards decorating the chest. He was never in the official military—had the photo made at a photo booth at the Hmong New Year celebration in Fresno—but his family knew he would be proud to have it displayed here. Song even arranged for some older ex-soldiers to perform a twenty-one-gun salute.

In the center of the room, Chou Lor's body lies on a low cot. He wears an oversize shirt and on his chest is balanced a pink cup, so that he may be given a drink with each of the ritual meals he is fed throughout the day. Always, there is at least one family member sitting beside him, guarding his body. Jimmy sits there solidly in a three-piece suit. Thao is in a black polo shirt, his eyes red and wet. Alice is a woman now in a long black dress, her hair straightened and curled at the ends as she gazes down at her father.

Ia is not particularly dressed up. She wears the same stretchy black pants as every other day, same V-necked shirt, except today it is pure black. Her surgical mask is too big for her face, the shield sagging down under her nose. Above, her eyes are heavy with exhaustion. At the farm, her rice is a golden ocean, a sea of perfection, thick and full and free of weeds—perhaps the best crop of all time. Only a few rows have been harvested, though, and mostly by helpful aunts. That is because Ia has spent the past three weeks furiously planning, haggling, and strategizing to make sure the funeral is as grand as it can be. All told, the ceremony and burial will cost $40,000. For Hmong in Fresno this is not unusual; many families invest in life insurance specifically so they will be able to pay for the loved one's funeral. Because there was no policy for Chou Lor, Ia and her children have also spent the past three weeks finding the rest of the cash necessary to cover the bills.

Still, all the decorations cannot disguise that attendance is light. The clean white chairs are mostly unoccupied. In the dining room across the breezeway, the Styrofoam boxes filled with meals for the mourners are stacked three high, waiting for a crowd that has not yet materialized. Dearest friends and truly loved ones are here, if for shorter periods than in normal times. But the clan members have again demonstrated, with their absence, where the family stands. Ia will roil over this for months to come. Today, though, she will not let bitterness claim her. As each valued guest arrives, she makes sure to cry with him or her for a moment. In the dining room, she urges people to eat, and eat more. The rest of the time, Ia sits beside Chou Lor at the front of the function room, making sure he is never alone.

Because the ceremony has been greatly abbreviated, by midday the first essential piece is already complete. This was the *Qhuab Ke*, the "Showing the Way" chant, an ancient song that tells the story of creation to explain to the deceased why he was born, why his body has died, and how his soul will reach the door to the sky so that it may move on to the land of the ancestors. The soul guide who performed the song sang his way through all the places Chou Lor lived on this earth: from Fresno back to the longhouse in Ban Vinai, and before that Sa Na Oua. Finally, to the smaller village where Chou Lor was born, before the war uprooted his family the first time. It was there that he would collect his *tsho tsuj tsho npuag,* his placenta, which was buried the day he was born in order that he could retrieve it now. Wearing this consecrated vestment, he would be shown the way to the ancestors and given the tools to get there.

Now begins a parallel song, sung by a long, curved instrument made of bamboo pipes called the *qeej.* The instrument requires a human player, but just so the person's breath, mouth, and fingers can bring the *qeej* to life. Its low, vibrating music is an encrypted language that speaks only to denizens of the spirit world. Whereas the singer of the "Showing the Way" chant explained to Chou Lor how to reach the land of the ancestors, it is the *qeej* that will actually guide Chou Lor's soul there.

The *qeej* is accompanied at times by a drum. The drummer spends much of his time on the sidelines, drinking shots of Jack Daniel's that another man pours for him between his parts of the song. But the *qeej* player is focused and deliberate. Even as a hired gun from a different clan, he seems to recognize that his sacred role is inviolable. He is an older man, nondescript in a worn maroon coat, and he curves his body down toward the *qeej,* letting it lead him in slow circles around Chou Lor's body. As the viscous music fills the function room, it builds a bridge between this tangible earth and the world beyond. To those who know and care, the sounds are a signal that Chou Lor's soul is finally beginning to leave. Soon he will be reunited with his father, and his father's parents, and all his lost siblings who were lucky enough to reach the land of the ancestors safely.

Perhaps no one knows or cares about this more than Ia. This is why she has drained every last bit of energy and money into making the funeral complete. With the song well under way, she rises from her chair at Chou Lor's side and is replaced by Alice. Her sons have assembled near the front of the room and will soon receive their father's final blessings, communicated through the *qeej.* But this is not for her. Ia moves to the far back corner of the room, where Chou Lor's coffin waits alone.

It is a heavy thing, made of honey-colored wood and varnished to an almost liquid gloss. The quilted bed is laid over with a large Hmong embroidery in black, with purple designs carefully stitched along every edge. Over that lie three strips of white cloth that are essential to the afterlife journey. At the head, a small pillow, simply for comfort. Ia stands beside the coffin and fixes her eyes on some middle distance within it. She lays her hand on the rounded edge and tears begin to fall. This is not the loud, performative sobbing she has done with guests all day. It is the soft weeping of unbidden heartache. She rides her palm along the rim of the coffin, stroking back and forth. When her name is called she does not hear. She has passed into an inner world, where she grieves alone.

As her sons bow to the *qeej* for the blessings it brings from their father, Ia knows that she has done all she can to ensure that Chou Lor's soul will be delivered safely. But at the same time she does not know, after this is all over, what will happen to her. Hers is not the hero's journey, wherein she conquers the beast and returns home in triumph. Chou Lor will ascend to the afterworld and reunite with his long-lost family. But when the funeral is finished, Ia will simply return to another round of life. This current tragedy will become a memory, written alongside all the rest. She will adapt to the new shape of her world. Naturally, she will find a way to survive, just as she has for every season that has come before.

EPILOGUE

The rice was a golden ocean, a sea of perfection, thick and full for the second season in a row. Ia had paid for her entire plot again, this time in December, a month early. Soon after, she had leased the bean land to a neighbor. Then when it had come time to plant the remaining five acres, she had consented to sublet a third of it to a woman who was slightly younger, still married. But the rest Ia had planted herself, all of it with rice. By the first week in October, a year after Chou Lor's funeral, the plants were taller than any of the women who had come to help Ia harvest her crop. From the road, only the roof of the shed was visible. Everything else—and everyone—had disappeared into the folds of yellow-green gold.

Then came the wind. It blew across the northern half of California, toppling trees onto power lines and sparking more wildfires to add to the 2.4 million acres that had burned in the state since June. In Fresno, winds reached forty-four miles per hour. The desiccated earth blew up into the air and turned the sky brown, prompting an official air quality alert that urged residents to stay indoors. Ia was at the farm, of course. The gales roared across her fields, and in anguish she watched as those beautifully tall rice plants were knocked flat. It happened not all in one gust, but over the course of minutes, in slow motion, the agony of it compounded by her knowledge that she was powerless to stop it. She cried out to Chou Lor in the spirit world,

319

begging him to block the wind. It only raged on. By day's end, one-tenth of her perfect crop was leveled.

If left standing, the plants would have given two, even three cuttings. Instead, the race is on to rescue whatever is ready now before it rots on the ground. For this job Ia has five women working today, all of them widows, all of them old enough to make Ia look young. They are friends of hers, but also just the kind of elderly ladies Ia always swears she will not hire: they are too slow to make the $80 a day she pays them worthwhile.

Now they will be even slower, with the field a knee-deep mass of vegetation. As they wade and dig to uncover the stalks of grain, they lose their footing and fall so many times it ceases to be funny. In the parts of the farm where the rice still stands tall and beautiful, Ia now sees a crop that must be put on hold to accommodate the triage. She can only hope it will wait.

The whole thing is that much more painful because Ia knows this may be her final season on the farm. Last year, after the funeral, her children all stepped up to help her harvest. Since then, though, they have united into a chorus telling her to quit. She should rest. Or travel. Visit relatives in North Carolina and Oklahoma. They assure her that Chou Lor's Social Security checks will pay her bills. If she wants more money, she can pick up day jobs on other people's farms. Or go to the Green Mountain and cash in on the marijuana boom.

Ia gradually loses the argument, begins to consent that she will give up the farm. Then her heart pulls her back in and she comes up with a work-around. She could hold the lease on the farm but sublet the whole thing, just so she doesn't lose the land. Or what if she planted only two acres? What if she paid the rent but took a year off to let the land rest? At times it feels like an addiction. Other times she recognizes that if she pushes forward without her children's blessings, the plan will fall apart. Even if Ia got her driver's license and was able to ferry herself to the farm every day, she would still need the kids to help plant in the spring and harvest in the fall. She can't do it alone.

They have all begun to move on. Song has a baby now. Jimmy wants to go back to school to become a physical therapist. Mee has a new job at the Gap. Alice graduated from high school in June. As soon as school was out, she asked Ia's permission to get married. Ia said no. Alice did it anyway. She says he's a good man whose father taught him to respect women, and never to hit. She moved in with his family in August, which means she is still in Fresno, but with new loyalties. She, too, has a new job, at the Walmart where Mee used to work.

In some ways, the most natural person to help on the farm would be Chai, but Ia has given up on that hope. Even after Donald Trump left office and President Biden promised a more welcoming stance toward immigrants, the election-year visa sanctions against Laos remain. Chai is still waiting simply to be allowed to file her paperwork, so that she may then begin waiting for it to be processed. Every day she dials her way through the list of phone numbers at the house at Creekside Ranch—Thao, then Ia, then Mee—until someone picks up and puts her on a video chat with her daughter. In four months, Emma will be two years old.

———

Even if the rice field is a windblown disaster, lunch is still a feast. The women push the trash on the table aside to make room for pork belly and two whole fish from the Asia Supermarket deli, as well as for persimmons, jujubes, and jicama just dug out of the ground. Mee fries up a mountain of chicken wings. Youa is no longer here, but Neng Her arrives with his new wife and puts a bag of passion fruit on the bench. Ia has brought both regular rice and sticky, each of which was harvested and roasted last week. By the time it's all ready, there is so much food on the table that the women must put their plates in their laps. Those who can't find a place to sit fashion a satellite table out of a piece of plywood and a bucket. As they eat, one big conversation is shouted back and forth across the shed.

For most of this past season, Ia did not eat at the farm. Usually her only companion here was Jimmy, and because she knows that he prefers McDonald's to Hmong food, she would just give him money for the drive-through and skip lunch for herself. It was too sad to eat alone, much less to cook for one. Today she doesn't take a plate. Instead, she picks at the food from around the edges—a pinch of fish here, a scoop of passion fruit there.

Still, being at the center of a feast again gives Ia a little jolt of energy, as if someone plugged her in while she wasn't looking. She makes sure all the women try both of her rices. When they marvel at its perfect, soft-but-not-too-soft texture, she talks them through each step of her intricate cooking process, which involves soaking, steaming, and turning the grains with a paddle.

But even as Ia finds herself at the center of the conversation, the old joy is not there. In the place beside her, where Chou Lor always sat, there is now a gray-haired widow. The woman's bottom eyelids droop down low to expose deep red rims, as if she has been crying for decades. Ia begins to weep.

The group's conversation turns to make a space for her sorrow. Between sobs, Ia tells them how hard this past year was, being alone at the farm, with no one to help her.

"Don't feel sad," says one woman. "We've all been there. We know what it's like."

"Yes, the first year is the hardest," says another woman. "If you survived this one, you'll survive next year. It will get easier."

"You stick with us," says a third. "We'll take care of you."

You stick with us. The very words Ia used to console another new widow at this same table, just four years earlier. The invitation cracks open Ia's gloom, just a sliver at first, but the others can see it in her face.

The first woman, who wears a devilish grin, tries to draw Ia out

322

more. "Just don't get remarried!" she calls from the little table. The women laugh.

"Exactly!" another woman chimes in. "Forget about husbands. You're just gonna end up having to cook for them. I'd rather be able to sleep all day if I want to." Neng Her, sitting beside the wife he married exactly a year after Youa's funeral, begins packing up their lunch in awkward silence.

Ia joins the fun, telling the story of a man who remarried shortly after his wife's death, only to have that woman die a month later, leaving him to pay for not one but two funerals in the space of a year. The women howl and throw out more stories about the perils of matrimony. Before Ia realizes it, she is right back in the mix.

Ia does not mention that she has a suitor who calls her from Minnesota every night. They were friendly as tweens in Sa Na Oua, and after Chou Lor's death, the man tracked her down and boldly told her that she should have married him instead all those years ago. Before long, the man was asking Ia to marry him now. She told him no: he is already married, and she has zero interest in being a second wife. Besides, remarrying would leave her children orphans, something she would not countenance even now that they are grown. She still answers the man's phone calls and entertains his affections. Every so often she will dress in a new Hmong outfit and have a photograph made, which she then posts on Facebook. New admirers surface. The attention is a balm.

Privately, though, Ia remains bound to Chou Lor. When she is alone at the farm, she calls to him over the rice, just as she used to call to her parents. Her children and friends caution her to stop, warning of the dangers, but she cannot help herself. She didn't know she would miss him so much. Kicks herself, too, for feeling it so deeply, after all the ways he hurt her. Over the summer, Ia learned that Chou Lor had been having an affair at work. For years, in fact. So entwined were he and his girlfriend that an acquaintance who also worked at the chicken processing plant initially assumed the woman was Chou Lor's wife. Ia had once suspected him of cheating, but when she confronted him, he denied it. Indeed, he responded by scolding her, saying, *If you don't trust in me, our marriage won't survive.* The wound of those long-ago words is now suddenly raw in the present. Ia gets angry at herself for wasting more of her life on this man even now that he is gone.

And yet it is so much easier for her to remember only the good times. The giant ache of missing him hurts far less than the thousand tiny injuries of betrayal and abandonment. That's why Ia will go to the cemetery laden with food to lay upon her late husband's grave. Why she will burn stacks of spirit money at her altar to make sure he is never poor again. When she feels the deep bone chill of her loneliness, she will point to the fact that Chou Lor is no longer by her side rather than say out loud that he, like so many others in her life, was never fully there to begin with.

––––––

After lunch, the women wrap back up with hats over their scarves and scarves over their hats to keep out the sun and the dust. Ia silently calculates how many extra twenties she will have to stack up and pay out before this wind-borne calamity is cleaned up. Normally, each worker would choose a row and harvest her way from one end of the field to the other. But the wind erased those careful lines, laying the rice down across the grooves of the furrows and the rises of the rows to make its own diagonal pattern. Instead of chatting their way down a predictable path, the women must bend over and work each stalk out from within the heavy blanket of green at their shins.

It is a cruel fate to be stooped down this time of year, as if they were planting all over again. Where a woman can find an opening in the leaves, she might sit and work from the ground for a spell. Mostly, though, they hinge from their hips. But without complaint. They are old enough that they remember all this from when they were young and in Laos: how the wind could rear up one day and blow down the crop, how there was nothing you could do about it except reach down and keep working. They know this pain, have made their peace with it. They know to abandon thoughts of the neatly laid rows that once were and instead follow the new, diagonal lines in their path across the field. They even know how to enjoy it—the conversation lasts all afternoon.

Earlier, Ia estimated that it would take at least two days to get through the mess. And yet by the time the sun is low and gentle in the west, the women have reached the barbed wire fence that separates the farm from the road. Behind them, the crop has been transformed into a million tidy bundles, laid out to dry on the bed of leaves from which they came.

Tomorrow some group of them will return and resume harvesting the rice that is still standing. They will cut until it's all in, and then it will be just Jimmy and Ia left to roast the grains and spread them out to dry in the sun. Ia will sell by the bucket from her garage, and at last the year will be finished. Maybe the final crop of her life.

Or maybe not. Today, as the women take a final break in the waning light of early evening, bundles of seed have already begun to collect on top of boxes and inside of old bags, conspicuously claiming the shed's far corner. There are bundles of a non-sticky rice with no name yet. Also *khao peh,* the favorite that everyone still remembers from the old days in Laos. When the grandmother rice comes ready later this month, Ia will gather enough seed to fill a feed sack.

Now Ia brings in six bundles from the field that was flattened by the wind. She collected them from the edges, where the plants managed to stay standing tall. Perhaps they possess some special inner quality that makes them more resilient than the ones that fell. Or maybe their endurance is simply a product of their location in the field, on the far side from where the gales blew in. Maybe next year Ia will use their seeds, and the plants that grow up will be knocked down by a new wind. But that would not be the end. Disappointment need not be the same as defeat. *Next year you can start all over again.* Ia's mother always told her that.

To make a place for the seed to dry out, Ia finds an old square of carpeting and lays it on the last level surface in the corner of the shed. The space the carpet makes is too small to hold the six long bundles, but it doesn't matter. While Ia gathers their golden heads in the middle of the square, to protect the seed, she lets the stalks stretch freely over the edges, fanning out in all directions like the rays of the sun.

ACKNOWLEDGMENTS

My greatest thanks go to Ia: for inviting me into her world with unceasing generosity, for sharing her life and emotions with bravery and candor, and for trusting me to tell her story to the world. Many times Ia and I have said that we long to be able to address the other directly, without an interpreter. Now more than ever I wish that I could give her my gratitude firsthand. Thank you, Ia, for opening your heart and letting me see inside of you. I will always admire your indomitable spirit.

Ia's continuous welcome was echoed by her family in Fresno, including those who were named in these pages and others who were not. I greatly appreciate how each of them showed me such hospitality, friendliness, and patience. Special thanks to Thao and Chai for allowing me to witness their trials over these years of long-distance marriage, especially during the times when fate tested their resolve. While Chou Lor is gone from this seen world, I remain grateful for his quiet kindness and his willingness to talk frankly about a difficult past.

In Laos, Pha Kao and his extended family received me with grace and warmth. Further, they did so at considerable personal risk, given the Lao government's prohibition of journalists like me visiting residents like them. For matters of safety I cannot name all those I met, so instead I'll simply say thank you to everyone who offered their time and their homes and their stories. Pha Kao, I am so grateful for your openness. I hope to return.

From day one in the field, Lor Xiong was my partner in reporting. She is a gifted interpreter who comes to her work with extraordinary skill, a powerful mind, and machinelike stamina. Moreover, she is a principled, compassionate person who not only embraced the emotional intensity of the conversations but often facilitated our journey deeper into topics of great intimacy. In ways both obvious and not, I couldn't have written this book without her. *Ua tsaug,* Lor.

Every dedicated writer deserves a talented editor. By great luck, I got two. Vanessa Mobley was the first to believe deeply in this project and championed it from the beginning. With passion and curiosity, she encouraged the nascent ideas to grow into the complex narrative they would become. With each step forward, the work was informed by both her sharp intellect and her commitment to doing right in this world. Coming to the manuscript when it was thought to be nearly finished, Alex Littlefield acted as a sort of book whisperer: seeing the soul of the story—at times better than I could—and gently coaxing out the elements required to make the story its fullest self. At every turn, he was an advocate both for me as a writer and for the book's best path to success—the kind of editor most authors wish for. Vanessa's and Alex's influences are woven through these pages from cover to cover.

Big thanks to my talented agent, David McCormick, for finding the book its home and for staying so unshakably cool even in the roughest times that followed. At Little, Brown, Mario Pulice brought tireless enthusiasm and creativity to ensuring the jacket design matched the words inside. Morgan Wu, Karen Landry, Nell Beram, H'Rina DeTroy, and the rest of the team were meticulous in their efforts to make this book top-notch. Behind the scenes, Seethong Yang provided fastidious translations and wise explanations, Mike Jerry cheerfully supplied countless transcriptions, and Rachel

Gostenhofer fact-checked with alacrity right up to the deadline (and beyond). Alex Hopp, researcher extraordinaire, saved me in the eleventh hour with his quick, thorough, joyous work.

While researching the information that underpins and enhances the story of Ia's life, I turned repeatedly to a group of powerful minds. For offering me their time and their thoughts over the course of several years, I am extremely grateful to Song Lee, David Lee, Cher Teng (Bee) Yang, Mai Na M. Lee, and Gary Yia Lee. Thanks to Mike Dwyer and Annie Shattuck for answering myriad questions, always with smiles. Thanks also to Ian Baird, Andrew Bartlett, Fritz Benson, Dia Cha, Yer Lor, Martha Ratliff, Pao Vue, friend and farmer Ia Yang, and the brain trust of LaoFAB.

Early on, I learned the long story of rice from these generous expert teachers: Susan McCouch, Ruaraidh Hamilton, Francesca Bray, Dorian Fuller, and Gene Hettel. My appreciation extends to the staff of the IRRI International Rice Genebank, and especially to Grace Lee Capilit, for accommodating many requests for archival information. Later in my research, I gained new understanding from conversations with Kue Chaw, Gary Crawford, Phil Hirsch, Mike Jackson, Bruce Linquist, Sai Chue Lor, Ken McNally, Laurent Sagart, Michael Victor, Kao Xiong, and Michael Yang of University of California Cooperative Extension. I was also helped by two kind spirits who have passed from this world, John Schiller and Mac Thompson. Tom Willey offered me the original seed for this story after he saw rice growing at the FIRM community garden on South Peach Avenue. Chukou Thao then patiently taught me the basics of what I was seeing.

As a journalist, I feel a duty to understand a topic deeply, represent the subject accurately, and write every sentence as precisely as I can. For this book, that required many years of traveling, including three trips to Laos. It also meant relying on the paid services of both trained interpreters for essentially all my time in the field and professional translators for a good share of my work in the office.

Because I could not have paid for all this myself, I'm lucky that I found a community of funders who recognized the value of this deep reporting. For their contributions, I'm grateful to the Seeds, Soil & Culture Fund, Nell Newman Foundation, Food and Farm Communications Fund, Small Planet Fund, and Munay Fund. On these matters I also received guidance and encouragement from Jonathon Landeck, Anna Lappé, and Hilde Steffey. Special thanks to Bob Scowcroft, my blessed mentor in figuring out how to make each step of this continually expanding endeavor happen.

Other people and organizations assisted this project by providing a creative space in which I could do the taxing, alchemical work of writing. Mesa Refuge in Point Reyes, California, hosted me at the very beginning and at the very end. In between, my dear friends Alex Frankel, Katy Mamen, Adam Wolpert, and Suellen and Allegra Lamorte offered me places of retreat in which to focus without interruption. The book is incalculably better for their generosity.

In 2019, a fellowship with New America supported the pivotal first year of actually writing down the words that would become this book. My fellow fellows offered critical perspectives on ethics and other topics, as well as wonderful friendships that last to this day. Likewise, the residents with whom I shared time at Mesa Refuge each gave to this book in individual ways. Thanks to Peter Barnes, Susan Page Tillett, Kamala Tully, Awista Ayub, and Clark Reeves for running the two programs that enabled such kinship. Also to the Food and Environment Reporting Network—especially Tom Laskawy and Sam Fromartz—for being my fiscal sponsor and longtime allies.

Authors Mark Arax, Lauren Markham, and Michelle Nijhuis were superb company and vital comfort over the many years of this project. Fay Dillof offered deep wisdom and the gift of a poet's relationship to language. Valerie Hamilton was always there with enthusiasm for the project, sharp insight into its many conundrums, and strong opinions when it mattered. Tucker Nichols brought his exceptional intellect to helping me see things from a new angle and finding a way forward—over and over and over again. I am privileged to have you all by my side.

Finally, I wish to thank my husband and daughter: For their love and their humor, without which I would have perished long ago. For their patience over these many years. Frankly, for their tolerance of my devotion to this project, but also for their ability to see the value in creative work like this. Even with the stability of a middle-class life in the United States, much of the time a woman must still choose between being a mother and being an artist. My beloved family has given me the space to be both at once. For that I am grateful beyond words.

NOTES ON METHODOLOGY

The first time I met Ia I was at her farm to visit someone else. I was harvesting rice with her neighbor Youa, to whom I had been introduced through a chain of people. That was how it worked: Finding a Hmong farmer to speak with about growing rice in Fresno was not a matter of looking on the Internet or picking up the phone. It relied on the old-fashioned web of personal relationships.

More than a year had already passed since I first came to Fresno for this project. I wanted to write a book about rice, and a farmer friend in the valley told me he had seen the plant growing in a community garden plot on South Peach Avenue. When I tracked down the Hmong woman whose plot it was, she explained that the planting—and the entire season of work that came with it—was for just one meal, at New Year's. As both a longtime gardener and a journalist who writes about agriculture, I was intrigued. I learned that other women were growing the crop on a larger scale, and that in fact there was an underground rice economy in the San Joaquin Valley. Of all places! I wanted to know more.

I met people, built relationships, and visited farms in Merced, Sanger, Clovis, and Fresno. I don't speak Hmong, and, with one exception, the farmers I met spoke not enough English for a deep conversation. So I mostly traveled with an interpreter, Lor Xiong. The farmers we talked to were women in their forties and fifties, some older. (While some husbands were involved in the farms, they were rarely there when we were.) Everyone was friendly, but most kept their guard up. Understandably: as several of the farmers explained, most had never had a non-Hmong American show interest in the details of their lives. I learned that often they and the neighboring farmers suspected I was an undercover agent of the government, coming to bust them for something. I tried my best to demonstrate that this was not the case, but still, in some instances I respectfully withdrew my interest.

Several months into the first summer I spent in Fresno, a well-respected medicine woman and shaman introduced me to Youa, who allowed me to visit her farm. One day during harvest, Youa, Lor, and I headed to the open-air shed in the middle of the fields for a lunch break. I always brought my own food, as did Youa, but today the farmer who grew rice on the adjacent land had prepared a bountiful meal and insisted that we share it. Through Lor, this farmer asked if I had ever tasted the beverage called *kua txhai,* which is made from the liquid left over after rinsing rice before it is cooked. When I said no, she poured me a yellow plastic tumbler full and watched my face with giddy anticipation as I drank. When I told her I liked it, she smiled hugely, then said something funny and laughed at her own words. Other farmers had also been warm, candid, even humorous, but this woman stood apart. Her face gleamed with its own brilliant light. She seemed ready for action, eager for some outlet that would receive all the electric life buzzing inside her.

After lunch, the woman pulled Lor aside and said, "Let me know if you two want to come talk to me sometime. I have stories to tell."

Lor asked for her name. It was, of course, Ia.

That was October 2016. Beginning when I visited the farm a week later, I would devote the next six years to learning who Ia was, both by listening to her unspool the story of her past and by witnessing her latest chapters take shape in the present. Without resistance, the book I had planned to write about rice receded into the background as the life of this remarkable woman took center stage.

———

For me, it was vital that Ia's involvement in this project not detract from her work. We mostly met at the farm, where Ia would proceed with whatever tasks were required that day and I would follow her doing the same, whether planting seed or picking beans or harvesting rice. As we worked, we talked. Lor walked beside us, interpreting and recording much of the conversation. Like this, the three of us spent hours, days, and eventually years together.

Working across languages is challenging. So much can be lost in the spaces between, especially when the poles are as far apart as Hmong and English are. From the start, Lor was an essential bridge. She went beyond merely exchanging words in one language for those in another, and depicted character and emotion. For instance, when Ia told a story with a stage actor's gesticulations and different voices for different characters, Lor brought some of the same animation to her delivery so I could take in the full range of Ia's humor. When I wished to express my concerns or gratitude to Ia, Lor recast my sentiments so they made sense in Hmong and spoke them using a solemn tone. And whenever I missed the point, Lor was sure to stop and offer me explanation and context. Altogether, this deep interpreting enabled Ia and me to know each other at a level beyond sheer questions and answers.

Because of this foundation, the interactions between Ia, Lor, and me gradually transcended what any of us might have expected when we first met. We laughed, we cried. We got sick in front of one another, and more than once slept side by side. Over the course of our time together, people we loved faced illness and death. Our children grew. And the three of us became friends. Many journalists would steer clear of such closeness, believing that bonding with a "subject" would endanger their ability to write clearly about that person. I see it differently. I believe that genuine relationships are what allow you to see a person and her experience at their fullest. From that intimacy, a new kind of story emerges. That was the kind of story I wanted to write.

Friendship notwithstanding, there was an unavoidable imbalance of at least certain kinds of power in Ia's and my relationship—that is, a professional writer writing a book about someone who has never read a book herself. Furthermore, I was writing about a community that is not my own. I reflected often on my position in relation to Ia, and explored from many different angles how to bridge any disparities between us. Some of the pieces came naturally: I listened vastly more than I talked; in the field, I mostly left myself behind and instead opened my mind to the world I was visiting. Over time, I had numerous formal conversations with Ia to apprise her of the potential risks she was taking by allowing me to write a book about her. I invited her questions about the process.

Time and again, Ia's response to my concerns was "I trust you." Those words—her words—always brought me back to the same fundamental recognition: Ia is a strong, powerful woman, and nothing defines her more than her sense of agency. I found that what ultimately guided our way in this project was the relationship we had built: she gave me her trust, and in response I vowed to honor that trust by telling her story honestly. The greatest respect I could give to Ia was to relate to her as a person, just like me, and portray her as I would anyone, in the full spectrum of her humanity.

I could not share the working manuscript with Ia; because the writing is literary, it comes out jumbled when interpreted live, and translation on paper is a slow, expensive process. Instead, I promised that once the book was finished I would find a way to have the story professionally translated, then recorded as an audiobook in Hmong. This way, Ia could experience the book in full and judge its merits for herself. As of this writing, that endeavor is under way.

NOTES ON SOURCES

The majority of the information in this book came from two sources: my observations in the field and Ia's accounting of her personal history. When possible, I cross-checked these sources however I could, most often by interviewing other people who were present when the events took place. This was challenging for a variety of reasons: Many people who were part of the past narrative have died or lost their memories to age. Other people's experience of past events was sometimes different from Ia's. And while I traveled to Pha Kao's village in Laos three times, twice with Ia, it was nearly impossible to follow up from afar. Because of the country's authoritarian government, people felt unsafe talking with an English-speaking American by phone.

Beyond those hurdles, the shifting nature of memory and relationships brought additional complexity to the process. As Ia and I discussed the main events of her life multiple times and from different angles, often the story was slightly different. I came to see this as natural. Neuroscientists have determined that our memories of events change each time we summon them. Likewise, Ia's relationship to me, to members of her family, and to herself appeared to shift over time, likely influencing how she felt about those memories and how much of them she wanted to reveal. I took this inherent variation within the stories as one more way to understand her.

To find the full breadth of what Ia told me, I had the English-language sections of our roughly 250 hours of recorded conversation transcribed. For an additional layer of understanding, portions of the Hmong-language sections were then translated by a professional or simultaneously reinterpreted by Lor Xiong, sometimes both. These multiple versions often revealed layers of meaning that helped elucidate what Ia had said and what it had meant. I then took all the pieces of information I had—multiple versions of the story, multiple interpretations of those versions—and triangulated them to find the clearest truth. When there was ambiguity, I pulled back and stuck to what was clear. Ultimately, much of the phrasing for Ia's personal history came from the words she herself had used to tell me the story. (And, it should go without saying, when I wrote that a person felt or thought something, it was because that person told me she or he did.)

A similar fluidity holds for the historical elements of this book. There is no such thing as a single, perfect history. There are cold facts—this person died on this day, this treaty was signed by these nations—but much of what we consider "history" is a matter of perspective. From the domestication of rice to the narrative of the Lao civil war, there are many different views on who did what and why. The violent conflict that took place at the Hin Heup bridge, described in the first chapter of this book, is a good example. As a journalist, not a historian, I sought to take in as much varied information as I could. From that, I distilled a telling of history that reflected the general perspective through which I understood Ia to see the world.

This led me to approach the Hmong community as my primary source of information. I turned to shamans, educators, and clan leaders, who graciously taught me about the culture and ritual that is the lifeblood of Ia's world. When reading, I went first to Hmong sources for depictions of Hmong culture, of the Lao civil war, and of the diaspora. Concrete information about the ancient history of Hmong people proved to be elusive, so I drew on a range of sources to compose a blended story of what was long ago.

In addition to studying the books and articles listed in the bibliography, I conducted interviews with dozens of experts on a range of topics. This would be true for most nonfiction books, and a more complete recognition of those people appears in my acknowledgments section. However, it's important to note that a greater than average portion of my research came from dialogue and learning directly with certain individuals, some of whom have never published an article or a book. Because a bibliography is not equipped to document those sources, I want to highlight the influence on my work that came from the writings and counsel of the following people: University of Minnesota historian Mai Na M. Lee; independent historian Gary Yia Lee; California State University, Fresno, lecturer and community leader Cher Teng (Bee) Yang; California State University, Fresno, professor and counselor Song Lee; and clan leader David Lee.

BIBLIOGRAPHY

Aamot, Gregg (Associated Press). "Hmong in Minn. Rally for Revered Leader." AP online, 20 June 2007.

"Agriculture Officials Urged to Help Farmers Boost Yields." *Vientiane Times,* 6 May 2016.

Amaro, Yesenia. "'Families Will Be Broken': Fear Grows as Trump Administration Moves to Deport Laotian Refugees." *Fresno Bee,* 27 Feb. 2020.

——. "It's an Immigration Crisis Few Know of. And Fresno County Might Be at the Center of It." *Fresno Bee,* 18 May 2019.

Amnesty International. *Hiding in the Jungle—Hmong Under Threat.* Mar. 2007.

Andelman, David A. "In Laos, the Confusion Is Expected to Leave a Blend of Communism and Nationalism in Control." *New York Times,* 25 May 1975.

——. "Laos After the Takeover." *New York Times,* 24 Oct. 1976.

Anthony, Victor B., and Richard R. Sexton. *The War in Northern Laos 1954–1973.* Center for Air Force History, United States Air Force, Washington, DC, 1993.

Arax, Mark. "The Child Brides of California: In the Central Valley, Hmong Men Continue the Tradition of Marrying Girls as Young as 12 or 13." *Los Angeles Times,* 4 May 1993.

——. *The Dreamt Land: Chasing Water and Dust Across California.* Alfred A. Knopf, 2019.

——. "Strategy for Survival: Lure of the Underground Economy (Series)." *Los Angeles Times,* 9–10 Feb. 1987.

——. "With Bagpipes and Feasts, a Hmong Is Mourned." *International Herald Tribune,* 8 Feb. 2011.

Armbuster, Shirley. "A Struggle in the Sun (Series)." *Fresno Bee,* 9–12 Oct. 1983.

Baird, Ian G. "Party, State and the Control of Information in the Lao People's Democratic Republic: Secrecy, Falsification and Denial." *Journal of Contemporary Asia,* vol. 48, no. 5, Oct. 2018, pp. 739–60.

Baird, Ian G., and Philippe Le Billon. "Landscapes of Political Memories: War Legacies and Land Negotiations in Laos." *Political Geography,* vol. 31, no. 5, June 2012, pp. 290–300.

Baird, Ian G., and Bruce Shoemaker. "Unsettling Experiences: Internal Resettlement and International Aid Agencies in Laos." *Development and Change,* vol. 38, no. 5, Sept. 2007, pp. 865–88.

Barclay, Adam. "Looking Up in the Uplands." *Rice Today,* vol. 6, no. 4, Oct.–Dec. 2007.

Bartlett, Andrew, *Dynamics of Food Security in the Uplands of Laos: A Summary of 10 Years of Research*. Lao PDR, Northern Upland Development Programme and National Agriculture and Forestry Research Institute, 2012.

Bekken, Deborah A., et al., editors. *China: Visions Through the Ages*. University of Chicago Press, 2018.

Bellwood, Peter. "The Checkered Prehistory of Rice Movement Southwards as a Domesticated Cereal—from the Yangzi to the Equator." *Rice,* vol. 4, no. 3, Dec. 2011, pp. 93–103.

—. "Examining the Farming/Language Dispersal Hypothesis in the East Asian Context." *The Peopling of East Asia: Putting Together Archaeology, Linguistics and Genetics,* edited by Laurent Sagart et al., Routledge, 2005.

Benson, Frederic C. "European Explorers in Northeastern Laos, 1882–1893." *Journal of Lao Studies,* vol. 6, no. 1, Dec. 2018, pp. 56–74.

—. "Indochina War Refugee Movements in Laos, 1954–1975: A Chronological Overview Citing New Primary Sources." *Journal of Lao Studies,* Special Issue, Mar. 2015, pp. 24–63.

—. "The Unraveling of the 1962 Geneva Accords: Laos 1962–1964." *Indochina in the Year of the Dragon—1964,* series edited by Stephen Sherman, Radix Press, 2014.

Bishaw, Alemayehu. *Poverty: 2010 and 2011*. American Community Survey Briefs, U.S. Census Bureau, Sept. 2012.

Blench, Roger. "From the Mountains to the Valleys: Understanding Ethnolinguistic Geography in Southeast Asia." *The Peopling of East Asia: Putting Together Archaeology, Linguistics and Genetics,* edited by Laurent Sagart et al., Routledge, 2005.

Boyle, David. "Water Experts Question World Bank's Role in Laos Dam." *Voice of America* news, 19 Oct. 2018.

Bray, Francesca. *The Rice Economies: Technology and Development in Asian Societies*. University of California Press, 1994.

Brown, Curt. "Alleged Plot by Vang Pao Called Act of Desperation: Some in the Hmong Community Say the General May Have Grown Impatient to Help Those Left in the Jungles of Laos and Thailand." *Star Tribune,* 7 June 2007.

Brown, MacAlister, and Joseph J. Zasloff. "Laos 1978: The Ebb and Flow of Adversity." *Asian Survey,* vol. 19, no. 2, A Survey of Asia in 1978: Part II, Feb. 1979, pp. 95–103.

Butterfield, Fox. "Communists Forging Gentle Laotians into More Spartan Society." *New York Times,* 16 Dec. 1975.

—. "Laotians Being Re-educated by Reds." *New York Times,* 5 Oct. 1975.

Cairns, Malcolm F., editor. *Shifting Cultivation and Environmental Change: Indigenous People, Agriculture and Forest Conservation*. Routledge, 2015.

Cano, Merce Monje, et al. *Hmong in Isolation: Atrocities Against the Indigenous Hmong in the Xaisomboun Region of Laos*. Unrepresented Nations and Peoples Organization, Apr. 2021.

Castillo, Cristina Cobo, et al. "Archaeogenetic Study of Prehistoric Rice Remains from Thailand and India: Evidence of Early Japonica in South and Southeast Asia." *Archaeological and Anthropological Sciences,* vol. 8, no. 3, Sept. 2016, pp. 523–43.

Castillo, Edward D. *Short Overview of California Indian History*. California Native American Heritage Commission, 1998.

Cha, Dia. "Hmong and Lao Refugee Women: Reflections of a Hmong-American Woman Anthropologist." *Hmong Studies Journal,* vol. 6, 2005.

—. "The Hmong 'Dab Pog Couple' Story and Its Significance in Arriving at an Understanding of Hmong Ritual." *Hmong Studies Journal,* vol. 4, 2003.

Chanda, Nayan. "Laos: Back to the Drawing Board." *Far Eastern Economic Review,* 8 Sept. 1976.

—. "Laos Gears Up for Rural Progress." *Far Eastern Economic Review,* 8 Apr. 1977.

—. "A New Threat from the Mountain Tribes." *Far Eastern Economic Review,* 1 Sept. 1978.

Chang, Te-Tzu. "Rice." *The Cambridge World History of Food,* edited by Kenneth F. Kiple and Kriemhild Coneè Ornelas, Cambridge University Press, 2000, pp. 132–49.

Chapman, William. "Laotian Refugees Fear Thailand Camp Dead End." *Washington Post,* 6 Aug. 1979.

Cheung, Siu-Woo. "Millenarianism, Christian Movements, and Ethnic Change Among the Miao in Southwest China." *Cultural Encounters on China's Ethnic Frontiers,* edited by Stevan Harrell, University of Washington Press, 1995.

Children of the Mist. Directed by Hà Lệ Diễm, Varan Vietnam, 2021.

"Citing Virus, Trump Moves to Punish Countries That Won't Accept Deported Citizens." *New York Times,* 10 Apr. 2020.

Clarke, Samuel R. *Among the Tribes in South-West China.* China Inland Mission, 1911.

Collins, Caroline. *Ours to Lose.* Cal Ag Roots Podcast #7, https://cirsinc.org/2018/08/13/episode-7-ours-to-lose/.

Committee for Planning and Cooperation, National Statistical Centre. *The Households of Lao PDR: Lao Expenditure and Consumption Survey 1997/98 LECS 2.* World Bank, 1999.

—. *The Households of Lao PDR: Lao Expenditure and Consumption Survey 2002/03 LECS 3.* World Bank, 2004.

—. *Lao Expenditure and Consumption Survey 2012/13 Result.* World Bank, 2014.

Cook, Sherburne Friend. *The Population of the California Indians 1769–1970.* University of California Press, 1976.

Cooper, Robert George. *Resource Scarcity and the Hmong Response: Patterns of Settlement and Economy in Transition.* Singapore University Press, National University of Singapore, 1984.

Craig, Geraldine. "Patterns of Change: Transitions in Hmong Textile Language." *Hmong Studies Journal,* vol. 11, 2010.

Cramb, Rob, editor. *White Gold: The Commercialisation of Rice Farming in the Lower Mekong Basin.* Palgrave Macmillan, 2020.

Culas, C., and J. Michaud. "A Contribution to the Study of Hmong (Miao) Migrations and History." *Hmong/Miao in Asia,* edited by Nicholas Tapp et al., Silkworm Books, 2004.

—. "The Hmong of the South-East Asia Massif." *Where China Meets Southeast Asia: Social and Cultural Change in the Border Regions,* edited by Grant Evans et al., St. Martin's Press, 2000.

Cullather, Nick. *The Hungry World: America's Cold War Battle Against Poverty in Asia.* Harvard University Press, 2010.

Cunnington, Paul. *Village Resettlement in Laos.* SOGES, 2011.

Decision on Criteria on Model Farming Family, Farming Village and Developed Farming District. Lao PDR, Ministry of Agriculture and Forestry, 16 Nov. 2017.

Delaware, Robert. *Vang Pao Documents* (declassified FBI documents requested through FOIA), https://www.muckrock.com/foi/united-states-of-america-10/vang-pao-documents-1166/#file-4804.

De Schutter, Olivier. *Report of the Special Rapporteur on Extreme Poverty and Human Rights on His Mission to Lao People's Democratic Republic.* United Nations Human Rights Special Procedures, 24 May 2019.

Diamond, Norma. "Defining the Miao: Ming, Qing and Contemporary Views." *Cultural Encounters on China's Ethnic Frontiers,* edited by Stevan Harrell, University of Washington Press, 1995.

Downing, Bruce, and Douglas P. Olney, editors. *The Hmong in the West: Observations and Reports: Papers of the 1981 Hmong Research Conference, University of Minnesota.* Southeast Asian Refugee Studies Project, Center for Urban and Regional Affairs, University of Minnesota, 1982.

Doyle, Michael. "Suspect in Alleged Laos Plot Had Friends, Influence on Capitol Hill." *McClatchy Newspapers,* 5 June 2007.

—. "Vang Pao Allies Seek Formal Waiver for Arlington." *McClatchy Newspapers,* 11 Jan. 2011.

—. "Vang Pao Influenced U.S. Policy Long After Vietnam War Ended." *McClatchy Newspapers,* 7 Jan. 2011.

Dwyer, Michael. *Territorial Affairs: Turning Battlefields into Marketplaces in Postwar Laos.* PhD dissertation, University of California, Berkeley, 2011.

—. "Upland Geopolitics: Finding Zomia in Northern Laos c. 1875." *Journal of Lao Studies,* Special Issue 3, Apr. 2016, pp. 37–57.

Dwyer, Michael, et al. "The Security Exception: Development and Militarization in Laos's Protected Areas." *Geoforum,* vol. 69, Feb. 2016, pp. 207–17.

Editorial. "Lao Government, Ethnic Communities Clash over Development Projects." *ASEAN Today,* 9 Apr. 2021.

Ehling, Matt. "The Neutrality Act and the Case of Vang Pao." *MinnPost,* 21 Aug. 2008.

Eisenhower, Dwight D. *Waging Peace, 1956–1961: The White House Years.* Doubleday, 1965.

Epprecht, Michael, et al. *Atlas of Agriculture in the Lao PDR: Patterns and Trends Between 1999 and 2011.* 2018.

Erickson, Doug. "Vang Pao Supporters March Outside Courthouse." *Wisconsin State Journal,* 19 June 2007.

Espiritu, Yến Lê, and Lan Duong. "Feminist Refugee Epistemology: Reading Displacement in Vietnamese and Syrian Refugee Art." *Signs: Journal of Women in Culture and Society,* vol. 43, no. 3, Mar. 2018, pp. 587–615.

Evans, Grant. *Laos: Situation Analysis and Trend Assessment: A Writenet Report.* United Nations High Commissioner for Refugees, Protection Information Section (DIP), May 2004.

Everingham, John. "Meo Tribesmen Resist the New Regime." *Far Eastern Economic Review,* 13 Feb. 1976.

Evrard, Olivier, and Yves Goudineau. "Planned Resettlement, Unexpected Migrations and Cultural Trauma in Laos." *Development and Change,* vol. 35, no. 5, Nov. 2004, pp. 937–62.

Fadiman, Anne. *The Spirit Catches You and You Fall Down: A Hmong Child, Her American Doctors, and the Collision of Two Cultures.* Farrar, Straus and Giroux, 1997.

Falk, Catherine. "Hmong Instructions to the Dead: What the Mouth Organ *Qeej* Says (Part One)." *Asian Folklore Studies,* vol. 63, no. 1, 2004.

—. "Upon Meeting the Ancestors: The Hmong Funeral Ritual in Asia and Australia." *Hmong Studies Journal,* vol. 1, no. 1, 1996.

FAO. *Asia and the Pacific Regional Overview of Food Security and Nutrition 2018—Accelerating Progress Towards the SDGs.* Food and Agriculture Organization of the United Nations, 2018.

Fenton, Nina, and Magnus Lindelow. *The Socio-Geography of Mining and Hydro in Lao PDR: Analysis Combining GIS Information with Socioeconomic Data.* Technical note. Lao PDR Development Report: Natural Resource Management for Sustainable Development, 2010.

Figiaconi, Fabio. "Are Laos' Land-Linking Dreams a Risky Bet?" *The Diplomat,* 6 Sept. 2019.

Fiskesjö, Magnus. "On the 'Raw' and the 'Cooked' Barbarians of Imperial China." *Inner Asia,* vol. 1, no. 2, 1999, pp. 139–68.

Franjola, Matt. "Meo Tribesmen from Laos Facing Death in Thailand." *New York Times,* 15 Aug. 1975.

Fujii, Lee Ann. "Research Ethics 101: Dilemmas and Responsibilities." *PS: Political Science & Politics,* vol. 45, no. 4, Oct. 2012, pp. 717–23.

Fuller, Dorian Q., Alison R. Weisskopf, et al. "Pathways of Rice Diversification Across Asia." *Archaeology International,* Dec. 2016.

Fuller, Dorian Q., et al. "Consilience of Genetics and Archaeobotany in the Entangled History of Rice." *Archaeological and Anthropological Sciences,* vol. 2, no. 2, June 2010, pp. 115–31.

Fuller, Dorian Q., and Ling Qin. "Declining Oaks, Increasing Artistry, and Cultivating Rice: The Environmental and Social Context of the Emergence of Farming in the Lower Yangtze Region." *Environmental Archaeology,* vol. 15, no. 2, Oct. 2010, pp. 139–59.

—. "Water Management and Labour in the Origins and Dispersal of Asian Rice." *World Archaeology,* vol. 41, no. 1, Mar. 2009, pp. 88–111.

Garcia, Dominica P. "In Thailand, Refugees' 'Horror and Misery.'" *New York Times,* 14 Nov. 1978.

Gender Development Association. *Lao PDR Challenges Facing Women's Development Since the 2nd UPR Cycle.* 2020.

Gerstein, Josh. "Laos Coup Plot Was a 'Fantasy,' Vang Lawyer Says." *New York Sun,* 26 June 2007.

Giam, Xingli. "Global Biodiversity Loss from Tropical Deforestation." *Proceedings of the National Academy of Sciences,* vol. 114, no. 23, June 2017, pp. 5775–77.

Gross, Briana L. "Rice Domestication: Histories and Mysteries." *Molecular Ecology,* vol. 21, no. 18, Sept. 2012, pp. 4412–13.

Hamilton, Roy W., et al., editors. *The Art of Rice: Spirit and Sustenance in Asia.* University of California, Los Angeles, Fowler Museum of Cultural History, 2003.

Hamilton-Merritt, Jane. "Flight from Laos." *New York Times,* 4 Sept. 1979.

—. *Tragic Mountains: The Hmong, the Americans, and the Secret Wars for Laos, 1942–1992.* Indiana University Press, 1993.

Hammond, Ruth. "The Battle over Zomia." *The Chronicle of Higher Education,* 4 Sept. 2011.

—. "Sad Suspicions of a Refugee Ripoff." *Washington Post,* 16 Apr. 1989.

Hartmann, John, and Shoua Yang. "The Promised Land: Socioeconomic Reality of the Hmong People in Urban America (1976–2000)." *The Journal of Asian Studies,* vol. 61, no. 2, May 2002, pp. 679–81.

Hartwell, Robert M. "Demographic, Political, and Social Transformations of China, 750–1550." *Harvard Journal of Asiatic Studies,* vol. 42, no. 2, Dec. 1982, pp. 365–442.

Hayden, Brian. "Rice: The First Asian Luxury Food?" *Why Cultivate? Anthropological and Archaeological Approaches to Foraging-Farming Transitions in Southeast Asia,* edited by Graeme Barker and Monica Janowski, McDonald Institute for Archaeological Research, 2011.

Hendricks, Glenn L., et al., editors. *The Hmong in Transition.* Center for Migration Studies of New York; Southeast Asian Refugee Studies of the University of Minnesota, 1986.

Henry, Rebecca Rose. *Sweet Blood, Dry Liver: Diabetes and Hmong Embodiment in a Foreign Land.* PhD dissertation, University of North Carolina, 1996.

Herndon, Nancy. "A New Life in the 'Land of Opportunity.' Relocated Hmong Refugees Make a Home for Themselves in Rural North Carolina." *Christian Science Monitor,* 11 June 1987.

Hillmer, Paul. *A People's History of the Hmong.* Minnesota Historical Society Press, 2010.

Hmong Oral History Project. Concordia University, Saint Paul.

Hobo Maps. "Summary of Laos Hydropower Projects." *Laos Hydropower Projects Info,* accessed Sept. 2022, https://www.hobomaps.com/LaosHydropowerProjects.html.

Hutt, David. "Confronting Property Rights and Wrongs in Laos." *The Diplomat,* 1 Aug. 2019.

Ing-Britt, Trankell. *On the Road In Laos: An Anthropological Study of Road Construction and Rural Communities.* White Lotus Press, Uppsala University, 1993.

Ivarsson, Søren. *Creating Laos: The Making of a Lao Space Between Indochina and Siam, 1860–1945*. NIAS Press, 2008.

Janssen, Peter. "UN Finally Tells the Truth About Laos." *Asia Times*, 1 Apr. 2019.

Jassier, Annie. "DeLIVERing an Introduction to Psycho-collocations with SIAB in White Hmong." *Linguistics of the Tibeto-Burman Area*, vol. 13, no. 1, Spring 1990.

Jenks, Robert Darrah. *Insurgency and Social Disorder in Guizhou: The "Miao" Rebellion, 1854–1873*. University of Hawaii Press, 1994.

Ju, Namu. "'Language as a Way of Speaking Back': An Interview with Mai Der Vang." *Writing on the Edge*, vol. 28, no. 2, Spring 2018, pp. 6–16.

Kamm, Henry. "End of Laos War Has Brought No Peace to Thousands in Meo Clans." *New York Times*, 13 July 1975.

—. *July 6 1975 Draft Submitted to Editors at the New York Times*. Henry Kamm papers. Manuscripts and Archives Division, New York Public Library.

—. "A Laos Army Met Defeat Before Battle." *New York Times*, 22 June 1975.

—. "Laos Said to Battle Internal Resistance." *New York Times*, 29 Mar. 1978.

—. "Laotian Aide Confirms Stationing of Vietnam Troops." *New York Times*, 23 Mar. 1979.

—. "Meo, Hill People Who Fought for U.S., Are Fleeing from Laos." *New York Times*, 28 Mar. 1978.

—. "Thailand Finds Indochinese Refugees a Growing Problem." *New York Times*, 1 July 1977.

—. "U.S. Involvement in Laos Is Virtually Over." *New York Times*, 20 June 1975.

Kang, Inkoo. "Vang Pao: The General Who Wouldn't Give Up the Battle." *MuckRock*, 17 Sept. 2012.

Karniol, R. "Laotian Resistance Emerges from Mist." *International Defense Review*, vol. 23, Mar. 1990.

Katibah, Edwin F. "A Brief History of Riparian Forests in the Central Valley of California." *California Riparian Systems: Ecology, Conservation, and Productive Management*, edited by Richard E. Warner and Kathleen M. Hendrix, University of California Press, 1984.

Katz, Cindi. "On the Grounds of Globalization: A Topography for Feminist Political Engagement." *Signs: Journal of Women in Culture and Society*, vol. 26, no. 4, July 2001, pp. 1213–34.

Kelly, Michael. "Letter from Ban Vinai." *Far Eastern Economic Review*, 15 Jan. 1987.

Kennedy, Tony, and Paul McEnroe. "The Covert Wars of Vang Pao." *Star Tribune*, 5 July 2005.

Kenney-Lazar, Miles. *Shifting Cultivation in Laos: Transitions in Policy and Perspective*. Lao PDR, Secretariat of the Sector Working Group for Agriculture and Rural Development, 2013.

Keyes, Charles F. *The Golden Peninsula: Culture and Adaptation in Mainland Southeast Asia*. Macmillan, 1977.

King, John Kerry. "Rice Politics." *Foreign Affairs*, Apr. 1953.

Kummer, David M. "The Physical Environment." *Southeast Asia: Diversity and Development*, edited by Thomas R. Leinbach and Richard Ulack, Prentice Hall, 2000.

Kurlantzick, Joshua. *A Great Place to Have a War: America in Laos and the Birth of a Military CIA*. Simon & Schuster, 2017.

Lao PDR, National Statistical Centre of the Committee for Planning and Investment, the Asian Development Bank, the Swedish International Development Agency, and the World Bank. *Lao PDR Poverty Assessment Report*. Poverty Reduction and Economic Management Sector Unit East Asia and Pacific Region, World Bank, Sept. 2006.

Lao People's Democratic Republic Poverty Assessment 2020. World Bank, Washington, DC, 2020.

"Laos Seeks to Become Regional Hub for Electricity Transmission by 2025." *Vientiane Times,* 14 Feb. 2019.

Lee, Gary Yia. "Bandits or Rebels? Hmong Resistance in the New Lao State." *Indigenous Affairs Journal,* no. 4, Dec. 2000.

—. "Diaspora and the Predicament of Origins: Interrogating Hmong Postcolonial History and Identity." *Hmong Studies Journal,* vol. 8, 2007.

—. "Ethnic Minorities and Nation-Building in Laos: The Hmong in the Lao State." *Peninsule,* vol. 11/12, 1985/86, pp. 215–32.

—. "The Hmong Rebellion in Laos: Victims or Terrorists." *A Handbook of Terrorism and Insurgency in Southeast Asia,* edited by Andrew T. H. Tan, Elgar, 2007.

—. "Minority Policies and the Hmong in Laos after 1975." *Contemporary Laos: Studies in the Politics and Society of the Lao People's Democratic Republic,* edited by Martin Stuart-Fox, St. Martin's Press, 1982.

—. *Opium and the Hmong.* 2015, https://www.garyyialee.com/topical-opium-and-the-hmong.

—. "The Shaping of Traditions: Agriculture and Hmong Society." *Hmong Studies Journal,* vol. 6, 2005.

—. "Transnational Adaptation: An Overview of the Hmong in Laos." *Hmong/Miao in Asia,* edited by Nicholas Tapp et al., Silkworm Books, 2004.

Lee, Mai Na M. *Dreams of the Hmong Kingdom: The Quest for Legitimation in French Indochina, 1850–1960.* University of Wisconsin Press, 2015.

—. "The Thousand-Year Myth: Construction and Characterization of Hmong." *Hmong Studies Journal,* vol. 2, 1998.

Lee, Regina. "Theorizing Diasporas: Three Types of Consciousness." *Asian Diasporas: Cultures, Identities, Representations,* edited by Robbie B. H. Goh and Shawn Wong, Hong Kong University Press, 2004.

Lee, Serge, and Jenny Chang. "Mental Health Status of the Hmong Americans in 2011: Three Decades Revisited." *Journal of Social Work in Disability & Rehabilitation,* vol. 11, no. 1, Jan. 2012, pp. 55–70.

Lee, Song. *Hmong Women Issues: Identity and Mental Health.* PhD dissertation, North Carolina State University, 2006.

—. "Mental Health of Hmong Americans: A Metasynthesis of Academic Journal Article Findings." *Hmong Studies Journal,* vol. 14, 2013.

Legacies of War. https://www.legaciesofwar.org.

Le Guin, Ursula K. "The Carrier Bag Theory of Fiction." *Dancing at the Edge of the World: Thoughts on Words, Women, Places,* Perennial Library, 1990.

Lemoine, Jacques. "To Tell the Truth." *Hmong Studies Journal,* vol. 9, 2008.

—. "What Is the Actual Number of the (H)mong in the World?" *Hmong Studies Journal,* vol. 6, 2005.

Lemoine, Jacques, and Kenneth White. *Kr'ua Ke (Showing the Way): A Hmong Initiation of the Dead.* Pandora, 1983.

Leonard, George J. *Story Cloths of the Hmong: The Hmong, the Mien, and the Making of an Asian American Art.* http://www.georgeleonard.com/articles/story-cloths-of-the-hmong.htm.

Li, Hui, et al. "Y Chromosomes of Prehistoric People Along the Yangtze River." *Human Genetics,* vol. 122, no. 3–4, Dec. 2007, pp. 383–88.

Lieb, Emily. *The Hmong Migration to Fresno: From Laos to California's Central Valley.* MA thesis, California State University, Fresno, 1996.

Lieberman, Victor. "A Zone of Refuge in Southeast Asia? Reconceptualizing Interior Spaces." *Journal of Global History,* vol. 5, no. 2, July 2010, pp. 333–46.

Ling, Huping, editor. *Emerging Voices: Experiences of Underrepresented Asian Americans.* Rutgers University Press, 2008.

Lofgren, Maj. William W., and Maj. Richard R. Sexton. *Air War in Northern Laos 1 Apr–30 Nov 1971.* United States Department of the Air Force, Directorate of Operations Analysis, CHECO/Corona Harvest Division, 22 June 1973.

Long, Lynellyn D. *Ban Vinai: The Refugee Camp.* Columbia University Press, 1993.

Lopez, Pablo. "TV Pitchman Behind the Plan to Create a Hmong Homeland Insists It's No Scam." *Fresno Bee,* 23 Oct. 2017.

Lovgren, Stefan. "Southeast Asia May Be Building Too Many Dams Too Fast." https://www.nationalgeographic.com, 23 Aug. 2018.

Ma, Sheng-mei. "Hmong Refugee's Death Fugue." *Hmong Studies Journal,* vol. 6, 2005.

MacDowell, Marsha. *Hmong Textiles and Cultural Conservation.* Smithsonian Institution, 1986.

—. *Stories in Thread: Hmong Pictorial Embroidery.* Michigan Traditional Arts Program, Folk Arts Division, Michigan State University Museum, 1989.

Magagnini, Stephen. "Hmong Flock to Vang Pao Funeral." *Sacramento Bee,* 5 Feb. 2011.

—. "Vang Pao—Hmong Leader Plans Laos Trip—Ex-General Is Aiming for Reconciliation." *Sacramento Bee,* 23 Dec. 2009.

Martin, Philip L., et al. *The New Rural Poverty: Agriculture & Immigration in California.* Urban Institute Press, 2006.

Mason, Bert, et al. "Fresno in Transition: Urban Impacts of Rural Migration." Julian Samora Research Institute, Michigan State University, 1996.

Matsui, T. "Rice (Oryza Sativa L.) Cultivars Tolerant to High Temperature at Flowering: Anther Characteristics." *Annals of Botany,* vol. 89, no. 6, June 2002, pp. 683–87.

McBeth, John. "Laos: The Government Under Guard." *Far Eastern Economic Review,* 24 Aug. 1979.

—. "Tracing a Gas Leak." *Far Eastern Economic Review,* 24 Aug. 1979.

McShannock, Linda. "Flowery Cloth: The Art and Artistry of Hmong 'Paj Ntaub.'" *Minnesota Historical Society Magazine,* Spring 2015.

Melo, Frederick. "For Hmong, Twin Cities Are Now Home. Mostly." *St. Paul Pioneer Press,* 8 Mar. 2015.

—. "He Promised a New Hmong Homeland. Now They Want Their Impounded Cash Back—for the Same Cause." *St. Paul Pioneer Press,* 20 Mar. 2018.

MERFI. *Dataset on the Dams of the Greater Mekong.* Bangkok, Mekong Region Futures Institute, 2021.

Messerli, Peter, et al., editors. *Socio-Economic Atlas of the Lao PDR: An Analysis Based on the 2005 Population and Housing Census.* Swiss National Center of Competence in Research (NCCR) North-South, University of Bern, Bern and Vientiane. Geographica Bernensia, 2008.

Michaud, Jean. "The Art of Not Being Scripted So Much: The Politics of Writing Hmong Language(s)." *Current Anthropology,* vol. 61, no. 2, Apr. 2020, pp. 240–63.

Michaud, Jean, editor. *Turbulent Times and Enduring People: Mountain Minorities in the South-East Asian Massif.* Curzon, 2000.

Miyares, Ines M. *The Hmong Refugee Experience in the United States: Crossing the River.* Garland Pub., 1998.

Morin, Stephen. "Troubled Refugees: Many Hmong, Puzzled by Life in U.S., Yearn for Old Days in Laos." *Wall Street Journal,* 16 Feb. 1983.

Moua, Mai Neng. *The Bride Price: A Hmong Wedding Story.* Minnesota Historical Society Press, 2017.

Moua, Wameng. "General Vang Pao, Hero." *Twin Cities Daily Planet,* 19 June 2007.

Nolte, Carl. "Sprawl, Clutter Define Fresno / Civic Corruption Has Splotched the City's Image." *San Francisco Chronicle,* 1 Sept. 1999.

Northwest Regional Educational Laboratory, Literacy & Language Programs, prepared by Stephen Reder. *The Hmong Resettlement Study: Site Report, Fresno, California.* U.S. Department of Health and Human Services, Social Security Administration, Office of Refugee Resettlement, 1983.

O'Dell, John. "Lao Agency Being Probed Closes Down." *Los Angeles Times,* 23 Jan. 1991.

Ogden, Mitch. "Tebchaws: A Theory of Magnetic Media and Hmong Diasporic Homeland." *Hmong Studies Journal,* vol. 16, 2015.

Ounkeo, Souksavanh (RFA's Lao Service). "Lao Government Troops Launch New Assault Against Hmong at Phou Bia Mountain." *Radio Free Asia,* 1 Apr. 2021.

Ovesen, Jan. "The Hmong and Development in the Lao People's Democratic Republic." *Hmong/Miao in Asia,* edited by Nicholas Tapp et al., Silkworm Books, 2004.

—. *A Minority Enters the Nation State: A Case Study of a Hmong Community in Vientiane Province, Laos.* Department of Cultural Anthropology, Uppsala University, 1995.

Parsons, James J. "A Geographer Looks at the San Joaquin Valley." *Geographical Review,* vol. 76, no. 4, Oct. 1986, p. 371.

Patten, Steve. "When Hanoi's Rulers Gobble Up a Neighbor—Thousands Flee Laos." *U.S. News & World Report,* 2 June 1980.

Peagan, Norman. "The Gradual Revolution." *Far Eastern Economic Review,* 10 Sept. 1976.

Peterson, Sally. "Translating Experience and the Reading of a Story Cloth." *Journal of American Folklore,* vol. 101, no. 399, Jan. 1988, p. 6.

"PM Calls for Tighter Security to Spur Development in Xaysomboun." *Vientiane Times,* 17 Dec. 2021.

Pollard, Jim. "New Questions Asked About Laos Dam Toll, Builder's Role." *Asia Times,* 19 Oct. 2018.

Pongsapich, Amara, et al. *Thailand and the Indochinese Refugees, Paper I: The Refugee Situation in Thailand.* The Institute of Asian Studies, Chulalongkorn University, 28 May 1987.

Quincy, Keith. *Harvesting Pa Chay's Wheat: The Hmong and America's Secret War in Laos.* Eastern Washington University Press, 2000.

Rack, Mary. *Ethnic Distinctions, Local Meanings: Negotiating Cultural Identities in China.* Pluto Press, 2005.

Radanovich, George P. (CA). "In Honor of Gen. Vang Pao." *Congressional Record* 142: 64 (9 May 1996), p. E739.

Ramsay, Deanna. "Phouvieng Phongsa: Examining Lao PDR's Trade Journey." *Trade for Development News,* 26 Nov. 2019.

Ranard, Donald A. "The Refugees and Their Carolina Roots." *Washington Post,* 29 Nov. 1986.

Ratliff, Martha. *Hmong-Mien Language History.* Pacific Linguistics, 2010.

—. "Vocabulary of Environment and Subsistence in the Hmong-Mien Proto-Language." *Hmong/Miao in Asia,* edited by Nicholas Tapp et al., Silkworm Books, 2004.

Reid, Anthony. *A History of Southeast Asia.* Wiley Blackwell, 2015.

RFA's Lao Service. "Lao Farmers Driven from Their Land by Foreign Concessions, Rising Costs." *Radio Free Asia,* 7 July 2021.

—. "Laos in Push to Inspect Dams Before Rainy Season Begins." *Radio Free Asia,* 22 June 2021.

—. "U.N. Expert: The Rich Get Richer in Lao PDR." *Radio Free Asia,* 9 Apr. 2019.

Rice, Pranee Liamputtong. *Hmong Women and Reproduction.* Bergin & Garvey, 2000.

"Rice Prices Set to Skyrocket in 2020." *Vientiane Times,* 14 Nov. 2019.

Richburg, Keith B. "Insurgency in Laos Seeking to Emerge from Anonymity." *Washington Post,* 11 Feb. 1990.

Rigg, Jonathan. "The Puzzle of East and Southeast Asia's Persistent Smallholder." *Journal of Rural Studies,* vol. 43, Feb. 2016, pp. 118–33.

—. "Rethinking Asian Poverty in a Time of Asian Prosperity." *Asia Pacific Viewpoint,* vol. 59, no. 2, Aug. 2018, pp. 159–72.

Robinson, W. Courtland. *Terms of Refuge: The Indochinese Exodus and the International Response.* Zed Books, 1998.

Roder, Walter. *Slash-and-Burn Rice Systems in the Hills of Northern Lao PDR: Description, Challenges, and Opportunities.* International Rice Research Institute, Los Baños, Philippines, 2001.

"Rubber to Top Laos' Agricultural Exports in 2018." *Vientiane Times,* 8 Jan. 2019.

Rujivanarom, Pratch. "Can Laos Afford to Be the 'Battery of Asia'?" *The Nation,* 25 Feb. 2019.

Rush, James R. *Southeast Asia: A Very Short Introduction.* Oxford University Press, 2018.

Sagart, Laurent. "How Many Independent Rice Vocabularies in Asia?" *Rice,* vol. 4, no. 3–4, Dec. 2011, pp. 121–33.

Savada, Andrea Matles, editor. *Laos: A Country Study.* 3rd ed., Federal Research Division, Library of Congress, 1995.

Save the Children. *Global Childhood Report 2019.* Save the Children International, 2019.

Saxon, Wolfgang. "Take-Over Ends Strife in Laos That Outsiders Had Intensified." *New York Times,* 24 Aug. 1975.

Saychai, Syladeth, and Guoqing Shi. "Resettlement Implementation Management Caused by Hydropower Development: A Case Study of Nam Ngum2 Hydropower Project in Laos." *Journal of Public Administration and Policy Research,* vol. 8, no. 2, Apr. 2016, pp. 12–24.

Schein, Louisa. *Minority Rules: The Miao and the Feminine in China's Cultural Politics.* Duke University Press, 2000.

Schiller, J. M., editor. *Rice in Laos.* IRRI, 2006.

Scott, James C. *Against the Grain: A Deep History of the Earliest States.* Yale University Press, 2017.

—. *The Art of Not Being Governed: An Anarchist History of Upland Southeast Asia.* Yale University Press, 2009.

Shaplen, Robert. "Letter from Laos." *The New Yorker,* 4 May 1968.

Sheehan, Tim. "COVID-19 Is No. 1 Cause of Death in Fresno County. See the August Surge in 4 Charts." *Fresno Bee,* 3 Sept. 2020.

Sherman, Spencer. "The Hmong in America." *National Geographic,* Oct. 1988, pp. 587–610.

—. "The Hmong's Blue Ridge Refuge." *APF Reporter,* 1986.

Soukhaphon, Akarath, et al. "The Impacts of Hydropower Dams in the Mekong River Basin: A Review." *Water,* vol. 13, no. 3, Jan. 2021, p. 265.

Spencer, Charles S. "Territorial Expansion and Primary State Formation." *Proceedings of the National Academy of Sciences,* vol. 107, no. 16, Apr. 2010, pp. 7119–26.

Stebbins, Samuel (24/7 Wall Street). "Despite Overall Sustained GDP Growth in US, Some Cities Still Hit Hard by Extreme Poverty." *USA Today,* 23 Apr. 2018.

Strategy for Agricultural Development 2011 to 2020. Lao PDR Ministry of Agriculture and Forestry, 19 Aug. 2010.

Stuart-Fox, Martin. "The French in Laos, 1887–1945." *Modern Asian Studies,* vol. 29, no. 1, Feb. 1995, pp. 111–39.

Sweeney, Megan, and Susan McCouch. "The Complex History of the Domestication of Rice." *Annals of Botany,* vol. 100, no. 5, July 2007, pp. 951–57.

Symonds, Patricia V. *Calling in the Soul: Gender and the Cycle of Life in a Hmong Village.* University of Washington Press, 2004.

Tapp, Nicholas. *The Hmong of China: Context, Agency, and the Imaginary.* Brill, 2001.

—. *The Impossibility of Self: An Essay on the Hmong Diaspora.* Lang, 2010.

—. *Sovereignty and Rebellion: The White Hmong of Northern Thailand.* Oxford University Press, 1989.

Termination Report: USAID Laos. United States Department of State, USAID, Laos Mission and Office of Laos Affairs, 9 Jan. 1976.

Thao, Mai See. *Bittersweet Migrations: Type II Diabetes and Healing in the Hmong Diaspora.* PhD dissertation, University of Minnesota, 2018.

Thao, Yer J. *The Mong Oral Tradition: Cultural Memory in the Absence of Written Language.* McFarland, 2006.

Thebault, Reis. "Fresno's Mason-Dixon Line." *The Atlantic,* 20 Aug. 2018.

Thompson, Don (Associated Press). "Hmong Leader Held on Coup Charges." AP online, 12 June 2007.

Thompson, Larry Clinton. *Refugee Workers in the Indochina Exodus, 1975–1982.* McFarland & Company, 2010.

Tuck, Eve. "Suspending Damage: A Letter to Communities." *Harvard Educational Review,* vol. 79, no. 3, Sept. 2009, pp. 409–28.

United Nations High Commissioner for Refugees. *Brief on Ban Vinai Refugee Camp.* United Nations Regional Office of Western South Asia, 1 Apr. 1985.

United States, Congress, House Committee on Foreign Affairs, Subcommittee on Asian and Pacific Affairs. *1979—Tragedy in Indochina: War, Refugees, and Famine.* U.S. Government Printing Office, Washington, DC, 1980. 96th Congress, 1st session.

United States, Congress, House Committee on Foreign Affairs, Subcommittee on Asian and Pacific Affairs, Congressional Delegation to Southeast Asia, December 28, 1978–January 13, 1979. *Refugees from Indochina: Current Problems and Prospects.* U.S. Government Printing Office, Washington, DC, 30 Apr. 1979. 96th Congress, 1st session.

United States, Department of Homeland Security. *DHS Announces Implementation of Visa Sanctions.* 10 July 2018, https://www.dhs.gov/news/2018/07/10/dhs-announces-implementation-visa-sanctions.

United States, Department of Justice, U.S. Attorney's Office, District of Minnesota. *Seng Xiong Sentenced to 87 Months in Prison for Defrauding Members of the Hmong Community.* 11 Oct. 2017.

United States, Department of State, Bureau of Consular Affairs. Nonimmigrant Visa Issuances by Visa Class and by Nationality, 2015, 2017, 2019.

United States, Foreign Broadcast Information Service. *Daily Report. Asia & Pacific.* Nos. 85–95, 96–105, 106–115, 116–126, June 1975.

UPI News Track. "Defense Wants to Question U.S. Agent." United Press International, 26 June 2007.

Van Driem, George. "The Domestications and the Domesticators of Asian Rice." *Language Dispersal Beyond Farming,* edited by Martine Robbeets and Alexander Savelyev, John Benjamins Publishing Company, 2017, pp. 183–214.

—. "The East Asian Linguistic Phylum: A Reconstruction Based on Language and Genes." *Journal of the Asiatic Society,* vol. 60, no. 4, 2018, pp. 1–38.

—. "Rice and the Austroasiatic and Hmong-Mien Homelands." *Dynamics of Human Diversity: The Case of Mainland Southeast Asia,* edited by N. J. Enfield, Pacific Linguistics, 2011, pp. 361–89.

Vang, Chia Youyee, et al., editors. *Claiming Place: On the Agency of Hmong Women.* University of Minnesota Press, 2016.

Vang, Geu. *Unforgettable Laos.* https://www.unforgettable-laos.com.

Vang, Lue, and Judy Lewis. *Grandmother's Path, Grandfather's Way.* Zellerbach Family Fund, 1984.

Vang, Ma. *Displaced Histories: Refugee Critique and the Politics of Hmong American Remembering.* University of California, San Diego, 2012.

—. *History on the Run: Secrecy, Fugitivity, and Hmong Refugee Epistemologies.* Duke University Press, 2021.

—. "Writing on the Run: Hmong American Literary Formations and the Deterritorialized Subject." *MELUS: Multi-Ethnic Literature of the United States,* vol. 41, no. 3, Sept. 2016, pp. 89–111.

Vang, Mai Der. *Afterland: Poems.* Graywolf Press, 2017.

—. "Poetry as Homeland: Reflections on Hmong American Exile and a Literary Future." *American Poets,* vol. 52, Spring–Summer 2017.

—. *Yellow Rain: Poems.* Graywolf Press, 2021.

Vang, Nengher N. "Political Transmigrants: Rethinking Hmong Political Activism in America." *Hmong Studies Journal,* vol. 12, 2011.

Vang, Susie Pakoua, and Mark Gross. "Rally for a Leader: 'The General Is Like the Sun to the Hmong,' Says One of Hundreds Who Showed Support for Gen. Vang Pao on Friday." *Fresno Bee,* 9 June 2007.

Vau, Terry. "Arrests of Oroville Residents May Have Triggered Alleged Laos Coup Plot." *Chico Enterprise-Record,* 26 June 2007.

Vento, Bruce F. (MN). "Citizenship for Hmong Veterans of the Vietnam War." *Congressional Record* 140: 7 (11 May 1994), p. 9997.

Vilavong, Buavanh, and Sitthiroth Rasphone. "Laos on Course to Graduate from Least Developed Country Status." *East Asia Forum,* 1 Jan. 2020.

Visser, Margaret. *Much Depends on Dinner: The Extraordinary History and Mythology, Allure and Obsessions, Perils and Taboos of an Ordinary Meal.* Grove Press, 1987.

Vue, Douacha Serina. *The Culture of Preservation and Its Impact on Hmong Funerals.* BA thesis, Whitman College, 2020.

Wang, Wensheng, et al. "Genomic Variation in 3,010 Diverse Accessions of Asian Cultivated Rice." *Nature,* vol. 557, no. 7703, May 2018, pp. 43–49.

Wang, Yanan. "The 'Open Secret' of Abused Hmong Child Brides Goes Public in Minnesota Lawsuit." *Washington Post,* 28 Sept. 2015.

Warner, Roger. "Peace at Last? No Thanks to the State Department…" *Huffington Post,* 22 Oct. 2010.

—. *Shooting at the Moon: The Story of America's Clandestine War in Laos.* Steerforth Press, 1996.

Weiner, Tim. "Gen. Vang Pao's Last War." *New York Times Magazine,* 11 May 2008.

Wen, Bo, et al. "Genetic Structure of Hmong-Mien Speaking Populations in East Asia as Revealed by MtDNA Lineages." *Molecular Biology and Evolution,* vol. 22, no. 3, Mar. 2005, pp. 725–34.

Whitaker, Donald P., et al. *Area Handbook for Laos.* Foreign Area Studies, American University, Washington, DC, 1972.

White, J. C. "Modeling the Development of Early Rice Agriculture: Ethnoecological Perspectives from Northeast Thailand." *Asian Perspectives,* vol. 34, no. 1, 1995, pp. 37–68.

Wiens, Herold J. *China's March Toward the Tropics: A Discussion of the Southward Penetration of China's Culture, Peoples, and Political Control in Relation to the Non-Han-Chinese Peoples of South China and in the Perspective of Historical and Cultural Geography.* Shoe String Press, 1954.

Wilkinson, Julia. "Letter from Ban Vinai." *Far Eastern Economic Review,* 24 Mar. 1988.

Williams, Ogden. *The Dark Night of the Hmong* (unpublished draft). June 1978.

The Working Lives and Struggles of Asian Americans and Pacific Islanders in California: Findings from the 2019 AAPI California Workers Survey. PRRI and AAPI Data, 18 Nov. 2019.

Xiong, Chao. "Son of Revered Hmong General Charged in Theft Case." *Star Tribune,* 3 June 2019.

—. "Supporters of Convicted Fraudster Who Promised New Hmong Homeland Demand Their Money Back, but Continue to Support His Cause." *Star Tribune,* 20 Mar. 2018.

Xiong, Yuepheng L. *English-Hmong/Hmong-English Dictionary.* Third edition, Hmongland Publishing Co., 2011.

Yang, Dao. *Hmong at the Turning Point.* WorldBridge Associates, 1993.

—. "Hmong Culture Is Hmong Soul." *The Impact of Globalization and Trans-Nationalism on the Hmong,* edited by Gary Yia Lee, Center for Hmong Studies, Concordia University, 2009.

Yang, Kao Kalia. *The Latehomecomer: A Hmong Family Memoir.* Coffee House Press, 2008.

—. *The Song Poet: A Memoir of My Father.* Metropolitan Books, 2016.

Yang, Kou. "Commentary: Challenges and Complexity in the Re-Construction of Hmong History." *Hmong Studies Journal,* vol. 10, 2009.

—. *The Hmong in Fresno: A Study of Hmong Welfare Participation and Self-Sufficiency.* EdD dissertation, California State University, Fresno, and University of California, Davis, 1995.

Yang, Pa Chou, and Se Yang. *Dab Neeg Hmoob: Myths, Legends, and Folk Tales from the Hmong of Laos,* edited by Charles Johnson, Linguistics Department, Macalester College, 1985.

Yang, Shoua. *Hmong Social and Political Capital: The Formation and Maintenance of Hmong-American Organizations.* PhD dissertation, Northern Illinois University, 2006.

Yau, Jennifer. *The Foreign-Born Hmong in the United States.* Migration Policy Institute, 1 Jan. 2005.

Zsombor, Peter. "Lao Villagers, Facing Eviction for Dam, Are Leery of Government Promises." *Voice of America* news, 28 Nov. 2019.